K

SS
E!

DATE DUE

JUN 1 6 2001			
7/23/07			
8/16/07			
FEB 0 6 02			

DEMCO 38-297

BREAK
THE
STRESS
CYCLE!

10 Steps to
Reducing Stress for
Women

Judith Sachs

Adams Media Corporation
Holbrook, Massachusetts

5/01

38002576

Published by
Adams Media Corporation
260 Center Street, Holbrook, MA 02343

ISBN: 1-55850-007-8

Printed in the United States of America.
J I H G F E D C B

Library of Congress Cataloging in Publication Data
Sachs, Judith.
Break the stress cycle! : 10 steps to reducing stress
for women / Judith Sachs.
p.   cm.
Includes index.
ISBN 1–58062–007-8
1. Stress (Psychology). 2. Stress management.
3. Women—Psychology. I. Title.
BF575.S75S23   1998
155.9'042'082—dc21   97–45179
CIP

This book is available at quantity discounts for bulk purchases.
For information, call 1-800-872-5627 (in Massachusetts, 781-767-8100).

Visit our home page at http://www.adamsmedia.com

Dedication

To my dearest taiji, aikido, and music buddies—you know who you are…may this book help you roll with the punches.

Contents

Part I
The Outer You:
Practical Techniques for Taming Stress

Part II
The Inner You:
Relax, Pamper, and Enjoy Yourself

Part III
The Outside World:
Getting the Help You Need from Others

Acknowledgments

Thanks to Julia Turofsky, Ph.D., at the Center for Applied Psychology at Rutgers University in Piscataway, New Jersey for her careful guidance.

Thanks to Phyllis Cooper, Ph.D., of the College of New Jersey, who gave me the opportunity to learn so much about the mechanics of stress and how to convey that knowledge to others.

Thanks to Dr. Michael Schwartzman, who provided a great deal of insight into the therapeutic process.

Thanks to my teacher, Susanna DeRosa, who introduced me to taiji, breathing, and meditation.

Thanks to my daughter, Mia Bruno, for allowing me to reprint her poem, "May This Hand Ward Off Your Evils."

And for sharing their stories, thanks to:

Karen	Cathy
Judith	Kathy
Ellen	Lynn
Jennifer	Jan
Isabel	Julann
Mary	Sarena
Jette	Maxine
Maggi	Valerie
Jeanne	Donna
Mame	Yvonne
Donna	Elaine

—and all the women who are slowly making their way toward the light.

Introduction Stress Is a Feminine Issue

Let me tell you a story.

Rabbit was a self-sufficient animal who lived quietly by herself, tucked away in her little warren behind a big sheltering tree. She worked hard all day, storing up food for the winter, and then returned to take care of her home and the three children she raised by herself.

Hedgehog was a rover and a loner, very affable and winning, always able to get the best of every situation using charisma and charm. The bristly creature was more concerned with comfort than planning ahead.

Winter was coming on fast, and Hedgehog suddenly realized how it felt to be all alone, with no family or home, with nowhere to go. It seemed rude to impose on anyone, but what are friends for? At last Hedgehog knocked on the roof of friend Rabbit's nice, cozy warren.

Hedgehog called, "It's awfully cold out here. Would you mind if I stopped in for a while?" Rabbit opened the door and regarded her visitor, not too sure about extending an invitation because the cave was small and her children needed tending. Besides, she had several projects to complete (as well as dinner to cook), and Hedgehog had all those prickly things that took up so much space.

But how could she refuse? She had known Hedgehog for a long time, and, after all, she did get lonely every so often. So she took Hedgehog in, and for the first few days, everything was fine. Rabbit would tutor her children in the early morning while Hedgehog slept late. Then the five of them would take a walk during the warmest part of the day, and when they got back, Rabbit would prepare their frugal daily meal. In the evenings, after the children were asleep, they would sit by the fire and talk for hours. Rabbit was a very good listener, and Hedgehog always had a lot to say.

But as the days passed, it became clear that Hedgehog had no intention of leaving. The warren was small, but Rabbit divided her space so that the visitor would have room. A week went by, then two, and it was clear to Rabbit that Hedgehog had really settled in. Every time she turned around, Rabbit had to dodge and make herself smaller so as not to be hurt by her friend's thorny protrusions. Her children were run ragged, trying to stay out of the way of the hulking guest. And every meal they ate, Rabbit realized, had to be a little less bounteous, because she had to conserve for the rest of the hard season and it was difficult, splitting all that food in five.

After a month, Rabbit was fed up. Hedgehog never did anything to help out—Rabbit did all the work. When she hinted broadly at how much there was to do, Hedgehog praised her for her diligence and cleverness. She was flattered, and at first, worked harder. But each successive day, when nothing got any better in their relationship, there was an even sourer taste in her mouth. She realized that she was doing everything and getting nothing. At last, Rabbit decided that she was being taken advantage of—and Hedgehog's extended visit really was an imposition.

She came up with all kinds of approaches. Kindly: "Don't you feel cramped in here? I'm sure you could find a much bigger cave for yourself." Manipulative: "People are talking about how dependent you've become. I know you hate having others think you can't fend for yourself. I'd miss you, of course, but I'd just have to get used to it if you left." Relaxed: "If I close my eyes, you'll go away." Demanding: "I'm sick and tired of waiting on you and sheltering you, you lazy slug. Get out by tomorrow morning." But to use any of these approaches, she had to confront the situation and actively do something about it.

Months later, bruised and bleeding from Hedgehog's bristles, starving from having to share her food, she spoke out. After breakfast one morning, she looked her boarder in the eye and said, "This just isn't working for me. I realize it will be hard on you, but I'd really like you to look for somewhere else to live."

Hedgehog regarded her with shock. "You're just hysterical, dear. How could you manage without me around, now that you're used to it? You have so much, and I have nothing. I'm staying.

After you've had a while to think it over, you'll agree this is what's best for both of us."

Rabbit is under a lot of stress. She feels anxious and put-upon. She works so hard, and what does she get for it? She feels guilty about asking Hedgehog to get out, angry that her visitor refuses to act within the bounds of common decency, and disgusted at herself for putting up with this mess. And yet there seems to be no way out. The daily grind just gets worse.

A lot of stress, huh? Do you ever feel like Rabbit? Do you *always* feel like Rabbit? Who is this Hedgehog, anyway, and what causes the conflict in their relationship?

Well, let's look at it a couple of different ways. We can say it's all Rabbit's fault, because she acceded too easily to her visitor's wishes. She does so much—she works, takes care of her family, makes things "nice" for everyone. Like put-upon women over the centuries, she doesn't know how to say "no" and gets walked all over. She's been taught to be polite, and inviting someone in is certainly within the realm of good manners, but she has no idea how to behave when the situation gets out of hand.

What about Hedgehog? Is he a dominant, abusive male? A female who has learned how to put herself on top? Or is this animal a victim, too, abandoned first by her own family and now, about to be neglected and discarded by her former friend? Rabbit seemed selfless at first, agreeing to take in a homeless orphan without a thought for her own well-being. Then, when she wants to end the relationship, Hedgehog points out how selfish she seems.

Or perhaps Hedgehog isn't a separate creature at all. Maybe she is the conscience of Rabbit. Perhaps she represents all those obligations and duties that we think we have to accomplish. And she'll never leave, because we're never finished with what we think we have to do.

This simple fable is filled with the discomfort and ambivalence most women feel about handling stress, and brings up a lot of significant issues related to giving, taking, overdoing, and putting yourself last. The good news is that these are all issues that can be tackled—and changed.

WHY WOMEN FEEL THEY HAVE TO DO IT ALL

Women are amazing—we are strong and resourceful, empathetic and compassionate, vulnerable and easily overwhelmed. This great stew of ingredients makes us susceptible to stress, possibly more so but certainly in different ways than our male counterparts. And in the nineties, we are under the gun more than ever before.

The *New York Times* reported in December 1996 that in addition to being homemakers, single mothers, grandmothers responsible for a child's children, and never-married individuals with all the responsibilities and emotional burdens those positions entail, women are now on the brink of tipping the balance in the working world. We are soon to become a majority of the work force of America. If there is a man in the picture, he may in fact perform many more household chores than men of previous generations. But here's the stressful news: even when a working woman has a partner, she still does 87 percent of the shopping, 81 percent of the cooking, 78 percent of the cleaning, and 63 percent of the bill-paying, according to a 1993 study by the Family and Work Institute.

Think of the Norman Rockwell archetypal picture of a stressed-out woman: she is wearing an apron, throwing up her hands, looking down at her unruly kids without a clue as to how to handle all the various problems they've caused her. How old-fashioned, you think. How far from my own reality.

But think again. Run the tape forward into the present day—*our* day—and you see the woman getting dinner on the table, then jamming her books into a backpack and running to an evening class. You see her bringing her toddlers to a day-care center so that she can get to work and help the family financially. You see her walking angrily into a divorce proceeding, or anxiously taking a cab to the hospital to have a baby on her own. Or you see her in a business suit, frowning at her computer, which has just gone down before a vital meeting. Or you see her racing across town to visit her mother in the hospital, then racing back to catch a plane across the country where she's due to report to her national supervisor, stopping off on the way to pick up her husband's shirts at the cleaners.

You see her, like Rabbit, doing everything, and blaming herself for not being able to subdivide herself into even more portions. Why can't she hold down a full-time job, redecorate the house, support her husband when he gets downsized, go rollerblading with the kids, find a nursing home for her ailing parents, volunteer for the school bazaar, and run a little craft shop out of her house in her spare time?

GUILT LEADS TO STRESS LEADS TO GUILT

Our super champion of the life show somehow always feels lacking, no matter how well she juggles her myriad roles and how much praise she gets for her accomplishments. And that is very stressful. She doesn't cut the mustard because there's so much mustard to cut, and it has to be cut right. The majority of women—of all ages—feel overwhelmed, overburdened, and guilty, guilty, guilty, not just for the things they can't fit in, but for the things they haven't accomplished to their satisfaction.

For many women, there's an ongoing, never-ending feeling of despair. Women with a sense of learned hopelessness feel that their life is destined to be terrible, and they *know* it's never going to get better.

Women have the external burdens—financial or legal problems, disaffected kids, dependent parents, a demanding job—and on top of those, they shoulder all the internal burdens—"I'm not good enough, smart enough, caring enough to even begin to tackle all the jobs I have to do."

What's the solution? Could we do it all if we had more time? Is that we don't apportion our time correctly? Is it that we just don't know how to let someone else take over? (Of course, we're certain that no one is as capable as we are, so we might as well do the whole thing and get it right.) Or is the real issue that we have no idea what would get us to stop the clock, just for a little while, so that we could relax and assess where we are and where we want to go?

WHAT IS STRESS?

Stress is our perception of an event or an experience as difficult, threatening, unpleasant, or challenging. It motivates us to become aware of our reactions and either change the situation for the better or succumb to it. Getting stuck in traffic produces stress (we want to get where we're going and we're thwarted), but so does getting married (it feels deliriously wonderful, but will the flowers arrive on time and will we stay in love forever?). Being bored is stressful, and so is having too much to do and too little time to do it in.

When we're forced to adapt to some circumstance or feeling either that we've conjured up inside ourselves or that others have forced us to deal with, the hypothalamus, or master gland in the brain, sends hormonal messages to our adrenal glands to produce stress hormones.

These substances—*adrenalin, noradrenalin,* and *cortisol*—help to increase the activity of the sympathetic nervous system. Consequently, when we feel stress, our respiration, perspiration, heart rate, and blood pressure accelerate, our blood vessels and muscles constrict so that we feel tense, and our pupils dilate and hearing becomes more acute (the better to see and hear the enemy!).

The pioneer of stress research, a doctor named Hans Selye, discovered as a second-year medical student that hospital patients—no matter whether they had a broken ankle or cancer—all displayed the same anxious, overburdened, exhausted feelings. The longer they had no control over their situation, were made to eat hospital food, take hospital meds on hospital time, go to sleep and wake up when told to do so, the more miserable they became.

Selye found that being stressed happens in three stages. First, we experience the *alarm* phase, when we become aware of some difficulty and the stress hormones are released. Then, we come to the *resistance* phase, where the body mobilizes itself to fight the stressor. Whichever organ system is the strongest rallies all its forces to do battle, until eventually, the *exhaustion* phase sets in. At this point, when the systems can't keep up under such enormous pressure, the person might become terribly ill, or even die. Stress-related illnesses, according to Selye, are "diseases of adaptation," because we are such malleable creatures. It's usually considered good to be adaptable, but in fact, this process can lead to our ultimate destruction.

Further research into the stress response has proved that Selye didn't have the process exactly right. Rather than exhausting our resources and stopping the production of "fight or flight" hormones, the body actually accelerates the outpouring of these hormones. The protective stress response becomes damaging to the system, depleting the immune system so that we can't resist any disease that comes along.

Luckily, however, you can control the stress reaction if you know its habits and patterns. As soon as you perceive something stressful going on, you can either allow it to overwhelm you (your muscles tense, your heart races, your palms sweat, you develop a knot in your stomach). Or you can stop stress in its tracks—by thinking about it differently, avoiding it entirely, or employing a variety of interventions to combat it that will be detailed in this book.

What you want is balance—you get stressed; you relax so that you can combat the next stress that comes along. The problem arises when you're stressed all the time. When every little incident is fraught with anxiety, when you can't have a conversation without flying into a rage, when you're trying to juggle twelve jobs in the time it takes to do two well, your stress level never gets a chance to diminish. Your radio dial is always tuned on high, and you feel strung out, wound up, and overwhelmed.

And that's when the danger sets in. Although the 1997 *Annual Review of Psychology* by Ronald Kessler states that it is "uncertain whether stressful life events promote psychiatric disorders," it is a proven fact that too much stress lowers the ability of the immune system to combat illness—both physical and mental. When the blood pressure remains high and the muscles stay knotted, you risk a heart attack or chronic back and neck pain. When you can't sleep at night because you're so worried about what went on during the day and what you're supposed to do the following day, you never get down to the deeper stages of sleep that allow the body and mind to heal.

Fortunately, you can learn to break the stress cycle anywhere along its path. You can take charge of your reaction and calm yourself down. The minute the boss walks into the room, and you look at his face, you can turn around your perception of him as mad at *you* to just plain mad. And if you see it that way, you wouldn't come up with the notion that he was going to fire you, and you'd never get sweaty palms.

The trick to managing stress, then, is to find a new way to look at life and yourself. The ten-step plan I outline in this book will help you do just that.

YES, VIRGINIA, THERE IS GOOD STRESS

One of the most interesting qualities of stress is that's it's an equal-opportunity oppressor. Biochemical changes occur in the mind and body whether you feel great or miserable. It doesn't really matter whether you are taking off on an all-expenses-paid cruise of the Mediterranean, or being approached by a mugger in a dark alley—your hypothalamus, pituitary, and adrenal glands do exactly the same rhumba.

When you have a lot of terrific things happening—moving to a new house, falling in love, getting your picture in the newspaper, speaking in front of several hundred of your colleagues at a conference—you are still under stress. This type of *eu-* (the Greek word for good) stress is certainly more pleasant to deal with than the lousy *dis*-stress that comes with getting fired, going through a divorce, or hearing that your child is going to jail. But your body handles the experiences the same way.

WHY STRESS IS DIFFERENT FOR MEN AND WOMEN

Do women really have more stress than men, or do they just talk about it more? It's true that women are better communicators—when something is wrong, they'll immediately get on the phone with a friend or stand at the office water fountain and complain. They cry. They rant and rave. And this response can be both positive and negative when it comes to managing stress: it allows the expression of the emotions, but sometimes takes them overboard and makes the experience worse than it might otherwise be.

Men, on the other hand, tend to smother stress. They put on a brave face and distract themselves so that they can overcome their panic or worry.

Let's examine the three ways of handling stress. When something rotten is happening in our lives, we can close our eyes and avoid it, we can fret about it and expand its meaning to crisis proportions, or we can sit down and come up with problem-solving strategies to deal with it. Men are more likely to avoid a problem—at least a short-term one—and get busy doing something else (having sex, going out for a drive in the car, and either playing or watching a sports event are primary distractions for men).

Women, on the other hand, are more likely to think about the problem, turn it over and over, discuss it with a friend, and kick themselves for what they did or didn't do in order to tackle it. This often results in prolonging their sadness or discomfort about the problem—and it doesn't solve anything. Women tend to engage in *polyphasic thinking*—they mull over dozens of things at one time instead of one thing at a time—which pulls them away from the sense of centeredness and focus that could act as a calming mechanism in their lives.

And women's predilection for empathy can increase the problem. We are usually affected emotionally not only by our own stress, but also by others' stress. We *feel* a child's pain; we get furious when a friend is laid off for no apparent reason. Many of us take on the stress of the world as though it were our own. And that means we are afflicted with many different types of stress than our male counterparts.

Women are doubly stressed—at home as well as at work—which is quite different from the male experience. When stress hormone levels are measured in the workplace, men's and women's levels tend to be about equal. At the end of the day, as men leave the hubbub of the office and come home to wife and family, their blood levels plummet. They are relaxed and comfortable as they start the home-based segment of their day. Even if the kids are screaming and the phone is ringing, and there are dozens of chores to be accomplished, men feel good. They're in their cozy retreat, and they're playing the role that gives them security and control.

For women, it's an entirely different story. The worker at the office gets into her car or on her train, and immediately begins thinking of everything she has to do when she gets home. On her way, she has to get to the market and pick up something for dinner, get her daughter in day care and her son at soccer practice, check on her invalid mother. Finally, when she gets home, she has to prepare the dinner, oversee the homework, field the phone calls. Her hormone levels are just as high—or higher—than they were at the office because she comes home to a second full-time job.

Another twist on this duality is that most women are incredibly invested in their relationships. According to a study done by Dr. William Malarkey, an endocrinologist at Ohio State University's Institute of Behavioral Medicine, women can't stand fighting with the one they love, and the distress colors everything else in their lives. Women's stress hormone levels rise after an argument and stay that way for twenty-four hours. The men in the study, having "vented" their anger, are able to get their stress hormone levels down within minutes.

It's understandable, then, that men fare far better than women when they're married. They get to enjoy the benefits of a coupled, familial relationship, whereas for women, wearing a wedding band turns out to be a lot more work, a lot more hassle.

But in the long run, women actually manage stress better than men. When dealing with really serious chronic events—the death of a spouse, or loss of a job—they rate higher in their ability to adapt. When the stress goes on for a long time, women shoulder the burden well. They report that when things remain bad and are out of their control, they are able to muster the energy to keep going, keep living, despite their feelings. Men, who may be able to handle the everyday nitty-picky problems pretty well, often fall apart when the stress seems unending.

Why is this? One reason is that women have a lot of great assets at their disposal. Women are more responsive to touch than men, so a massage or back rub or just plain old handholding can start to calm a woman down more easily. Women tend to react more quickly to pain than men—and although this would seem to be a mark of weakness, what it actually means is that we start taking care of ourselves sooner to alleviate our discomfort before a crisis hits. Women tend to exhibit lots of stress-related symptoms such as colitis/irritable bowel, mitral valve prolapse, migraines, and TMJ, but we'll go to a doctor to have our problems checked out; men, on the other hand, hold themselves together on the outside, but the infrastructure may be crumbling without their knowledge. Such ignorance can lead to a heart attack or stroke.

We may come to the third alternative for handling stress—problem-solving—only after exhausting the possibilities of the other two methods. In other words, we can learn from negative coping what *doesn't* work, and then move on to some concrete steps, such as those suggested in this book.

Women tend to be molders of their own fate and with the right motivation and guidance, can learn to handle stress-related problems successfully. By taking charge of our stress as only we can, we have the potential to heal whatever ails us.

IS IT ALL IN THE HORMONES?

Women are constantly ragged about their hormones. When they get weepy or irritable, men ask if it's their time of the month, or alternatively, whether they might be pregnant. When they're older, they get asked if they're going through the change of life. When women act nervous or upset, scared or tense, their hormones are blamed once again.

Actually, the production of estrogen and progesterone, which are responsible for mood changes over the menstrual cycle, are protective when it comes to stress. Women's gonadal hormones have been shown in many studies to inhibit the production of stress hormones. This means that younger women in their reproductive years are protected somewhat from the ravages of the stress response, but after menopause, their reactions and hormonal output come to equal that of men.

It's not surprising, since our sex hormones are triggered by the same master gland in the brain that sets off the stress hormones, that when we're under a lot of pressure, our menstrual cycles get out of whack—we may miss periods, have excessive cramps and bleeding, and have difficulty getting pregnant if we're trying too hard.

A lot of life events that occur only to women center around some great hormonal change. Think about how your body matures at puberty—the first menses and the budding of tender sore breasts can be very hard on many girls. Then there's the stress (both good and bad) of becoming pregnant and carrying a baby to term. This is followed by postpartum pressures, when the body valiantly attempts to get back into hormonal balance. Midlife, too, can be a challenge for some women, particularly if they suffer from hot flashes, vaginal dryness, or other markers of menopause.

But it's important to remember that it's not just the biochemical blasts you're getting that make you feel stressed out. Puberty is a time when your life is in total flux and you are alternately deliriously happy and miserably lonely; pregnancy fills you with the joy of bringing new life into the world and also reminds you that there is a small human being totally dependent on you; menopause can offer the excitement of a new job or life after divorce, but at the same time it may be the first occasion you have to ponder the meaning of aging and death.

Stress is multifaceted—clearly, it's not all hormonally based. Whether you excrete a lot or a little adrenalin, no matter how fast your heartbeat gets, laboratory measurements can't register the fine, subtle shadings of response that we have when we're stressed out.

SYMPTOMS THAT MEAN YOU'RE STRESSED

When you tell someone that you're "totally stressed out," what do you mean by that? You feel tense and anxious, your stomach is in knots, and you're either too hot or too cold. Your heartbeat and respiration come quickly—maybe you can't seem to get enough air when you breathe. You may have clammy hands, headaches, an increased urgency to urinate, diarrhea or constipation (or both), or a tense neck, or you may stammer or have difficulty framing your thoughts into words.

And all of that is just physiological. Your behavior may change as well. Maybe you become forgetful or confused; you just can't pay attention to details. Your sleeping, eating, exercising, and lovemaking patterns become erratic or vanish completely. You go on crying jags, or find yourself snapping at everyone for no apparent reason. You blame others for your rotten mood, and you blame yourself for being so hard to get along with. Your self-esteem slips to new lows.

As your mind spirals around various anxieties and problems, the connections the brain makes to all the body's systems start unraveling as well. One of the worst stress reactions is the decline of your immune system. You spend a tense afternoon in your lawyer's office hammering out custody details and voilà, you spend the next four days in bed nursing a cold. Then the tax bill comes from your accountant, and suddenly your allergies flare up. These feelings and events are all related.

The accumulation of stresses over the days, weeks, and months wears down the ability of the body to produce those substances that normally protect us from foreign invaders (such as bacteria, viruses, fungi, and the whole array of antigens floating around us at all times). One particular element that keeps us healthy is immunoglobulin-A antibody, and according to several studies, this is precisely the stuff we don't make enough of when we're stressed. A study at Carnegie Mellon University in Pittsburgh shows that we double our risk of catching cold when we're perennially under stress. Researchers asked healthy adults to fill out a questionnaire that rated the amount and quality of stress in their lives. All participants were then given nasal drops that had cold viruses in them and the group was quarantined for five days. Forty percent of them—those with the highest stress ratings—became ill. In other similar tests, the participants' saliva was measured for that magic elixir, secretory immunoglobulin-A. The less they made, the greater the likelihood that they would catch cold.

The stomach is a particularly good place to study stress management because we actually have a secondary nervous system, known as the *enteric nervous system,* right there. This network of neurons, neurotransmitters, and proteins works independently of the brain and central nervous system to produce a variety of feelings. When you feel distress and anxiety, the brain in your head tells your adrenal glands to release stress hormones, and these in turn stimulate the gut's brain. Colitis and irritable bowel syndrome are symptoms of problems in this secondary brain.

So it's vital to your general health to learn how to calm down. More than just feeling "okay," you can actually take care of some chronic physical complaints at the same time.

THE GRAVE NEWS ABOUT LONG-TERM STRESS

Colds, headaches, stomachaches, and allergic reactions are unpleasant, but they won't kill you. Stress, however, is more insidious than a cold or a bout of diarrhea. Long-term, unrelieved stress can create such a decline in the responsiveness of the body that heart disease and cancers may develop. And because being chronically ill for long periods of time is extremely stressful, a vicious cycle may develop that can makes it virtually impossible to heal.

Heart disease is the number one killer of men over 50 and women over 65. There are dozens of contributing factors—certainly a high-fat, low-fiber diet, no exercise, and poor preventive health care are the most common offenders. Overproduction of the stress hormones and hyperstimulation of the sympathetic nervous system increase your risk of heart disease. When you experience the "fight or flight" syndrome—feeling that you must either run away from or combat the enemy—you raise your serum cholesterol, decrease your vascular flexibility, increase your blood pressure and cardiac output. If you're always stressed, you're doing this all the time, putting a terrible burden on your cardiovascular system.

Women are at high risk not only for heart disease, but also for a number of different cancers—breast and colon cancer topping the list. Certain families are rife with genes that are out of whack and set off wild cell growth that leads to tumors that can kill. One possibility as to why certain people get cancers and others don't is the theory of the carcinogenic personality—someone who is helpless, hopeless, pessimistic, and self-hating. In truth, heredity counts for a great deal, as does our polluted environment. But whatever the cause, fear of the illness, the illness itself, and the treatments for it are incredibly stressful.

Any long-term illness, from heart disease to cancer to AIDS to arthritis to kidney failure to COPD (chronic obstructive pulmonary disease), can change you totally. Your life very often centers around being a sick person—because that's how the medical system sees you and treats you. The trick is to retain your identity in the midst of your illness. You are not a cancer, you are not a lung that can barely take in oxygen—rather, you are a woman with a life and interests that may range from gourmet cooking to whale watching.

Everything is interconnected. If you're feeling blue, you won't think as clearly, you may get a migraine, and you will have trouble cheering yourself up. Physical, mental, emotional, and spiritual stress links together and overlaps.

But by the same token, fix your mind-set about how you feel and what you're going to do about those feelings, and the whole picture gets rosier.

ARE YOU ADDICTED TO STRESS?

We complain about how lousy we feel because of the burdens we carry around each day, and how we'd love to chuck it all and run away to a desert island. But how many of us would actually survive without the stress to which we've become accustomed?

The truth of the matter is, you may already be physiologically addicted to stress. Although it's damaging to be pouring out stress hormones, it's also exciting. As a result, your brain is incredibly stimulated—when you're stressed, you get a rush that's hardly comparable to anything else in your life.

Then, when the episode is over, you crash. True, you're not harried and tense anymore, but you probably feel washed out and limp. Instead of being pleased that you've conquered the stressful experience, you're actually bummed out. So what do you do? You go looking for another experience that will, once again, take you over the top. Then you feel up, all systems go, your pistons firing one after another.

How can you tell if you're addicted? Generally, you have a problem:

- If you're always on the lookout for conflict in your life
- If you get angry quickly at the least little thing (true, you don't consider it "little," but others, more rational than you, do)
- If you're always in a hurry
- If you work too much, and actually spend more time working than you do at leisure activities or home with family and friends
- If you blame others and yourself for things never being right

- If you need to control every situation
- If you're unhappy even when things are going "okay"
- If you come down with a lot of minor ailments like headaches, backaches, and stomachaches
- If you abuse alcohol, nicotine, or other drugs
- If you constantly feel overwhelmed
- If you look older than you are (come on, be objective now!)

An addiction to stress, like any other addiction, can be broken. But you have to acknowledge your craving before you can start to do something about it. It's all right to say out loud that you need your stress, as long as you're motivated and committed to learn how to manage it. Like a wild animal, stress isn't dangerous when you can train it to lie down and roll over.

AGGRESSIVELY STRESSED, LAID-BACK AND BORED, OR MOTHER TO THE WORLD?

In the 1960s and 1970s, when stress research was in its infancy, investigators found it convenient to label people's personalities as stress-prone or stress-free. All of the early research was done on men, because men were the ones keeling over from heart attacks, and the largely male medical world was determined to fix the problem. (Women can suffer from heart disease for years, but typically don't experience a lethal attack as a first symptom.)

The researchers determined that certain individuals were Type A's, characterized as aggressive, hard-driving, hard-working, angry men, and others were Type B's, who were seen as laid-back, easy-going guys, generally calm in the face of disaster and not susceptible to stress.

In the 1980s, these descriptions were found to be lacking. Obviously, people's reactions to stress are a great deal more varied and idiosyncratic. And at this point, women were given equal opportunity to be stressed out and were included in the previous categories as well as two new ones. Harriet Braiker, author of *The Type-E Woman*, identified a third kind of stress-filled individual as the person who tries to be "Everything to Everyone"—the over-doer—and other researchers coined the "Type AR" woman, who was anxious and reactive. She catastrophizes every incident that occurs—which means that the most benign event is interpreted as the end of the world. Her stress response never takes a break, and she is beside herself most of the time.

As we learn more about our adaptations to stress, these types show themselves as a lot more varied than previously thought. Naturally, none of us fall into just one category. At certain times, we may have feelings and reactions that are typical of any of those four types just mentioned. And there are other criteria for your stress triggers, depending on the sort of person you are. Whatever your basic personality, you will see benefits as well as risks when it comes to stress. Because we have within us the possibility for change, we can use the qualities inherent in our personalities to manage the stress we do have.

THE MOST COMMON PERSONALITY TYPES AND THEIR STRESS PATTERNS

You may be:

- *A Leader.* If you are usually self-confident, competitive, and on track with your life, a woman whom others look to for mentoring and guidance, you probably have a lot of stress, but you manage it well. The downside is that you may be prone to hypertension and heart attacks. The upside is that you may be so driven to get back on track and renew your life, you recover quickly from trauma and tragedy.

- *A Thinker.* If you take each situation that occurs and dissect it intellectually, you will only be stressed in situations where emotion is really more appropriate and you can't literally "think" your way out of things. Your stresses will be challenges, but you enjoy working hard for your rewards.

- *A Feeler.* You not only feel deeply for yourself, but for everyone around you. Each situation you encounter is fraught with trauma or tragedy—because you put it there to begin with. When you empathize with everyone in the world, you do make more trouble for yourself, but others love you for it, and that boosts your self-esteem.

- *A Comfortable Joiner.* You are relaxed to begin with, although you may lack focus and direction. You let other people suggest pathways, and you follow along most of the time, because you see no reason to buck the tide. You can become bored and lackadaisical, and you may have little sense of self-worth, which can be very stressful. On the other hand, when you learn to take charge of your life, you can be very nurturing, patient, a good judge of others, and someone who evolves slowly as she grows.

- *A Sensitive Sister.* If you take everything personally, if you cannot stand criticism because it makes you feel like a failure, you are simply too touchy for your own good. The fact is that whatever happens is not always your fault, and you can alleviate a lot of stress in your life by forgetting about blame, especially the blame you put on yourself.

- *A Star.* If you are a star, you want to be the center of attention at all times. You know how to rally people to your cause, and exactly what to do to get the ball on your side of the net. You may care a great deal about how you look (both in terms of your physical appearance and also how you're perceived in any situation). For this reason, you may create stress where it doesn't even exist. But getting the accolades of the crowd may calm your inner demons and may be worth the effort to you.

- *A Helper.* If you recall the reactions of the Rabbit from our story at the beginning of the chapter, you'll understand the Helper. She is self-sacrificing and put-upon, and she just can't say no, no matter how much she has to do. This can make her feel as though she has no control over her life, that life is manipulating her as though she were a puppet on strings. But when she learns to manage stress, she can be altruistic, open and giving to others, and able to accomplish many tasks well.

- *A Worrier.* Are you constantly overwhelmed with stress, always thinking the worst, always sure that the sky is falling? The Worrier relives every awful event and usually embellishes the details so that they become more horrifying and difficult. And she anticipates disaster when she thinks about the future. But as she learns to take hold of herself and practices stress management techniques, even she can reduce her stress levels. She can become a very aware individual, clear about her own reactions and able to stop them in their tracks, before they accelerate.

You may find that you fit a few patterns—or all the patterns at different times. No matter our type (or combined types), we are all prone to stress—we just have different triggers for it. Most women are always under routine stress because they play so many roles and therefore feel hassled and crunched for time and space. But the more you know who you are, the easier it will be to manage the stress you've got.

Complete the following questionnaire to find out what your stress triggers are:

Are You Stressed?

I find that I...	ALWAYS	SOMETIMES	NEVER
1. Move, walk, and eat quickly	❏	❏	❏
2. Find it hard to keep from finishing others' sentences	❏	❏	❏
3. Feel guilty when I do nothing for several hours	❏	❏	❏
4. Feel guilty when someone else completes one of my chores	❏	❏	❏
5. Think about what went wrong at work three days ago	❏	❏	❏
6. Shrink back if someone challenges me or my ideas	❏	❏	❏
7. Think about my kids getting in trouble while I'm at work	❏	❏	❏
8. Try to do two or more things at once	❏	❏	❏
9. Worry that I'll be alone if I don't seem to agree with others	❏	❏	❏
10. Find myself pounding the table to make a point	❏	❏	❏
11. Worry that others won't like my ideas	❏	❏	❏

I find that I…	ALWAYS	SOMETIMES	NEVER
12. Say yes to everyone, even if I don't feel like doing what they ask	❏	❏	❏
13. Try to get everyone to come over to my way of thinking	❏	❏	❏
14. Habitually clench my jaw or grind my teeth	❏	❏	❏
15. Blame myself for any personal defect or emotional difficulty	❏	❏	❏
16. Try to smooth over any difficulties with my spouse, kids, or boss	❏	❏	❏
17. Find that I can't really enjoy myself unless I'm doing something for someone else	❏	❏	❏
18. Find that I analyze situations instead of experiencing them	❏	❏	❏
19. Let others express their opinions, because what I'm saying just isn't that important	❏	❏	❏
20. Keep trying to schedule things tightor and tightor co that I can get more done	❏	❏	❏

If you answered "Always" to more than ten questions, you are under a great deal of stress and badly need to start on a program of stress reduction. If your "Always" score is between five and ten, you would do well to work on several different methods of healing yourself.

If you answered "Sometimes" to more than ten questions, you are doing pretty well at managing, but could certainly stand to relax more. If your "Sometimes" score is between five and ten, you are right in the normal range—we all react strongly to certain triggers at certain times.

If you answered "Never" to more than ten questions, you are very healthy. Keep up the good work. A "Never" score between five and ten is pretty good, too!

Remember, too, that as you adapt to stress and learn to cope more effectively by using the ten steps outlined in this book, your basic type may change or combine with another type. They are all part of you—don't be afraid to acknowledge them.

EMOTIONS LIKE MAGIC POTIONS

Women are not just busy with chores and activities; they are also striving to make sense of some very large issues that are extremely emotionally charged. Unlike routine stressors, the big events and feelings are never really taken care of—they're ongoing and tend to cause both anxiety and elation.

Take a minute to think about how these forces affect you. Are you pleased because you're a creative person who feels a lot of love for others? Are you busy overcoming some tough life influences but now feel on the road to success? Are you caught in between rage and happiness most days, so that sometimes you feel split between two distinct personalities?

We can sketch the most important (not necessarily in descending order of importance):

- *Creativity.* You would like very much to add something to this universe. Whether you feel your forte is artistic (writing, music, art) or intellectual (discovering the cure for cancer, reading all the Great Books), or simply being a genius at calming a child's rage or coming up with the perfect birthday present for a friend, you know that you have some unique spark no one else shares. The more you can cultivate this attribute, the more you can rely on it when you're feeling overwhelmed.
- *Love (romantic and other).* You have the ability to look beyond your own concerns and take in the warmth and affection of others. You may be married to someone who "clicks" with you, you may watch your sleeping child and feel the blessing of being connected, you may open your heart to your best friend who does the same for you, and you may cherish your parents even as you see their faults and foibles. Your open heart and ability to care for others makes you bigger and better than you

could ever be on your own. And knowing that you have so many out there rooting for you means you have support when you're in need.

- *Success.* You don't have to have money to be successful, although it's a nice bonus. Your idea of success undoubtedly has evolved over the years. When you have real purpose in your life, and a set of goals you'd like to achieve, you know that you're successful—even if you don't get to the top of the heap in society's estimation. If you don't set your sights on one specific goal, you have a lot more chances to achieve things you never thought possible. Success can be a fickle master, because if you're always dissatisfied with not having your version of it, you don't ever get to appreciate the successes you've already garnered—and that can make you mad and sad.

- *Life influences.* Maybe it was a trip to Rome when you were in college; maybe a teacher who turned you onto Chinese philosophy or the cello. Maybe it was a homeless person lying on a city street who made you feel you had to do something to make the world an easier place to live in. Or maybe it was a rotten, abusive marriage that you escaped from, thankfully leaving you free to start over. Things happen to you, but what's more important is that you shape them so that they become the warp and woof of your life's fabric.

- *Hopes and fears.* Luckily, we can always dream. Unfortunately, some of those dreams are nightmares. We can't let ourselves get bogged down by either one. When you learn to manage stress, you see that you have good reason to hope and less cause to fear. Your spirit gets stronger as you let it tackle harder challenges.

- *Femininity/sexuality.* The attachment we have to our femininity is partly what gives us our unique sense of self. Our sexuality is a driving force throughout life that can add vitality and energy to each day, regardless of what difficulties we may be in the midst of. When we are admitted into the close-knit (though sometimes jealous and backbiting) society of women at puberty, we know exactly what it is that makes us powerful and makes others look to us for comfort, support, and pleasure. Nurturing our feminine aspect can go a long way toward alleviating stress and tension in a situation.

- *Mothering (or lack of it).* Everyone has a mother, although we don't always get the amount or kind of mothering we crave. Whether we relate closely to the person who brought us into the world, whether we mourn her (because she's not there now or never really was), or whether we've selected a substitute, this person is a rock in the foundation we build as women. We need someone who listens objectively, who gives us advice or withholds it because she knows we can decide for ourselves, who laughs and cries with us, and who, in a pinch, can be called on to hand over the cookies and milk (literal or figurative).

- *Vanity.* Much as we hate to admit it, we're all pretty vain. We compare ourselves to advertisements of women who look nothing like us, we agonize over pimples at puberty and wrinkles at menopause. Vanity isn't a bad thing—it's part of what gives us a sense of self-worth, and makes us want to look better so that we can feel better, too. If we can temper our vanity with a little reality, it can give us the strength we need to get through bad times.

- *Rage.* We all have the right—perhaps the obligation—to feel righteous anger. But if we don't express it, and it boils inside, it can turn to rage, and this is a very destructive emotion. Understanding that we have the capacity to tear off and scream and protest against injustices done us is a useful step in the journey toward self-knowledge. But we don't have to use that ability. Controlling our rage and applying it only when absolutely necessary goes a long way in any stress program.

- *Happiness.* And this is the crux of the matter. We all want happiness and aren't really satisfied unless we have it—and how often is that? If we were happy all the time, it wouldn't seem like bliss, but rather like going to the market for milk—same old same old. Striving to be happy isn't much of a goal; the idea is to find the happiness in each moment, even if it's not conventionally terrific.

The big pieces of the puzzle keep shifting as you grow and change. But when you put them to work for you, you can sometimes see the smaller stressors in better perspective.

How Do You Feel?

There is no "right" answer to any of these open-ended questions. They are merely to provoke some interior thinking that may start you on the path to being more aware of your strengths and joys as well as your weaknesses and stresses.

1. How do you feel right now?

2. What are you thinking right now and how can you relate that to your feelings?

3. How would you describe yourself?

4. How do you see your future?

5. What kind of work do you like?

6. What kind of leisure do you like?

7. When do you feel most yourself?

8. How have you changed since puberty? In what ways are you exactly the same as you were as a teenager?

9. What kind of people do you respect?

10. How are you different from or similar to your mother? To your father?

11. What goals do you have for yourself?

12. What are your greatest strengths?

13. What are your greatest weaknesses?

14. In what way might you work on those weaknesses to modify them so that they could be managed?

15. What would you be proud to have written on your tombstone?

THE OUTER YOU, THE INNER YOU, AND THE OUTSIDE WORLD

Stress bombards us from all quarters—which means that we have to strike back on the same field. *Break the Stress Cycle* will give you the battle plan you need to manage and cope with the stressors in your life, and to enjoy the fulfillment and creativity of using your mind, body, and spirit to heal.

Let's look first at what happens on the outside. The *outer you* has dozens if not hundreds of obligations, as wife, mother, child to an elderly parent, Girl Scout leader, town selectwoman, chauffeur, party-giver, laundry-doer, etc. You have to fit in all these jobs and do them responsibly every day, even when you don't want to. So on the outside, you have to discover ways to:

- Decide what's really crucial and in what order the tasks should be done; and manage your time so that you're not rushed
- Change negative coping patterns that may be holding you back—being a workaholic, neglecting your health, mismanaging money
- Let others pick up the slack—because you can't do it all
- Set goals that you can really meet—today, tomorrow, and five years from now

Once you've taken care of the practical details that can make the "outer you" function smoothly, you can move inside. The *inner you*, which remains unseen by most people who know you, may have to cope with feelings of inadequacy, sadness, confusion, rage, or jealousy. So on the inside, you need to retool the way you react to stress. You can:

- Learn how to relax and pamper yourself
- Learn how to breathe again
- Get centered with meditation
- Increase your capacity for sensual and sexual experience

And then, when the outer and inner you seem to have some balance, you can add on the support of *the outside world.* When you stop believing that you are an island unto yourself and allow others in, you can alleviate a great deal of stress. Sharing burdens is a skill women must learn. So you can:

- Make sure that your family pitches in regularly
- Seek professional help if the previous stress-management steps aren't making enough of a difference for you

You can use good and bad stress, inner and outer stress to your advantage when you realize that you can handle them—perhaps not immediately, but over time. There are many ways to deal with every type of challenge you have to meet, whether it's an acute problem, like your child coming down with chicken pox on the first day of your new job, or a chronic one, like going into bankruptcy.

The ten-step program that follows will give you the tools you need to chill out, calm down, and soar ahead.

THE TEN-STEP STRESS/SUCCESS PLAN

1. Identify the stress
2. Modify behavior
3. Delegate responsibility
4. Plan reasonable goals
5. Find a passion
6. Learn to breathe
7. Meditate
8. Increase sexual pleasure
9. Enlist family support
10. Get professional help

Ten steps. That's all you have to take to make your stress manageable! And you don't have to take them all together—you may implement one at a time, adding on elements of others as you wish. The three-level attack of the steps, however, is important—it's vital that while you're working on the outer you, you also get in touch with the inner you and, in addition, enlist support from the outside world.

Practice is the key element in the stress-management program. Each step will offer several skills you can learn that will help to accomplish the step itself. The more you practice these skills, the more capable you will be able of meeting small and large challenges in your life, and consequently, the more stable, content, and energized you will become.

These steps are tools that anyone can have available—but as with any activity you want to master, you must do a little every day to build stamina and proficiency.

HOW TO USE THE TEN-STEP PLAN

Start by glancing down the steps and see which ones in each category seem most like you. You should begin by taking one step from the outer you and one from the inner you. For example, you may be a goal-oriented individual, so Step 4 might jump out as a good place to start. Maybe you figure you breathe all the time, so it can't be too tough to pick up the specialized breathing techniques—in that case, Step 6 is the place you want to start.

Read only those steps and begin to practice the skills outlined for you. Make sure that as you approach a stressful situation, you take a little time seeing how these two steps can be called into action to reduce your feelings of pressure and discomfort.

Keeping a journal is a very helpful way to find out exactly what you did and how you felt in any given situation. Write down the ways in which you've used the techniques and whether they worked or didn't. If they made a difference, bravo! If they didn't help, don't despair. There is no quick fix for stress—it takes a lot of time to alter ingrained reaction patterns. This program can't "cure" what ails you, and it will take a real familiarity with all the steps before you can start to heal some of the thornier problems you'll encounter.

When you've got your first two steps under your belt, select two more, one from the outer you section, and one from the inner you. Add these on for daily practice. Again, use a journal to check yourself and chart your progress with the four steps.

At this point, you should also start to add on the more advanced steps. You will probably have realized on your own that Step 9 is essential now, because you can't do it all by yourself—trying so hard to be Superwoman is part of the reason you may be stressed out to begin with. You need others to help you along the way.

Now you can add on the final steps in each section. Undoubtedly, the ones you select last are those that seem the most foreign to you, and that you may assume won't be as helpful. On the contrary, doing something you've never done before, like meditating or behavior modification, may change your whole attitude toward stress. Because you have a beginner's mind and have no old habits to unlearn, these steps may in fact take you in a direction you never anticipated. And that can feel very good indeed.

If you have tried and practiced all the steps and still feel crushed by the stress in your life, it is time to consult a professional. The last step of this program encourages you to reach out when you need to and to select a therapist who may be able to give you some guidance and hope that you could not find by yourself and start you on the road to self-mastery.

Remember to have fun with these steps—play around with them to your heart's content. Don't get bogged down in details, but instead, allow yourself to improvise around the set techniques. You know, when you first learn to play the piano, you have to get the fingering and the notes correct. But after that, you can allow your imagination and your spirit to take over, so that music flows from *you*, regardless of where your fingers sit on the keyboard or what notes you play.

The same is true of this program—make it your own, and then have a ball with it!

Part I

The Outer You: Practical Techniques for Taming Stress

On the outside, it all looks so simple. You get up, you do what you have to do, and you ignore the things you can't or don't really want to fit in. You work a job, you manage a house or apartment, you interact with loved ones—both those you're related to and those who are connected because of bonds that developed over time.

But it's not that easy, is it? You get bogged down in the middle of one task and can't get on to the next. You try to do everything, or get overwhelmed and don't do anything. You feel like you're slogging through an endless swamp, and you don't even know what you want to find when you get to the end of it. What should be an easy task turns out to be like Sisyphus's rock—as soon as you haul the thing to the top of the mountain, it rolls back down and you have to start from scratch. And each time, it's a little heavier.

There *are* ways out of this quagmire. In this section, you will learn the basics of self-management: how to set priorities and budget your time, how to delegate responsibility, how to achieve reasonable goals, and, perhaps most important, how to change the behavior that has so far led you down the High Stress trail. With these essential skills at your fingertips, you will be able to cope better and relish each moment more.

Step 1 Identify and Prioritize Your Stresses

Marge started getting up at 5 A.M. after her second child was born. At first, she did it because it was nice to have the house to herself and to have the luxury of sitting with a cup of tea, sketching the sunrise or just watching it. Her husband, Alan, told her he envied her this nice respite before the hustle and bustle of daily life began. But after a few months, she stopped enjoying the quiet. The annoying little drill sergeant in her head was ordering her to get cracking and do something with all this extra time. So she cut to the chase and started her day at five. She certainly had enough to keep her busy.

She'd fold the dry clothes from the previous night's laundry, put in a new load, make bag lunches for herself and her husband, feed the dog and cats, and then get to her desk to do a little work. She'd glance through the paper as soon as it came at six, but looking at what was going on in the world just made her anxious.

"I was juggling so many roles at home, at work, with my parents and Alan's, feeling guilty about having two kids in day care, and I couldn't say no. Whenever someone asked me to be on a town committee, I'd say, 'Sure,' thinking I could manage it. If some lady in my church said she was desperate for someone to organize a bake sale, I'd feel pressured into it. I guess I didn't think I deserved to rest at all. And every time I added a new chore to my full platter, I got these looks from my husband. He was really upset with me, and claimed that even on weekends or late at night that I wasn't ever there for him—whatever that means. I said, hey, look, see, I'm here! But that would just make him sulk.

"Alan's five years younger than me—sometimes I think he's such a kid. Well, we were both pretty immature before the kids were born and our parents wanted us to be accessible all the time. In those good old days, we used to take day-long bike trips or go to the shore or stay up real late and go listen to jazz in bars. But we never do that stuff anymore—our conversation is strictly from the how-to-get-things-done school of communication. I'd say we're still in love—jeez, I don't even know what that word means anymore—and we do have some kind of glue sticking us together, even if we don't talk about sharing goals and world views and all that lofty stuff you talk about when you're young.

"It's just that…sometimes I feel so pressured, I feel like I'm the only one here. Like I'm disconnected from him as well as everyone else. We live our life together like we're making battle plans—you go here and do this, I'll go there and do that. Whew! As you can imagine, romance doesn't enter into it.

"And work stresses me, too. My job isn't stable—I'm an administrative assistant at a VA hospital, which means I never know when I might be laid off or have to take a salary cut. I also have a really temperamental boss. Some days he's tickled pink about my work; other days, he threatens to replace me with a temp and save the government a bunch of money, not that my salary and benefits are so princely. So I feel like I have to please him all the time, which is ridiculous, but that's how I am. I never thought I'd end up as a paper pusher. I've always loved drawing because I can pour my emotions out on the page—in school, I was sure that I would do something with art. So here I am, nowhere near what I really wanted to do with my life, and I feel cheated.

"The next area of stress is my kids. I wanted to be a mother so much, and when they came, I was depressed. Really depressed. The noise and crying and mess and no sleep. It was like, 'Is this all? Can I handle it if I don't love them to bits every minute?' I feel like I hardly know them, and that makes me feel so guilty. I have this niggling suspicion that I would be a better mother if I had the luxury of not having to work. I'd have some idea of who they were and they'd know me and come to me first.

"But that's not how it is. The sitter saw them both take their first steps, and the older one talks a mile a minute to her, but barely gives me a word. Like every working mom, I'm split about staying home and going out of my mind (I know that I would!) or working to pay for their day care. Is that a double bind, or what? I finish up a hard day at work, pick them up at the sitter's, strap them in their car seats, and one's bawling and the other needs a diaper change—and I realize I have to go to the market to get more. There's no break between the job and home—I feel the tension mounting when I leave the office and get in my car.

"Sometimes I have palpitations in heavy traffic—I imagine maybe I won't get to the sitter by 5:30, she has to go somewhere, and I'll arrive and my kids will be gone. Just thinking that makes me frantic.

"Then there's the parent problem. (Do I sound like I'm complaining a lot?) My mother-in-law's on dialysis, and every day's a new crisis. She gets bad in the middle of the night, and says she can't breathe, and my father-in-law rushes her to the emergency room. My own mom is frail and lives alone in the city—she refuses to move to a senior housing complex, and she's terribly depressed and lonely most of the time. We end up spending weekends driving back and forth between the parents, trying to make sure the kids have their naps and get fed.

"I feel like crying a lot of the time. I'm only 33 and I feel so old! I didn't think life would have so few perks. I need to organize myself better and take it easier. Maybe there's stuff I could cut out of my life—but what? It all seems urgent and important—even though it means nothing to me."

There is no pause in the action, no time away for a breather. All the things that might give Marge a break—her early morning reveries, her kids at the end of a long day, her love of drawing—have become additional burdens to her. The quiet time in the morning is now taken up with chores; the children are out of sight and out of her emotional reach most of the week. And she can't give them her undivided attention because of her needy in-laws and mother. Her marriage seems functional, but just barely, because she's not present and accounted for when her husband wants to be with her.

What to do? When Marge started having palpitations, she felt really scared. It made her realize that *nothing* was as important as how she ran her life. And she wanted to stop running her life—it would be better if she walked it. So she decided to make some changes. . . .

The first step is the hardest.
—MARIE DE VICHY-CHAMROND,
MARQUISE DU DEFFAND

IF YOU CAN, LET GO; IF YOU CAN'T, DEAL

There is no simple solution to the issues that make up your life. Just when you think you've licked one problem area, you move ahead and discover there are three new ones you have to handle. As you live longer in the world, you accumulate experiences—some that may be a wonderful and others that can be exceptionally stressful.

I've explained before that the stress cycle can be halted anywhere along the line. One particularly effective means of dealing with the pitfalls of stress is to walk away from it. This is, of course, not as easy as it looks.

If your child comes home and reports that an older kid took his lunch money, you can't ignore the problem. If your elderly father tells you he's fed up with being sick and is thinking about suicide, you will move heaven and earth to see that he gets help. Although these situations are very stressful and fill you with anguish, you can't avoid them.

On the other hand, you can let go of some of the garden-variety stresses that have previously turned your stomach into knots. You don't have to have a fit over too much starch in your shirt collars, lousy drivers, a neighbor who wants you to trim a tree that shades his property, gaining five pounds, or losing a night of sleep. All of these unpleasant experiences can be shrugged off when you begin to practice the ten-step plan in this book.

Because, in the great scheme of things, *they are not that important.* By dividing up the very crucial from the not-so-crucial, and then by subdividing once again to get the top priority separated from the very crucial, you will begin to find ways to save time and reduce stress.

Let us start with taking an inventory of where you are and what you actually do. Start by making a wheel that will indicate what your roles are—then block in the time you have to spend on each part of your life.

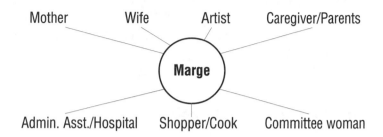

Mother   Wife   Artist   Caregiver/Parents

Marge

Admin. Asst./Hospital   Shopper/Cook   Committee woman

All of these seven roles have within them subroles with specific duties:

Mother: Nurturer, Disciplinarian, Playmate, Organizer, Listener

Wife: Partner, Friend, Lover, Organizer, Listener

Artist: Visualizer, Creator, Emotional Mediator

Caregiver/Parents: Listener, Organizer, Nurturer, Cheer-bringer, Health-Care Proxy

Administrative Assistant: Listener, Organizer, Thinker, Phoner, Speaker, Team Player

Shopper/Cook: Organizer, Decision Maker, Creator, Crowd Pleaser

Committeewoman: Speaker, Organizer, Note-taker, Phoner, Petition-Writer.

It is interesting to see that "Organizer" and "Listener" are part of almost every role that Marge plays—and if you look at your own life, you may find the same is true. If you're doing a couple of essential things well in this one role, you can let some others go. As you scan your roles and the obligations connected with them, see what you can and can't control, and then start winnowing down the list. Maybe you don't have to spend an hour nurturing your parents on the phone tonight because you'll see them at the hospital tomorrow; maybe you can skip the committee meeting where no important decisions will be made, and instead go to next month's meeting, where policy will be set.

There is one very important omission from this chart. Before anything else, Marge is a *woman* and a *person*. She has to eat, sleep, go to the bathroom, have doctor's appointments, go to the movies, smell flowers, make love, smile, cry, and do all those other things that can get shunted aside when she's trying to play so many other roles. How can she make time for what's essential? How can you?

There are dozens of things you can eliminate from your day—and from your life. All you have to do is use your organizational skills to figure out where you're wasting valuable time.

HOW TO MAKE THE BEST USE OF TIME

Dost thou love life? Then do not squander time; for that's the stuff life is made of.
—BENJAMIN FRANKLIN

If other people are using your time, it's not your own any more. This means you have to make some judicious choices as to what you'll cut out.

- *Telephone.* If it rings and you're right in the middle of something, don't answer or let the machine pick up. You can set phone hours that are convenient for you and get back to whomever it is when you're available.
- *Television.* Limit your viewing, or at least combine it with exercise. You can ride a stationary bike or rowing machine, or stretch on a mat in front of the set.
- *Errands.* Do them all at once in one swoop around town. Whenever possible, allow other people to come pick up things from you instead of you going to them.
- *Shopping.* Try to avoid getting into stores on weekends or right after work. Shop first thing in the morning when no one is around and avoid the lines. You might also consider catalogue shopping, which you can do on the phone or by mail. These days, many supermarkets have "on-line shopping," where you select items on-line and the store delivers without extra charge if you spend over a certain amount. You can save at least an hour each time (not including driving to and from the market) if you shop by computer.
- *Kid's homework.* Don't sit with them to prod them into action; instead, encourage them to try to work things out and promise you'll be available if they really need you at the end. If there

are some problems they think they can't do, go over all of them at once.

- *Separate work and home concerns.* When you're at the office, don't keep calling home—and vice versa. If you must split your attention, do it at one time of day, say after lunch, when you answer your e-mail or return phone messages. If you really need to speak with the sitter or your mom or your husband, do it then.

ARE THERE REALLY ONLY 24 HOURS IN A DAY?

We all say, "I just don't know where the time went." If you don't know, it's time to find out.

It's a good idea to keep a time diary (just as people often keep a food diary when they're trying to adjust their caloric or fat intake). Let's actually review your daily routines to find out where your time went. The following list is a suggestion—you will have to make your own to conform to your schedule. When you are so busy you feel that you have to do several things at once, you probably aren't doing any of them particularly well.

ACTIVITY	TIME SPENT	ACTIVITY	TIME SPENT
Eating	_____	Drinking	_____
Sleeping	_____	Exercise	_____
TV	_____	Telephone	_____
Computer/e-mail	_____	Reading	_____
Personal hygiene	_____	Studying	_____
Working (job)	_____	Meetings	_____
Hobbies	_____	Meditation	_____
Conversations	_____	Shopping	_____
Household chores	_____	Driving/commute	_____
Listening to music	_____	Movie/video	_____
Paperwork (lists)	_____	Cooking	_____
Waiting on line	_____	Sex	_____
Procrastinating	_____	Nothing much	_____
		Total hours:	_____

After you've kept this list on a typical day, a light day, a really heavy day, and a weekend, sit down and count up your minutes. You may be astounded at the time in your "procrastinating" or "nothing much" column. Now it's time to set some priorities—see if you can cut a few minutes here and there on activities that are not really important, or aren't helping you manage your stress.

Work on repatterning your days and nights, then complete the lists again in a few weeks.

Obviously, in real life, you don't count minutes—you just live. When you're really into what you're doing or thoroughly enjoying yourself, time doesn't even enter the picture. But this exercise will force you to be economical about the things that have to get done, so that you can give more of yourself to the things you'd like to do.

Time the destroyer is time the preserver.

—T.S. ELIOT

TIME BITES

In a recent survey of how people of all ages, of many professions and different walks of life actually used their time, it was found that no one—not even the unemployed—had any free blocks of time.

What people did find were pockets of time—little "time bites" of fifteen minutes here and a half-hour there. Never enough to make a five-course meal or to complete a thousand-piece jigsaw puzzle, but just enough time to watch a rerun of a sitcom on television. This, of course, is why the clever media folks structure programs with breaks every ten or fifteen minutes.

Instead of wasting more time, it's possible to take these pockets and get some real action accomplished. You may not be able to pre-pare a banquet, but you can pre-prepare parts of dinner (many cook-books break their recipes into segments of intensive labor, after which you can let the ingredients rest for several hours and finish right before you eat). You may not be able to finish a puzzle, but you can get through an exercise tape or do some yoga postures. You can always fit in a little check- or e-mail writing, or sit down with a chapter of that book you say you never have the time to read.

When you decide to manage time, you are cutting off a big chunk of your stress. The hardest thing is to choose between activities and to know when to do what. We know that the best way to handle stress is to chop it into its smallest components. If you are going crazy because of so many demands on your schedule, you simply have to take the schedule in hand and be its boss instead of letting it be yours.

There really is time in your day—it may just not be apportioned the way you'd really like it. Stop being so fussy and consider what you have a gift. Then go spend it on something meaningful to you.

Time will rust the sharpest sword,
Time will consume the strongest cord;
That which molders hemp and steel,
Mortal arm and nerve must feel.
—SIR WALTER SCOTT

MAKING MAPS

It's an old stereotype, but women get lost and ask directions at the nearest gas station. Men would rather jump off the Brooklyn Bridge than admit defeat, so they tend to wander around until they find a landmark they know, and then proceed to their destination.

Better than either solution, however, is to have a map. If you start out knowing where you're going and have reference points along the way, you feel confident, and you remain on top of the situation. You travel fifty miles, decide whether to continue straight or veer off on a side trip, then go another fifty and stop for something to eat and to look at the scenery. You have your ultimate goal in mind, but you can always make choices along the way—to linger in a city you really like, to go out of your way to visit a friend, to abandon your original plan and go somewhere else—or to turn around and go home.

This is as true in life as it is on the highway.

Let us say you are having trouble getting your six-year-old daughter to go to bed on time at night. You begin with nagging and demanding, and you each get furious, butting your heads against the problem without getting anywhere. You change course and allow her to stay up really late one night—and of course, she's dead tired the next day and can't function. You change course again, and offer a reward—if she goes to bed without fussing four nights in a row, she can stay up on a weekend night.

If you begin without a map, you may get lost, and that's not a terrible thing—but you can avoid a lot of hassles if you know where you're going before you begin. A little planning goes a long way and saves on frustration, anger, and stress.

TIME SPENT ON STRESSORS

Just as you made a diary of things you do and time you waste, so you can make lists of your stresses in order to identify and prioritize them.

The hardest part will be dividing the stressors into two categories: the crucial and the less crucial.

ABSOLUTELY URGENT	LESS IMPORTANT
Mother's dialysis	Car trouble
Divorce	Shirts ruined at cleaner
Death of favorite neighbor	Didn't get invited to party
Selling the house	Child adjusting to new school
Broken leg	Dog has fleas

All right—the lists look self-evident. But if you are honest, you will admit that there are times when you judge the party invitation or problems with your car as top priority. (Naturally, if you can't get to work because you need a valve job you can't afford and you're in danger of getting fired, you must move "car trouble" to the other side of the page.)

You can surely see other differences between the two lists—you can physically *do* something about your dog's fleas and your shirts; if you wait long enough, you'll be invited to someone else's party; children adjust to new situations better than adults. But you have to wait for a broken leg to heal just as you do a divorce; your mother won't suddenly regrow a kidney and get off dialysis.

The great "Serenity" prayer, adopted by Alcoholics Anonymous, begins: "God grant me the serenity to change what can be changed, to accept what cannot be changed, and the wisdom to know the difference."

As you get better juggling stresses, your eyes will see them differently, and you will begin to judge them objectively, giving them appropriate weight and the type of attention they deserve. When you are really in the swing of stress management, you will actually be able to ignore some stresses completely until such time as you've taken care of those at the top of your list.

COPING WITH TIME PRESSURE

We are all familiar with negative coping techniques because we resort to them on a regular basis: we may cry, scream, blame someone else, blame ourselves, reach for a drink or a cigarette, or sit and stew over the problem and alienate ourselves from others who are trying to help.

Positive coping techniques are abundant, but sometimes, in a pinch, it's too hard to do something really good for yourself. Keep this list handy and try each technique at least once. (You can also use them in combination.)

- Set limits—learn to say "no"
- Stay in the present moment—don't beat yourself up about the past or future
- Live each day as a new day
- Smile (even when you don't feel like it—it's catching)
- Keep a journal
- Admit when you're wrong and when you're right
- Listen attentively
- Plan alone time and really use it
- Stop rescuing people
- Take breaks

Finally, keep in mind that you are the only one responsible for yourself—if you expect someone else to make it "all right," it will never happen. Making a commitment to being your own mentor and guide will help you cope with the toughest problems.

You are eternity's hostage: A captive of time.
—BORIS PASTERNAK

TIME TO LET GO

When you're completely pressured, when the day seems to eat up the hours you need, this is the best time to stop what you're doing (probably ten things at one time!) and let go. There are several proven skills you can practice that will make a huge difference in the way you feel the next time you're overwhelmed. The following exercises are physical routes to relaxation; for mental and spiritual routes to the same destination, see Steps 6 and 7.

Relaxation Response

Herbert Benson, the director of the Body/Mind Institute at Harvard Medical School and Beth Israel Hospital, found that when certain conditions were present, anyone could alter normally involuntary physiological responses.

You can do this, too. All you need is a quiet environment, a comfortable seat (either cross-legged or in a straight-backed chair with your feet flat on the floor), an object you can concentrate on (this could be a word such as "peace" or "one," or your breath going in and out), and a passive attitude, letting whatever may happen, happen.

Inhale through the nose, exhale through your mouth. Close your eyes and sit quietly, focusing on your word or breath. Sit for five minutes the first few days, building up to ten and then fifteen minutes.

Take your pulse before and after this exercise. You may be astonished at the results.

> . . . [He] shows his intelligence, if any, by his ability to discriminate between the important and the negligible, by selecting here and there the significant steppingstones that will lead across the difficulties to new understanding.
> —HANS ZINSSER

EXIGENT TENSION REDUCERS

If you are going out of your mind, about to scream or throw something, you need a quick release.

Clench your fists, hold for a count of ten, then release. Do this five times.

Inhale, then blow the air forcefully out your mouth. Repeat five times.

Drop your head into your neck, then slowly roll it around, first to the right, then to the left. Keep breathing as you circle.

Stop wherever you are and use your imagination to place yourself somewhere else—a beautiful, peaceful location like the seashore or on top of a mountain. See yourself in this scene.

SKILLS FOR BETTER PRIORITIZING

Organization

Know where everything is. If necessary, set aside a few days to get yourself together. Organization is a lot more than a Filofax and a household system—it involves the way you think about yourself and your many jobs.

Organize yourself. Decide that from today on, you will get to bed before 11 P.M. and rise before 7 A.M. If you're starting up an exercise plan, give yourself an extra half-hour (that means a 6:30 wake-up) before the rest of your day begins. You also need to organize yourself around making shopping lists, going shopping, and cooking foods that will get your stress levels stabilized.

This is not as hard as it sounds. A well-structured day—even a nicely balanced wake-up, including some meditation, visualization, or a brisk walk or jog—will give you the motivation to eat better, respond more calmly to stress, and stay on top of your many activities.

Organization lets you breathe. As soon as you come out from under your piles of "stuff" that sit around, you have room to maneuver. Periodically, throw out what you really don't need. It means getting your kitchen in shape for the most efficient means of moving around it and finding things when you absolutely have to get a meal on the table. It means going through your kids' rooms (preferably with your kids) and getting a system for clothes, books, toys, schoolwork, etc. And it means going through your own desk so you can discard projects that you've abandoned.

You also need to organize your day. This means you have to first decide you know what's *important* enough to write down. Time-savers for the early morning rush might be:

- Taking your shower, laying out your clothes, and making lunches the evening before
- Making a list of errands and chores for the following day
- Setting the coffee or tea system to start perking while you're in the shower
- Giving everyone a chore—one person feeds pets, another gets breakfast foods on the table, another grabs up the dirty laundry from the previous day and dumps it in the hamper or starts a load of wash.

Trash Day

This exercise in getting rid of problems is a wonderful release. First write down each problem and worry you've got on a small piece of paper. Fold each one individually and make a stack of them. Then, one at a time, take them over to the wastebasket. After you've read your problem aloud, spend ten minutes coming up with a solution, even if it's just short-term. Then, let go of it. You don't need it any more. You've dealt with it, just by thinking about it, and you can now tear it in half, and in half again—then discard it.

You may want to have trash day once a week, just to clear out your head.

The more you relinquish your stressful patterns, the more positive coping skills you'll be able to use. And then, you'll find, it's much easier to make a commitment to changing your behavior. That's the next step.

Step 2 Modify One Behavior

L ois looked at the cake and turned away. Then she did a double take. She could have *sworn* the cake winked at her. Was she going out of her mind? She held her breath for a minute and turned around, looking at it again. Why had she allowed Karin to bring it over for the meeting so early in the day? Now she had to sit with it, a viper in her kitchen, until the girls got here.

She went back to the den to read, but found her mind wasn't on it. In a little while, she got up and went to the desk in the corner, where she'd stashed a package of peanut-butter crackers. When they were finished, she realized she was ravenous, and opened the bottom drawer in the TV cabinet, which held the emergency chocolates. And once she was finished with those, she was on edge, so agitated, her hands shook. It wasn't fair! She tried so hard and she'd eat just three tiny meals a day, and then she'd get a phone call like the one from the lawyer's office about her divorce this morning, and it would set her off.

"By the time the gang came over, I was on a binge. I'd eaten nearly everything in the refrigerator and all the food I'd hidden around the house. That was a lot, and it should have satisfied my hunger, but I couldn't stop thinking about what everyone had brought to the meeting tonight and the leftovers I could have when they were gone. There would be twelve women—if they all left a part of what they brought, that meant twelve different dishes."

That night, after the group left, Lois ate herself into a stupor. She was dizzy and nauseated, and fell down before being able to reach her bed. She knew, finally, that she had to get help.

"Yes, I was obsessed. I was miserable and angry at my estranged whatever you call him—I certainly wouldn't dignify him with the label of 'husband'—but I had more respect for myself than to lose control like this. I was sick of myself and determined to do something about it.

"I'd never talked to anyone but my sister, Betsy, about my reactions to stress. Because she's an alcoholic and has been going to AA meetings for five years, I know she understands. She was really sympathetic—but tough on me—and said this was the time. I *had* to go to OA meetings (Overeaters' Anonymous) or I was going to kill myself with food.

"So I went. I have fought compulsive eating all my life. Whenever I'm really stressed, like before exams when I was at school, when I'm going on a job interview, when I got married, when my mother died, and now, with the divorce crap hovering over my head, I just dive into food. My mouth becomes the focus of my whole day—I look at it in the mirror, I run my tongue around it, I put lip gloss on my lips, I swallow a lot. It's a visceral physical release—like I want to scream and yell a lot of obscenities, so to cover it up, I shove something inside it and start chewing. It only helps for a while, though. As soon as I've swallowed whatever it is, the anger and fear and sadness well up again and I have to shove it down with more food.

"I was incredibly skeptical when I started out at OA. I couldn't stand the idea of getting up in front of people and talking about my 'eating problem.' But I found a lot of really interesting women there, all from different backgrounds, all with the same type of issues as mine. I felt like maybe there was something here for me, too. At first I just sat back and listened. I got a buddy, and I'd call her every night to talk about what I'd done during the day and what I'd eaten (and what I wanted to eat, but didn't). I liked the idea of 'letting go' of my hassles and giving them over to a higher power. I'm not a religious person, but somehow, that made sense to me.

"Slowly, I started changing. I wrote down everything I was going to eat the day before I ate it. I bought a new set of measuring cups, and they became my higher power. I cleaned out all the areas where I used to hide food and put something else there. I brought into the house only the food I intended to eat for the next two days. Every time I was in a horrible mood, I went to a meeting instead of to the convenience store for a stash of candy.

"Yes, I slipped a few times. My behavior around food was so ingrained, I was amazed. I would dream about swimming in melting ice cream or chewing on an all-day chocolate chip cookie. I'd wake up sweating.

"I guess the thing that finally hit me after going to all the meetings and getting as nutsy about eating right as I had been about eating wrong was that I actually *needed* to scream and cry. I wasn't *supposed* to cover up the bad feelings and choke down the sobs with food. When I really expressed my anger in words, I didn't have to think about stuffing myself or comforting myself with a substance. Over a period of six months, I found times during the day when I actually didn't think about food at all. I was delighted to see that I had a real brain that reacted to stressful situations by handling them rather than denying them.

"Changing my behavior around food changed my attitude about eating; changing my attitude made sticking to the healthful behavior easier. You don't get one without the other. There are still times when I get these cravings, but I drink a glass of water or take a long walk or go to a meeting, and then I'm fine. I think I'll be fine now forever, and guess what—I really enjoy eating again! It's not a crutch but, instead, a way to nourish myself."

You may not be fighting compulsive eating the way Lois is, but if you are currently using coping mechanisms that increase rather than decrease your stress, this step will be a crucial one for you. Whether you use alcohol or recreational drugs or sleeping medications when you're overwhelmed, or take a cigarette, or drink endless cups of coffee, or pull your hair or chew your nails, or watch too much television or engage in compulsive gambling or lying, or self-destructive relationships (sexual or otherwise), you must know that you are not stuck. You don't have to keep doing what you've been doing just because it's the only way you know how to function right now.

You can change your behavior, just as Lois did. All you have to do is change your mind first.

> *Many people believe that by simply improving*
> *a problem, they are taking sufficient*
> *action...But don't set your goals too low.*
> *Aim for full freedom from your problem.*
> —JAMES O. PROCHASKA, JOHN C. NORCROSS,
> CARLO C. DICLEMENTE, *CHANGING FOR GOOD*

WHY WOMEN INVOLVE THEMSELVES IN DESTRUCTIVE BEHAVIORS

As I mentioned in the introduction, it's a common pattern for women to take stress inside and make it such an intricate thread in the fabric of their personality that it becomes normal, expected, terrible but unavoidable. In a valiant effort to ward off the effects of feeling rotten or angry or depressed or overwhelmed, many women grasp at any comfort that will take them out of their distressing moments. If you feel furious at the world, impotent at your job, and completely out of control in your relationships, you long for a way to take back the reins.

For Lois, eating was certainly not a way to nourish herself; rather, it was a punishment and reward rolled into one. It was her way to take charge of life. Her hidden foods, her compulsive need to cram things down her throat, her disgust with the way she felt and looked were all part of the vicious cycle in which she was trapped. She felt bad, so she ate, which made her feel worse, so she ate to feel better. She filled up the empty void inside with food, not realizing that she was really digging a deeper pit into her rage and depression each time she binged.

This is also true for you if you are relieving tension by doing something unproductive for the body, mind, or spirit, even though you know that you shouldn't. When you first experiment with a negative behavior—lying, drinking, drugging, gambling, promiscuous sex, hitting your child—you convince yourself that it just happened once, and you used it for a reason, and you won't have to do it again. But the next time you're under pressure, you remember how easy it was to take the burden off. And each time you use this behavior to stop the racing thoughts or quell the bad emotions, it works. Eventually, it becomes a pattern. Doing the same negative behavior over and over becomes routine, and the onus of whatever you're doing eventually fades. The normalcy of habit takes over, and because it provides momentary respite from stress or depression, the activity is welcomed and accepted.

---

*Life is its own journey, presupposes its own
change and movement, and one tries to arrest
them at one's eternal peril.*

—LAURENS VAN DER POST

THE STRESS OF COPING

If you have a sore on the right side of your foot, you lean to the left when you walk to take the pressure off. When you are very stressed-out, you'll reach for anything that will alleviate that type of pressure. The feelings are unbearable, so you want to get rid of them as quickly and painlessly as possible.

The coping mechanisms that people develop spring from a deep well that contains within it elements of our past, our personality, the people who influence us, and our beliefs about what we can and can't accomplish in life. So for some, being depressed drives them to drink, for others to binge eating, for still others, to taking it out on their kids. Certain coping mechanisms evolve early in life because they are the best method we can come up with to help ourselves—for example, Lois found that eating was the only thing that would calm her down when she was a child and felt lonely or hurt. But when we outgrow this mechanism, it becomes self-defeating rather than helpful. There are dozens of negative behaviors we've done for years that take the stress off—and yet, ironically, performing them adds a great deal of stress to our lives.

Even when we rationalize or deny our problem behavior, underneath, we feel guilty or anxious about what we're doing, and that sense that we are making things worse brings us even more stress.

How do we stop it? Some people need therapy to get them on track. Others need a momentous, perhaps life-shattering event that acts as a wake-up call. At a point when we are in danger of doing real damage to ourselves or others, we come to our senses and realize that we have to change.

WHY CHANGE BEHAVIOR?

Because change is so difficult, many people give up before they start. Their mantra, repeated dozens of times is, "I *can't* change. This is me; this is how I act; this is all I know."

Can't is a funny word—it rolls off the tip of the tongue, and people use it constantly. It has powers beyond the linguistic. The more you say it, the more you believe it.

On the other hand, *can* is much more difficult to say because it involves commitment. It has a kind of teeth-gritting determination to it that often seems beyond the capabilities of normal, stressed-out women.

But the desire to change must take hold before change can occur, and that is what turns the *can't* to a *can*. If you start out with determination, carving a path for yourself and making sure you have alternative strategies and specific ways to implement them, you can stay on track as you begin attempting to alter behavior.

The key to successful behavior change is to take it slowly, one small element at a time. Do everything in moderation. Cold turkey approaches are evidently necessary if the behavior you're trying to change is killing you (alcoholism or drug addiction), but nearly everything else, including smoking cessation, works better if you first modify rather than eliminate your behavior.

WHAT IS BEHAVIOR CHANGE THERAPY?

According to behavior theory and therapy, the actions we perform are controlled by environmental contingencies and our personal learning history. If you got your mouth washed out with soap every time you used an obscenity or were caught masturbating, you learned that there was something shameful about sex—talking about it or doing it. Your behavior might have gone overboard as you dared your parents to punish you, or you might have held it all inside, thinking the forbidden but feeling guilty whenever you indulged in it.

In this type of therapy, behavior is examined in the context of the individual and his or her environment. Rather than spend years lying on an analyst's couch, you can do something concrete to make a gigantic difference in what you do and the way you do it.

This is a rational, reasonable method of reducing stress—look at the underlying beliefs, not the emotional traumas. With behavior change, you can bypass the difficult feelings and do something constructive to change them.

Behavior is triggered by impulses in the brain, and the brain itself responds to the various chemicals it produces. Some of these chemicals make us feel positive, eager, and energetic. Others make us feel miserable and hopeless. When we impulsively commit an act that we know from past experience and social expectation is "bad," such as stealing or committing adultery, we punish ourselves with a flow of neurotransmitters that increase guilt or deaden pain.

But when we actively change that behavior to something we consider "good," like giving money to someone who badly needs it or ending the affair, our brain gives us a literal pat on the head by allowing serotonin (the neurotransmitter that fills us with a sense of well-being) to flow. We feel good. And that becomes our incentive to keep up the good work. We continue the positive behavior because we like the way it makes us feel and expect to feel that way again in the future when we do this behavior.

USE COGNITIVE AWARENESS TO RELABEL YOUR THOUGHTS

Why do we have to persuade ourselves to do things in a way that will brighten our lives? This is where the cognitive awareness comes in. Most of us are programmed to listen to old "tapes"—the memory of a critical parent, a teacher who humiliated us in front of the class, a boyfriend who berated us for everything we did. As long as we believe the old voices, and don't counter with any new statements of our own, we are doomed to repeat the words and the actions that go along with low self-esteem and poor self-image. Those key words, "should," "must," "always," "never," "ought," usually come unbidden as an automatic reaction to a stressful situation. But when we change our thinking, we can alter our behavior.

If you tell yourself that everyone is out to get you, or that you're fat and ugly and that's why you can't get a date, or that you have no self-discipline and that's why you can't stick to your diet—sure enough, all those will become self-fulfilling prophecies. When you seriously believe that you can't change your behavior, you really can't.

Cognitive awareness highlights your negative thinking patterns. It makes you aware of the odd tricks and stubborn beliefs that we cling to. "I couldn't exercise today because I had to drive my daughter to school," or "a couple of puffs on a cigarette won't hurt me because I never inhale," are two examples of *stinking thinking*—that is, making your thoughts permit the behavior. If you always react in the same, automatic way with a thought such as *I'm a loser, I'll always be fat*, you have nowhere to go but down.

We think the way we do because of a personal belief system that we have honed over the years. See how this type of negative thinking can change reality:

> *I have no control over my eating.*
> *I'm so fat that not eating what I want now will not help anyway.*
> *There is no other way I can feel better except to eat.*

Obviously, with this type of information flowing through your brain, you can't make a move in a positive direction. Your thoughts may not only be negative, but may lead you in a self-defeating circle. For example,

> *I have to eat when I'm a little blue—I have low blood sugar.*
> *If I don't keep some candy or snacks around the house and office, I could have a fainting spell.*
> *The weaker I feel, the less work I can do—my boss could fire me.*

This amazing chain of thought leads from eating to compensate for depression to saving one's job! Though it makes no sense at all, it's something many of us do routinely in order to justify inappropriate behavior. The maladaptive thinking—automatic, negative, or self-defeating—keeps you stuck in old habits.

In order to turn your head around, you must follow a detailed course of action:

1. Become aware of your negative feelings.
2. Identify each inappropriate thought.
3. Look at the real facts of the situation and compare them to your feelings about what happened.
4. Test the new premise to be sure it holds true.

5. Stop thinking in black or white—there's always a middle ground.
6. Put the picture in perspective: other people are involved, not just you.
7. Come up with a rational solution to your problem.

In order to become aware, you have to break down the ideas into their individual components. Let's say your boss has just told you that he's sending your immediate supervisor to the annual meeting to present the new project that you've just worked so hard on. You go home that evening and start to raid the refrigerator as the negative thoughts overwhelm you:

He hates me because I'm fat.
I shouldn't be seen in public.
No one pays any attention to my ideas—all they see is my body.

In order to stop your bingeing in its tracks, you must first see that you are soothing yourself with food because you're "hungry" for the appreciation you deserve.

Once you've become aware, you can identify what's the matter: you think this is a personal affront rather than a business decision. From here you can look at the real facts—your supervisor will be at the conference anyway and they'll save money on a plane ticket and hotel room; also, no one else at your level in the company does these presentations. You can then test the hypothesis that no one listens to you by talking to the boss about another idea of yours, or asking other employees whether he reacts in a similar way to their ideas. This will help you to see a middle ground in between your black-and-white feelings about rejection and acceptance. Now you can put the situation in perspective and perhaps come up with a rational solution: asking for written credit for your project at the meeting.

The next time you are impelled to eat to assuage your bad feelings, stop and identify the element in the event that just occurred that triggered your hunger. Link it with the emotions you feel—are you sad or mad, angry or frustrated, etc.? Examine your thinking in the light of these feelings—what are you really trying to say?

Relabel the event, dealing only with what actually happened. Substitute rational responses for your irrational ones, then think about something else for a while.

When you have figured out how you think, it will help you re-evaluate the way you behave.

Meet is it changes should control
Our being, lest we rest in ease.
—ALFRED LORD TENNYSON

HOW TO SUCCEED AT BEHAVIOR CHANGE

There are a few prerequisites for doing well at this—and anyone can accomplish them. In order to make a commitment to change, we must:

- Know what we want
- Stop blaming others and events for our behavior
- Control our emotions
- Improve our self-esteem by doing something active that will make us proud of ourselves
- Make changes slowly, one day at a time, one element at a time
- Expect obstacles and be prepared for setbacks
- Reach a plateau without feeling that we have to give up

If you chart your behavior, you can't lie to yourself. You can't say you consumed four carrots instead of the whole bag of potato chips, or that you ran three miles instead of lying in the hammock for an hour.

Keep the following record for a week—*without making any attempt to change or modify your behavior.* If you're a smoker, for example, write down exactly when and why you took that cigarette. Did you do it because your best friend criticized your new haircut, or because you had a cup of coffee and you always smoke when you drink coffee? Did you do it out of boredom, habit, panic, or some other reason?

Make sure you note the times of day when you are most prone to succumb—usually first thing in the morning or last thing at night, during stressful moments, when you're waiting for someone or something to happen, or during a break, especially when socializing with other people.

Before you take that cigarette, ask yourself if you really need it, or if there is some other activity (drinking a glass of water, walking around the block, calling a friend) that might do just as well.

When you know exactly *when* you are at your weakest and you know exactly *why* you're falling back on the negative behavior, you have a greater chance of stopping midstream.

It is essential, if you are currently feeling pretty down on yourself, to do something that will increase your self-worth. You could volunteer in a literacy program, tutor a teenager after school, or do some shopping for an elderly person in your neighborhood. The kind of warmth and praise you will get will slowly begin to change your own view of yourself.

Probably the most important factor in succeeding at behavior change is forgiveness. You cannot do it all at once; you can't expect yourself to turn into a paragon of healthy, stress-free living overnight when you've been struggling with these issues for years. Be kind to yourself, and accept your limitations. But continue to expect great rewards as you learn more about the process of change.

THE SPIRAL OF BEHAVIOR CHANGE

James O. Prochaska and Carlo DiClemente, pioneers in this field, tell us that change is a process. Not only can you not change overnight, you can't even maintain change the first time—or the fourth time— you implement it. You must be patient and persistent, and eventually you will accept the new behavior as the norm. But you must travel many steps before you reach that goal.

Precontemplation

In this stage, you're clueless. You don't know that you're an alcoholic or a binge eater or a liar, and you have no idea that you're hurting other people and yourself. Even when your best friends tell you, you don't believe them because you're in denial. You minimize the problem and say you could give up this behavior tomorrow if you chose. But you should ask yourself, are you really just involved in this behavior because you prefer to act this way, or are you well informed about the pitfalls and dangers of this behavior and willing to be responsible for any consequences? The answers to those questions may spur you to move onto the next stage.

Contemplation

You are aware that you're doing something that may not be in your best interests—some days, you actually can say that you have a problem. This causes a certain kind of grieving—you regret the person you've been and you mourn the easy ways you've used for years to combat your depression, anxiety, or tension. There's a sense of loss when you think about giving up every comfortable tactic that you use to make yourself feel better.

Contemplation implies serious thought and decision-making. You have to balance out the way you've been taking care of yourself and the way you'd like to care for yourself in the future. Although you have no immediate plans to change, you think that maybe, someday, you could alter your behavior around this issue.

Preparation

In this stage, you admit that you are doing something that hurts you, and may hurt others as well. You make plans to change your behavior soon—perhaps in a month. Finally, you're confident of your ability to start the process, although you feel confused about how to begin. You hope for one magic first step you could take that would make the whole thing fall into place. Maybe, in preparation for healthier living which you intend to start doing in the near future, you might move your bathroom scale into the kitchen or buy a new set of exercise clothes. You should also set a date on which you're going to begin your process of change. Put it on the calendar with a big star.

Action

You've made a definite commitment, and you're starting right now. The first week can be the hardest because it involves a radical restructuring of the way you think about your problems and what you do to combat them. It also involves a lot of trepidation about the risk you are taking—by changing, you could fail, and then what would you do?

When you go into action, you may clear out the house of snacks, cigarettes, or alcohol. You might tell everyone close to you that you've started a new plan for living and you'd like their support. You might follow a meal plan designed by a doctor, or only eat when there is someone else to eat with you so that you can't binge or snack. When you are finally in action, you feel tentative but proud of yourself—you know you're on the right road.

Maintenance

After you have kept up your new behavior for six months, you can consider yourself on maintenance. This period also encompasses times when you fell off the wagon—perhaps losing control and eating crazily at a wedding, bumming a cigarette from a friend, or going to a bar and getting drunk after your mother died.

Maintenance is not the end of this process. As anyone knows who has ever been on a diet or tried to start an exercise program, or to quit smoking—you eventually stop taking baby steps forward and you get stuck. Plateaus are a natural, inevitable part of the process.

But we hate plateaus because they remind us of how fallible we are and how easy it is to flip back to the old, comfortable ways. You get tired and disgusted of being so "good" all the time when it doesn't really get you anywhere. You start up the patterns of irrational "stinking thinking." Hey, you say to yourself, if I'm working on time management, eating right and exercising, avoiding confrontations with my boss, and really listening and talking openly with my partner, I should be stress-free. Right?

Wrong. There is no cure for stress, and the more you learn about change, the more you understand this. But when you first begin the process, you can be overwhelmed by your plateaus. As a matter of fact, you may be so stymied by not going forward at a steady clip that you throw up your hands and fall all the way back to a precontemplation stage, where you deny you ever had a problem—or ever tried to change your behavior.

The behavior change process is often more dependent on repetition than on cognitive awareness or good feelings. The spiral that takes you from one stage to the next and then back to the beginning gets smaller each time you go through it, until finally, you stay on maintenance. Though you may have setbacks, you don't relapse again.

At certain revolutions all the damned
Are brought: and feel by turns the bitter change
Of fierce extremes, extremes by change more fierce.
  —JOHN MILTON

QUIZ: Why Do You Do What You Do—and Could You Change It?

Ask yourself the following questions. Although there are no right or wrong answers, carefully review your responses when you finish the quiz. If your responses indicate that your behavior is out of your control, you may wish to consider consulting a professional for help (see Step 10).

1. Do you discuss your behavior with others? Do you ask for their opinion or advice about it?

2. Do you perform your behavior in front of others, or is it something you always do alone?

3. Do you have certain rituals associated with your behavior? (A cup of coffee or phone call triggering the need for a cigarette; purchasing one particular food that triggers a binge?)

4. Do you perform your behavior when you're feeling depressed or pressured, when you feel really good, or both?

5. Can you go a day without performing this behavior? How do you feel at the end of that time?

6. Has your involvement with this behavior ever caused harm or embarrassment to anyone else?

7. What negative consequences do you foresee if you stop this behavior? If you continue this behavior?

8. What positive consequences do you foresee if you stop this behavior? If you continue this behavior?

9. Can you think of something else you could substitute for this behavior?

10. Have you ever made an attempt to stop doing this behavior? What was the outcome?

REMINDERS AND REWARDS

In order to get yourself on the road to behavior change, you must learn what triggers your negative behavior, what interventions will keep you away from that behavior, and what incentives will impel you to stick to your chosen path.

There are certain occasions when it's more likely that you will fall back on old, familiar habits:

- When you're really stressed at work or home
- When you're bored
- When you feel lonely and misunderstood
- When you've been working very hard and feel you *deserve* a break (cigarette, drink, sex, etc.)
- When you feel helpless and out of control
- When you experience any strong emotions, even positive ones.

In order to curtail the immediate negative response to your feelings, you'll need to come up with some reminders, or interventions, that will to stop you from doing this behavior:

- Try snapping a rubber band on your wrist or turning a ring on your finger when you feel impelled to revert to old behavior
- Keep a chart or diary of your behavior
- Give up your old haunts—places you used to drink or smoke with friends, places where you buy lottery tickets, or fast-food restaurants or candy stores if those are your problem behaviors—and stay away from friends who participate in this behavior with you

You may come up with a variety of incentives or rewards to keep you on your new path. Make sure you have a reasonable goal in mind to earn this reward (i.e., being on your new course for a month, overcoming certain major temptations):

- A new CD or book you've been wanting when you get to the end of your first week of change
- A new wardrobe or shopping spree to celebrate a commitment to a healthier body
- A night at a bed and breakfast with your signficant other
- A trip to a spa on your own, to pamper yourself

SETTING A QUIT DATE

It's well known in addiction treatment that if you stop abusing drugs cold turkey, you go into withdrawal. This true of most prescription drugs, too, and it's certainly true of behavior. It feels rotten not to chew your fingernails, or eat an entire quart of ice cream, or have a drink, or lie, hit your child, avoid an obligation (or fill in the blank!) when you need a release. You feel deprived and punished if you have to do without, and this makes you want your behavior more than ever.

The idea of *modifying* behavior, and changing it over a period of time, however, gives you the opportunity to see what it feels like to have just a little less of what you previously had. As you cut down gradually, you understand that it was not the behavior itself that was so important, but the use of it to alleviate stress and anxiety.

Eventually, as you modify the activity, you come to a plateau. You can only divide a cigarette into so many puffs. Finally, you have to give them up.

Once again, it's time to mark your calendar. Your quit date, just like your start date, is completely up to you. (If your problem has to do with eating, obviously, you are not ever going to *stop* this behavior. Rather, you will stop doing the self-destructive behaviors you do around eating, such as hiding food, bingeing, purging, and eating alone, that have become a repetitive pattern.) And you will find yourself asking the questions that will lead you to better coping mechanisms for your stress: How could I get more love? How else can I feel useful? What can I do if I'm bored?

You can give yourself four weeks to modify behavior and cut down, or six months (although your gung-ho enthusiasm usually diminishes proportionally over time). On the date in question, you will toss out all cigarettes and empty packs, or you will drain all the liquor bottles, or throw out the hidden food or coffee equipment. If you have the fortitude and stamina, this particular trash day will feel great because it will come at a point when you're absolutely ready.

Tell a few select people you've done it, and accept your deserved praise. Just remember that it is quite likely that you will fall off the wagon—but you are now strong enough to climb aboard again and begin your spiral of behavior change with more grace and humility than you did the last time.

SUBSTITUTING POSITIVE BEHAVIORS FOR NEGATIVE ONES

After you've removed the maladaptive behavior, you have a hole. And a hole craves to be filled up. Since it's just as easy to make a good habit as a bad one, your new task is to find great substitutes. There are dozens of positive, life-affirming ways that people manage stress, and any one—or several of them—will take the place of the behavior you've abandoned. You will simply substitute this new behavior for one old one.

When you want to binge, or drink, or have an illicit affair, think about the nature of this behavior. What does it really do for you? What else you could do that would be interesting, time-consuming, and fun? You want to do more than distract yourself—ideally, you'll find several pursuits that become real passions. For example:

- Play the piano
- Go for a walk or jog
- Read a book
- Call a friend
- Cook a healthy meal
- Make love
- Knit
- Listen to music
- Do a puzzle
- Surf the Internet

When you're developing new hobbies, you will understandably think about your old predilections. Sometimes you'll regret the old knee-jerk reactions, and sometimes you may hate yourself for committing to this beneficial change. But if you're honest with yourself, you'll admit that you feel better, less stressed, more in accord with others, than you used to. Change works if you work it.

SKILLS TO CHANGE THOUGHT AND BEHAVIOR

Make a Commitment

After a while, as you realize exactly what stresses you the most, you'll understand that you have to make a change. Once you know that you must modify your behavior, you have to commit to changing it. Whatever you say you're going to do, do it.

There will certainly be hurdles you'll have to overcome to get to where you want to be—the path will never be completely smooth—but you can change if you decide to. By making this choice, you take your goals out of the wishing category and turn them into reality. You don't have to hope and dream that one day you'll learn karate, or stand up to your boss—you will actually do those things.

Don't Procrastinate

When you have something that must be done, and you just can't bring yourself to do it, you start up a cycle of anticipation and guilt that adds on more stress to your already stressful life. It's very difficult to grit your teeth and stop smoking or end a destructive relationship or talk about money with your spendthrift partner, but it's actually harder on your system to hold off and not do what you intend to do.

One reason that we procrastinate is that we're afraid of failure. If you don't try something difficult, you don't have to find out whether you can do it or not. But if you intend to make a change in your life, the best way to start is by jumping in and doing it. Of course it's scary, but as long as you stick to your old mantra of "I can't," or even "I can't right now," you will never get anywhere.

The time is now. Make the effort.

Watch Yourself Be Yourself

The way out of maladaptive coping, first, is to sit back and be an observer of your own life. When you're upset and you start to cry or you reach for a drink or you go and mope in your room and won't talk to anyone, you aren't helping yourself. But these behaviors are ingrained—they feel like the right thing to do because you do them routinely; they are your comfort when you are feeling low.

Keep a journal of your good moments and bad ones, and write down exactly what your instinctive reaction is. Like the first time you hear your voice on a tape recording or see yourself on a video, you probably won't believe it's you. But as you become more aware of your knee-jerk negative behaviors, you will be better able to substitute actions that help you out of your trouble.

Step out of Emotion into Action

Every time you scream at your kids for leaving a mess, you're acting out of passion. The same is true every time your philandering boyfriend calls and you allow him to persuade you that you're the only one and he wants to see you tonight. It's a mindless response that comes from your desire to have whatever you want when you want it.

The next time you are in a stressful situation, first be the observer, and then the actor. By counting to ten (or better, waiting a full twenty-four hours) before you react blindly, you break the cycle of negative emotional responses. You give yourself time to think clearly and rationally about what needs doing now.

Forgive Yourself

It's not easy to change, and at least a part of the time, you will lapse back into your old, comfortable patterns. Don't look at this as failure. What you are attempting in your ten-step program is a lifelong commitment, and it takes a while to get on track. Forgive yourself for backsliding; take one day (one hour, one minute) at a time.

Get Professional Support

If, like Lois, your problem is compulsive eating, it's important to get professional help as you dedicate yourself to thinking differently about food. You may wish to call the National Food Addiction Hotline (1-800-872-0088) to get a referral to a support group in your area. You can also ask your physician to recommend a nutritionist, who will do a thorough history to find out what you eat, how and when you eat, what your food preferences and dislikes are, and how much exercise you do (to see how many calories you typically burn). She may also ask you to have a checkup with some routine lab tests before giving you a diet to follow. You'll also be able to call this professional to talk about your progress and to work out any problems that may spring up along the way.

If your problem is smoking, you can call Smoke-Enders (1-800-828-4357) to be referred to a seminar in your area or to implement a self-start home program of tapes, workbooks, and get access to a twenty-four-hour helpline.

If your problem is drinking, Alcoholics Anonymous has chapters and meetings everywhere, at all times of day or night. Check your Yellow Pages under "Alcohol Information" for this listing as well as for treatment centers in your area.

There are additional hotlines in the resource appendix at the back of this book and also in your Yellow Pages. Whether you are struggling with gambling, drugs, compulsive sexuality, abusing your children, or dealing with a wide range of other problems, help is there for you—reach out and touch it.

Step 3 Delegate Responsibility

V alda is a high–powered executive wearing herself thin in an attempt to stay on top of her job. She says that stress used to be her middle name; now she's so identified with it, she feels it's become her first name.

"I started out as a designer, working on hats and belts for Jo-Jos, a major presence in the fashion industry. I worked for them five seasons, always rushing to put out the new look, knocking myself out, working impossible hours, putting my personal life on hold—and you know what? After a while, I didn't care. Boring. I found it less interesting each season. Then I started to worry. So what was I if not a fast-track designer? I went to my supervisor and asked for a promotion. Hey, you should never ask because you might just get what you wish for. And the headaches that come with it.

"She said no, there was nothing for me, so I went elsewhere as a designer. I worked around for a few years, but I gravitated back to Jo-Jos when I turned forty. The supervisor I'd worked for was gone, and now they wanted me as a manager. I thought I could hack it.

"I was older than all the kids in the department, head of the accessories department with eight employees to supervise, in addition to designing belts and bags. This is a young person's field—there's really nowhere to go but director of design, and there's only one of those. I was on a real treadmill, going to shows, traveling twice a year to China and Taiwan to oversee production.

"The hours were 8 A.M. to 6 P.M., plus I had to take work home and work on weekends. And the lists in my head! I would start up out of bed in the middle of the night, thinking I have to do this or that. I have to tell Susie to cut that red leather or John to order that hardware for the handbags. Everything in my department was *my* baby, my hands-on opportunity to shine. You know, I'm not the maternal type—I never wanted kids. I was an artist, pure and simple. Whatever my projects were at the time, those were my children. And I would knock myself out for them.

"I could do the work. That wasn't the problem. I could even manage people. I started out great guns, giving them hell when they needed it, being a Boss. But I didn't have a barometer of when to crack down and when to be nice. I would also get bogged down in their problems. It was so damn political. The employees had their own personal grievances—I didn't want to be bothered with them, but I got sucked in. And the resolution, whatever it was, was always not great for somebody.

"People were disgruntled, and even though they didn't blame me, I'm not the sort of person who lets things roll off her back. It all stuck to me, and I was too self-critical to shake it off.

"If you're conscientious, you get a feeling about the company you work for that you can't let them down. That's what happened to me. I wasn't me anymore, I was a leg or a heart or an eye of Jo-Jos. And that's dangerous—because when you're the kind of person who has to do well, you feel that if you just worked a little harder, if you just spent a few more minutes explaining a job to the person who has to do it, if you just hired the right people and fired the right people, that it would all come out all right.

"And you know what? It might not anyway. That's a hard lesson to learn. You get such a big ego about making the ship run smoothly, but you can't do it all. To me, stress is like carrying a suitcase through Kennedy Airport. When you start out, the weight is okay and you scarcely feel it. But after you've walked down all those ramps on all those concourses, you start to feel the strain. And the longer you walk, the heavier it gets until finally, you have to stop. You're carrying exactly the same weight, but it gets beyond your ability to handle.

"My health started falling apart—I was tired all the time and had a battery of the weirdest symptoms you could ever imagine—hair falling out, feeling sore everywhere, incredible fatigue, emotionally weak and depressed. I went to different doctors, finally found out that

I'd had parasites—some giardia and amoeba that I'd picked up in the Far East—and this was the end product of their infestation. Even after I got the bugs out of my system, it took me a year to recover.

"I thought about quitting. I was literally sick and tired. My husband encouraged me to get off the treadmill, so I decided to work part-time for a while in order to get my health back on track. I honestly thought the company would fall apart without me as a constant presence, but after a few months, I realized that the readjustment I'd made hadn't changed things at all. Jo-Jos was still as insane, and I was still getting my work done (in about a third of the time), but I didn't have to manage anyone.

"When I went back full-time, it was with a new appreciation of what other people in the department could do. I think of myself kind of like an engineer—I'm artistic but I know how to fit things together. I've always been fascinated by the body—how it looks, how clothing looks on it, how the pieces all mesh. So now I'm fitting together all the really important pieces of my life.

"My husband and I bought a cabin in the Adirondacks and we go there as often as we can, and I spend extra time there in the summer. I don't have as much control over my department, but in a way, I have more control over me—and that makes the work go better than it used to. I'm learning that work isn't everything. And it always gets done, even if you don't do it yourself.

"You can get so burned out that you have no idea you've lost your spark. It's that bad. You know, I'm a perfectionist and really high energy—and employers love that. They'll exploit it to the hilt. So you have to take care of yourself and eventually say, yeah, the company's paying my salary, but they don't own me. Nobody owns me but me."

Valda's aches, pains, and stress-related symptoms were fortunate alarm buttons. If she hadn't started to take care of herself, she might have fallen into the work picture that many women experience: flogging themselves to work harder even when their minds and bodies tell them they've reached a dangerous impasse. And the types of stress-related conditions that can kill—heart disease, some cancers, autoimmune diseases—strike without warning.

Valda knew when to slow down and change direction, and her awareness of the fact that others could perform adequately was a big revelation, one that possibly saved her life. If you're in a high-pressure job (whether white collar, blue collar, or pink collar), you have to admit that others can do what you do—perhaps not the same way, perhaps not as well, but so what? You are not alone, and you're not the savior of the world—or even of your company.

Responsibility, n. A detachable burden easily shifted to the shoulders of God, Fate, Fortune, Luck, or one's neighbor. In the days of astrology it was customary to unload it upon a star.

—AMBROSE BIERCE

TRYING TO SEPARATE WORK AND HOME LIFE

We define ourselves by our work. Whether you are a doctor, teacher, carpenter, homemaker, artist, bookkeeper, computer analyst, or horse trainer, you show yourself to the world in great part as an emblem of your profession. What you do with your time when you work, whether you earn a great deal of money at it or no money at all, is to fashion a type of mastery and expertise in a craft that no one else can touch. You do it your way, and you do it so well that it's difficult to introduce yourself without mentioning your work.

Of course, the interesting thing about women's work is that, as the old saw goes, it's never done. According to a 1993 Families and Work Institute national survey, 56 percent of American women with children between the ages of six and seventeen worked year-round outside the home, and 43 percent of those with kids under six did as well. These women spend an average of 41.7 hours a week at their full-time job. After that workday is done, however, most women have a second full-time job waiting at home. This one isn't paid, and it's often not really appreciated—but it has to be done, so women do it.

Women tend to take their stresses with them wherever they go. In a study done of Volvo car employees in 1990, men and women managers were tested to see how well they could unwind at the end of a workday. The stress hormone, norepinephrine, was measured at intervals through the day to see how the men and women responded to acute stress. After 6 P.M., the men's blood pressure and stress hormone levels had decreased sharply. However, the women's levels actually rose as they started out the door to go home. When asked how they felt, women reported being tired and pressured; the men, on the other hand, anticipated a relaxing evening and were feeling pretty good.

Women who work usually work hard, and this means they are constantly at a stress level that endangers their hearts and minds. But interestingly enough, having a job that is fulfilling and satisfying tends to counter the bad cardiovascular effects of stress—in other words, the *dis-stress* that the women feel about never having a chance to rest is turned into *eu-stress* when they do something well or feel competent in their life work. (This is not generally true of blue-collar women, as we'll see later.)

If having stress as a worker is a given, then there must be a way to make that stress work for you. Across the board, studies on working women show that it's *beneficial* to your general health to be employed. As to how beneficial it is, this depends on other factors, such as whether you're married and your spouse helps around the house, whether you're a parent and have adequate child care, and what, exactly, you do to earn your way in the world.

It all comes down to how you balance the pressure versus the rewards of your job. And that's not always such an easy balancing act.

In order that people may be happy in their work, these three things are needed: They must be fit for it. They must not do too much of it. And they must have a sense of success in it.

—JOHN RUSKIN

THE EXECUTIVE TWIST

The types of stress that you might feel on your job are intricate and varied. For example, if you're in academia, and you have papers to grade and research and teaching to do and articles to publish, you tend to have a constant cloud over your head. The work is never-ending and never finished.

If you're an architect, you have deadlines to meet. You have to come up with an initial proposal, meet with a client, create and revise blueprints, work with contractors and builders, oversee many types of laborers, and remain in charge. Eventually, the work is finished, but you may be juggling several projects at once—or, you may worry that you'll never be hired again.

Whatever type of job you do, if you're white collar, you have more control over your work situation than if you're blue collar. You have more flexibility in terms of clocking in at the office; you can take time off for family emergencies or outings; you are able to influence your work situation and get those in charge to listen to you. Your stress, although high, is often tolerable because you feel you can develop your own abilities, use the knowledge and experience you already possess, learn new things on the job, and figure out your own methods of doing your work in the most efficient manner. Independence and variety come as perks of the job, as does leadership potential.

If you're blue collar, however, you are already struggling with low pay (which may mean that you have to work two or three jobs, particularly if there is no other breadwinner at home), and you may feel under the gun all the time. You are bound to a desk or machine, or in a position where you serve others (in a restaurant, hair salon, or gas station, for example); you suffer from too much routine and are stuck with boring tasks you already know how to do. You don't have the chance to develop new skills or learn on the job.

If you're a receptionist in a busy office, your time is not your own. You are a slave to the phone, to the visitors who come to the door, to the boss and the mailroom assistant alike. You have to take breaks and lunch hours when you're told, personal phone calls (if permitted) must be kept to a minimum, and it's often difficult to get a minute to run to the bathroom. You don't get to make many decisions on your own, and this robs you of that wonderful feeling that you make a difference, or that your presence would be missed if you weren't around.

And of course, you don't make enough money to hire someone to take care of your kids or clean your house—which means that your total work load (job plus home work) may be staggering. Many women say, "I wish I could split in two," and mean it.

But splitting isn't the answer. What we really need is to come together, to focus more and self-divide less. If we don't, it can spell trouble.

---

*I don't like work—no man does—but I like
what is in work—the chance to find yourself.*
—Joseph Conrad

HOW TO RECOGNIZE IF YOU'RE BURNING OUT

The phenomenon of "burnout," a serious psychological condition resulting from unrelieved work stress, is a serious problem with severe consequences. A job that used to have meaning and purpose is suddenly deadly; the stresses of working at it begin to outweigh the rewards of doing it.

To burn out you must first be on fire. So what may happen is that you get a promotion or a new job, and you're gung-ho for the first year, filled with plans and methods to enliven and improve not just your own situation but the company itself. As you tackle various obstacles over the next year or so, you realize that no one else wants what you want. Your memos are ignored; doors are slammed in your face. Or, what's worse, your enthusiasm wanes by attrition, because no one makes a fuss or pays any attention to your demands for change in the workplace.

Eventually, you give up. You don't care. You get frustrated and bored. Your energy reserves, once sky-high, are now depleted, and you hardly think it worthwhile to come in every day. Whereas you used to give 110 percent and work from dawn until 7 P.M., now you can scarcely drag yourself in to the office, and though you may even work longer hours, you don't get anything done.

You're pessimistic about the outcomes of your project, and sometimes even fear—but secretly hope—that you may be fired. You feel like you're walking a tightrope, and the next crisis will push you over the edge. Every once in a while, you just don't feel like coming in, so you call in sick. Eventually, you really *are* sick because your immune system stops protecting you from infection and illness. Your family gets on your case—what's the matter with you? they ask. Why can't you just do your job and straighten up and fly right? You have a terrible sense of isolation—no one understands you, not at work or at home.

Here are some of the risk factors for burnout:

- Your perception of stress shifts—what used to be exciting and challenging is suddenly overwhelming and ponderous
- You can't deal with problems you used to solve easily
- You don't care enough to work with others: your support system breaks down
- You get no relief from parts of the job that used to give you pleasure and fulfillment

- You become obsessed with frustrations of your work
- You feel pessimistic and self-doubting all the time
- You have a sense that your job problems will never end—you feel like a trapped animal
- You have begun to suffer a multitude of stress-related physical disorders: headache, heart palpitations, chronic colds or sinus problems, dizziness, nausea, etc.

And job burnout is worse when compounded with family pressures:

- Your marriage or partnership is shaky, or you are going through a divorce or separation
- You have experienced the death of a close relative or friend
- You have difficulty communicating with your kids—or your kids don't relate to you anymore because they see you so infrequently

As you start to burn out, you may try to escape in a variety of negative ways. Maybe you feel you just have to have that drink as soon as you get in the door, and one glass of alcohol turns into four. Maybe you start smoking more, or consuming cup after cup of coffee when you're annoyed and frustrated. Burnout can become totally entwined with other problems such as alcoholism, drug abuse, or mental illness.

The sooner you admit you're in crisis, the sooner you can get help. Although women in the workplace often find it difficult to say that things have gone beyond their ability to cope, the admission can be crucial. Like Valda, sometimes you have to retreat a few steps so that eventually you can leap forward.

HITTING THE WALL—GETTING HELP WHEN YOU'RE IN CRISIS

> *A burden in the bush is worth two on your hands.*
> —JAMES THURBER

Hitting the wall means many things to many people. For some women, it's finding that you're in tears on the way to and from the office every day. For others, it's discovering that you no longer care about anything you're doing at work. And for still other women, it's a physical

HOW TO WARD OFF BURNOUT

- Take a long weekend off. Schedule nothing but time for yourself and leisure time with your family. Make a deal with yourself to explore your problems and all possible options fully.
- Make a list of your life roles—this will be tangible proof of all the many things you do in many spheres. You are not only a worker on the job, but possibly a wife, mother, child, gardener, writer, musician, chess player, community organizer, gourmet chef, etc.
- Stop identifying with your job. You are not A Bookkeeper, but rather, an individual who knows how to do bookkeeping. If you are so intertwined with your position that you only see yourself as a function, then whatever failure you have doing that task will be a personal failure. Separate yourself from what you are and you will soon find that you can separate yourself from your job pressures, too.
- List three things you enjoy and seldom do; list three things you hate and always do. Then take the time you once spent on the stuff you loathe and use it to do the things you love.
- Give yourself a few options for dealing with the situation you're in. It may not be feasible financially to quit, but you might think about cutting back your hours or going on flextime. You might consider seeing a career counselor and beginning the process of searching for another position. You might opt to take some adult-ed classes at night in a field that's always interested you. You might check within your organization and see if you could be transferred to another department.
- If you are too depressed to make any changes to help yourself, you should see a therapist or counselor (see Step 10).

warning sign—you may feel mentally and emotionally as if you're falling apart. Real somatic symptoms such as chronic headaches, stomachaches, or flus indicate that your body is under such stress that it no longer functions properly.

When you are in crisis, you need to ask for some time off so that you can figure out what to do next. This is an incredibly tough step for many women to take. According to a new book by Arlie Russell Hochschild, *The Time Bind: When Work Becomes Home and Home Becomes Work*, the trend has become *more* hours on the job as opposed to fewer ones. Women are fed up with having to do the second-tier chores of housework and child care, and they find it more rewarding to stay in the workplace where they are at least valued in terms of a paycheck and benefits.

But if you're burned out and turned off to life in general, it is essential that you pull back and re-evaluate what you're doing and why you're doing it. If you work in a large company or a government-sponsored facility, there are human resources for counseling and life management. All visits are supposedly confidential and should not in any way jeopardize your job status.

If you're in a smaller company or you work for yourself, you may not have these benefits available. But you can still help yourself. (See the sidebar "How to Ward Off Burnout" for some vital tips.)

STRATEGIES IF YOU'RE THE BOSS

If you are the boss, this means you have to figure out where you stand in relation first, to your work, second, to your employees, and third, to the company or corporation you work for.

Here are some important strategies:

Really Listen

Your employees may not complain in words, but they may be quite eloquent in the way that they stop connecting to one another, compete with each other, get into hassles over small details, or find ways to sabotage projects. Don't stick your head in the sand and hope the problems will go away. If you are aware enough to pick up the dissension in the ranks, you must manage it before it gets out of hand.

Make Time for Open Communication Between You and Your Staff

If you set aside an hour a week where everyone can put something on the table—complaints, ideas, concerns—and it's made clear that everyone gets an equal say and equal consideration, you'll find you have a group of diligent, hard-working individuals on your side.

You may want to try the following exercise in your department:

Ask everyone to come up with four sources of stress on the job and have them write down their ideas anonymously on index cards. Perhaps you'll find a few similar entries, like "I hate it when someone is telling me what to do when I'm in the midst of doing it." Or you might find, "I hate it when my supervisor makes a nasty comment about my work when I thought it was really good."

Read the cards aloud and go around the circle, asking what coping strategies could be used to combat the difficulty. The range of suggested tactics might include avoiding the supervisor, calling a colleague and complaining, going outside for a cigarette, bringing it up at a staff meeting, or making an appointment with the supervisor after work and having it out. Let the responses generate a free-wheeling discussion about positive and negative methods of coping with work stresses, and make an agreement among everyone present for the following week to use only positive strategies and see how they feel at the end of that time.

Mix Criticism with Praise

Everyone has to be told they've done well at some time. And everyone needs correction. But you need to understand how to balance the two, particularly because employees talk to one another and will undoubtedly compare notes. When you're praising, make it specific rather than a general wash of delighted enthusiasm. When you're criticizing, don't get personal or sarcastic or nasty about it. Do it in a way that exposes the problem and offers a possible solution. You should also leave the door open to the employee to allow him or her to solve the problem.

Use Your Influence to Redesign Jobs

Let each person take on the responsibility he or she handles best. For example, some people are great with interpersonal skills—let them do the phone work and take meetings. Others are wonderful researchers, and still others are crackerjack salespeople who can close deals. Whenever possible, be sure you allow people to do what they like best and what they do best.

Offer Employees the Opportunity to Take Charge of Their Work

Naturally, you have to prepare the way and explain the project. But then assume that those who are working on it are self-starters and can handle the job themselves. If you're always looking over their shoulders and pointing out what you would have done, you undermine their authority and don't get the best results anyway. Everyone in the organization should have some unsupervised chores and decisions they can make on their own.

Consider Flex-time

Everyone these days is doing at least two jobs, and women with children are in a real bind if the sitter or the school calls with an emergency. As much as you can, allow employees to create a workable schedule so that they don't feel like robots. There are all kinds of ways to make up forty hours a week, and many firms are now happy to consider working off-site or from a home office.

Consider an Exercise Room or Employee Lounge

Sitting at a desk for eight hours a day is killing to mind, body, and spirit. The largest corporations now encourage their staff to join their fitness club and they are given incentives (such as convenient parking spaces) for attending health-related programs on the job. The use of the employees' physical space may seem like small potatoes—in fact, having somewhere to go so they don't feel tied to their office and desk may be vital.

Employees feel more comfortable when they have perks like being allowed personal phone calls and having a refrigerator for lunches and snacks. This type of consideration from an employer makes for a better attitude about work in general.

STRATEGIES IF YOU'RE THE EMPLOYEE

If you're an employee, or if you work for yourself and are both boss and employee, you have many people to answer to. Remember to answer first to yourself if you wish to keep your stress on the job as low as possible. Ideally, you would like the good things you do to preserve your sanity and autonomy to spill over into good things you can do for your boss or company.

Here are some very important strategies:

Realize What It Is about the Job or Your Performance of the Job That Bugs You

Spend a few days observing yourself, and write down what it is that makes your stomach knot up or your anger quotient rise. Don't deny the fact that you are frustrated and furious. The more aware you can be of those elements that are stressful, the more strategies you'll find (see Step 1) to handle them.

After You've Set Your Priorities, Make Sure That Others Know Your Mind

It's one thing to figure out what you feel is important and should be done first; quite another when you're in a business situation to translate this information to your colleagues and to those in charge. It is far better to say what you think than to hide it. You'll find that others respect your no-nonsense approach and may even begin to emulate it themselves.

Shift the Focus from "What's Wrong with Me?" to "What Can I Do about the Situation?"

This makes you a problem-solver instead of a hand-wringer. It also takes the burden off your shoulders and makes it a concrete concern that may be handled by you alone, or by you in conjunction with other individuals.

Separate the Demands of Your Job from the Demands You Put on Yourself

It's not personal, rather it's a task to be accomplished. The sooner you realize this, the easier it gets. You may be a perfectionist, but you don't have to knock yourself out just to set a world record. Maybe you have a thing about time (getting things done before they're due or waiting until the last minute and "cramming") or versatility (being the one who can complete any task, no matter what your job description). Maybe you feel you have to take on an unreasonable number of chores just to say you could. Now it's time to give yourself a break. Slow down, breathe, and consider why you are doing the work in the way you're doing it.

Listen to Your Body

A racing heart, a knot in your stomach, or a chronic headache indicates that you are highly stressed and are in danger of burning out. Stop before you get sick.

Create Reasonable Expectations

It's not helpful to demand the world either of yourself or anyone else—they will always let you down if you do. See what's possible and ask for that, then set a new goal, and then another one. Eventually, you will get what you want out of each situation.

Cut Out Overtime

No matter how they beg, no matter what you think you can accomplish in just a couple more hours, *Don't do it.* You have a life—go live it!

Make Time for Decompression

Many companies offer a fitness center or quiet space. If you have these on the premises, take advantage of them before or after work or during your lunch break. If you have no such area, make one for yourself. You can always retreat to a back hallway to meditate and breathe for a few minutes—this type of escape can mean the difference between coping and being overwhelmed by your job pressures.

Develop a Good Support System

No matter what your position, make sure you have allies who will stand by you. A united and sympathetic group will make it easier for you to deal with work and personal problems and to get help when you really need it. Beating the sense of isolation is paramount, especially in a big corporation where it's easy to get lost.

Our privileges can be no greater than our obligations. The protection of our rights can endure no longer than the performance of our responsibilities.

—JOHN F. KENNEDY

BEING A WOMAN ON THE JOB

Women on the job have the same burdens as men, but we perceive them differently. Like men, women have a heavy work load (in these days of downsizing, we may be doing the amount of work that would have been shared by two or three employees ten years ago), time pressure, deadlines, and responsibilities. But when surveyed about the ways in which they approached their work, women managers and clerical workers both tended to say that they found it difficult to communicate problems to their superiors and thought that they had to work harder than their male colleagues if they wanted to be praised for their work. Because they sensed a real pull between home and career, many women had conflicts about the amount of time and energy they could devote to the job.

Work satisfaction was highest among male managers, next highest among female managers. The clerical workers, with little or no autonomy and variety to their jobs, were often bored or burned out. But more than any other group, the female clerical workers felt a sense of community and support at work. And this, as it happens, can be a key to how women manage stress.

> *Make [your employers] understand that you are in their service as workers, not as women*
> —SUSAN BROWNELL ANTHONY

THE NEED FOR SOCIAL SUPPORT

You have to have people on your side. And at work, having loyal allies can mean the difference between your job running smoothly or poorly. It can also spell disaster for your personal sense of well-being if you feel that others are out to get you, or that they just don't care enough to stand up for you if you need assistance.

The incidence of the "good old boys'" club is tough to emulate in the world of women. Guys tend to act like guys together—when they're out having a beer or talking about cars or sports, their socioeconomic levels magically evaporate and the barriers between bosses and employees break down.

Women have been trying, in the past few years, to establish women–in–business networks, and the results are promising, at least at the executive level. It's a good thing to have a group you can hang out with once a month—this is an opportunity to air problems you may not be able to discuss with anyone in your workplace. And you may hear of solutions that have helped other women.

These networking groups are vital, particularly because women managers generally lose out on getting support in their own work situation on their way up the ladder. These individuals (who rated highest for Type-A behavior of all their male and female colleagues) had done something consciously or unconsciously to set themselves apart. They may have met with a lot of competition from both male and female colleagues, or they may have jumped from the clerical pool to a white-collar job, thus incurring the wrath and jealousy of women who used to be their pals and equals.

How can you preserve your energy and eliminate your sense of isolation? How can you persuade yourself that you have potential allies who can help you out, and if you do delegate responsibility, that the whole project won't slip out of your hands (and your control)?

Very often, you can't. And it's a considered choice. But as Valda found out, her health was jeopardized when she remained aloof and alone. It was only after she discovered the value of group work, team building, and a more laissez-faire attitude toward supervising that she began to enjoy what she was doing—and she started healing physically as well.

> *A councilor ought not to sleep the whole night through, a man to whom the populace is entrusted, and who has many responsibilities.*
> —HOMER

KEEP YOUR LEISURE TIME FOR YOURSELF

When you only have so much time in a day, you can mete it out any way you like, but it will not expand to fit your needs. So what you have to do is preserve some special blocks that are all yours and cannot be interfered with.

"I want to take some time off." Interesting phrase. Time *off* of what? Obviously, it's off of the job. The idea of leisure is expressed as the negative correlative of the main course, which is work. But what if the job were seen as the appetizer and dessert, and the time you had to yourself (however small) was the entree? If you look at the list of things that women enjoy doing when they "take time off" (see Step 5), you will note that they are simple pleasures—reading, taking a bath, gardening or knitting, talking to friends on the phone. But these are the very activities that enhance our feelings of security and identity.

If we see ourselves as workers first and women second, we are giving ourselves very short shrift. It is vital that we switch the picture around and make our responsibilities to ourselves paramount and those obligations we have to others secondary.

Very hard to do. According to Dr. Hochschild, we get more rewards in the workplace as we work harder and devote ourselves to the company more avidly. We work hard so that we can have a sitter or day care center or sleep-away camp for our kids; we work hard so that we can have "personal shoppers" buy presents for us and oversee surprise parties for our husband's fiftieth birthday, or clean our house, or help our kids with their homework. When we abdicate our own personal time, others have to stand in our place. We fit so easily into the three-piece work suit. But it's harder to tie on the apron and be "Mommy" or "wife" or "child of an elderly parent," because the chores we have to complete in those roles are often poorly rewarded or not rewarded at all.

So let's try to recapture the part of ourselves that we grew up with—the "me" lurking underneath the job-doer and the invaluable asset to the company.

As soon as you pass off at least some of your work role to others, you leave yourself freer for other opportunities that may come along. Give yourself the chance to find out your purpose for being on this earth and waking up each morning. (*Clue*: The answer is a lot more complex than the title you put on your income tax form.)

All work and no play makes Jack
a dull boy.

—JAMES HOWELL

QUIZ: Do You Have to Do Everything?

Answer Yes, Most of the Time, Rarely, or No to the following questions.

1. When you have generated a new project at work, can you portion it out to others, or do you feel you must be hands-on every detail from inception to completion?

2. If your project involves many different facets (writing a proposal, making a sales pitch, coming up with marketing ideas, etc.), do you outline the entire thing yourself first, before passing each piece off to the specialists who will do the work?

3. When your supervisor gives you a job, do you do it immediately, putting it first, before finishing your own work?

4. Do you feel a lot of guilt and anxiety if you don't get something accomplished in the time period in which you promised it?

5. If your pencils need sharpening or your letters need stamping, do you do it yourself, instead of asking an assistant to do it?

6. Do you ever realize that you haven't gone to the bathroom or taken a drink of water all afternoon?

7. Do you come in early and stay late most days? If you've had a day out of the office for any reason, do you feel you have to do two days' work in one when you return?

8. Do you ever find yourself daydreaming at work about escaping from your responsibilities? Or, about thwarting a superior's plans?

9. What is your idea of an "easy" day at work?

10. If you could change one thing tomorrow about your work situation, what would it be, and how would you go about making this alteration?

If you answer "yes" or "most of the time" to the first eight questions, you are too eager a beaver. And you will see that the answers to the last two questions reflect your insistence on doing everything yourself.

Start to use the skills described below and wait three months, then take the test again, this time starting with questions 9 and 10. See how your answers to these two questions will now alter the answers to the first eight.

SKILLS TO LEARN FOR DELEGATING RESPONSIBILITY
Relinquish Control

Very often, we feel we have to do everything because we are insecure about losing control. Our great idea might be smashed or, at the very least, weakened and made unrecognizable if we let others horn in on our territory.

The control issue is particularly hard for women who were socialized to be "nice" and "compliant" as little girls. Suddenly, being part of the big, bad working world makes them go overboard in their attempt to be no-nonsense and tough as nails.

What's needed, of course, is an ability to let go of some—if not all—of the work that you are less suited for so that you can get your own jobs accomplished efficiently. If you can see yourself as an observer on the scene rather than a master puppeteer, you will probably find it easier to sit back and reap the benefits of what you originally sowed.

Count on Others and Make Them Accountable

Other people are really very competent. And the more challenging work you give them to do, the more responsibility they have, the better they'll do it. When you praise (and offer constructive criticism when necessary), when you show someone how to do a job and then say, "Now you're on your own," you increase capacity for independent thought and labor. When they are accountable for their own actions, they immediately rise in their own estimation.

In effect, counting on others gives you choices you didn't have when you mistrusted them. By passing on responsibility, you make others more powerful so that they can act autonomously without coming to you for every little thing. You create a better work force by training people conscientiously to take over their portion of the work and leave you free for newer, bigger, better endeavors.

See the Competence in Others

They won't do it the way you would. They may not do it exactly as you like it done. But if the work is getting done, that's fine. Remember how Valda was amazed when she started working part-time and the company didn't fall apart. It is humbling to realize that you are not the linchpin in the whole works. And as high up as you may be in the organization, there is probably someone who is actually smarter and faster than you, regardless of her position. Spend some time admiring the feats of your colleagues, and be grateful that you work with other people who may challenge you to do your own job better.

Develop Overseer Abilities

Whether you are a big boss or a person at the bottom of the corporate ladder—whether you work for yourself or have a partnership with one or two other individuals—it's a great learning experience to be a mentor. When you can show someone else how to do a task— maybe how to load a new program into a computer, or how to make a piece of jewelry, or how to write a great speech—and then stand back to let your assistant try it, you give a gift. Don't hover; don't correct. Let the other individual find her way. Remember when your kids were learning to walk and they kept falling down? You wanted desperately to prop them up and hold their hands until they got the knack of it. But the only way to learn is to make mistakes.

This goes for you, too. Don't try to be so perfect. Don't try to do everything, and trust your colleagues' ability to take the load off you.

Step 4 **Plan Reasonable Goals**

"In the bad old days," says Kiley ruefully, "I used to spend my days in constant anxiety. I had an almost addictive relationship to my first husband, and I would do whatever he asked so that he wouldn't leave me. What he wanted, that was what I wanted—I never even thought about my own feelings. I also had a constantly panicked feeling about how he spent all our money and how we'd never have enough to pay the bills each month. And how I would have to make it all right, even if it killed me."

It took Kiley, now fifty-eight, years of therapy to discover who she was and what she wanted. "I had such a traditional Catholic upbringing. I was just supposed to suffer my lot in life and not make waves. But therapy changed me. I know now that the stress I feel is up to me to handle. Sure, I fret and worry over things, but I have a continuity of relaxation inside me now. I look ahead to all the good things, so I've got a much more stable outlook on life than I used to have.

"Like my current marriage. My second husband is a melancholy sort of guy, but I don't glom onto his troubles the way I used to with my first husband. I say, okay, he's going to get me down if I let him—so I just won't. I appreciate the wisdom and common sense he brings to our relationship, but I don't want his feelings to rub off on me. I'll go do my own thing for a while and then come back to see how he's doing. That's okay with him—he's very supportive.

"I still worry about money because I'm a freelance writer, so I never know where the next check is coming from. My husband works for Nordstrom, so his salary and benefits are vital to us. But not enough, of course. I used to get sick to my stomach over money—now I function under the assumption that it's not Nordstrom or Doubleday who's the provider. St. Paul said it best: 'Keep your hand to the plough and God will take care of the rest.' I truly believe that. Once we wanted to take this trip to Mexico to see our daughter and it cost $950, which we didn't have. And the very next week, I got an unexpected royalty check for $965. You see! It works.

"My religious background was important to me and still is—I think it lets me maintain my balance and it really does give me a sense of peace. I can anticipate a great future and sketch out a design for it because I really believe there's Someone up there helping me. Of course, my design is flexible—just in case God has some different ideas!"

Kiley has a structured plan for her life, and it unfailingly helps to keep her stress level under control. "I've been keeping a journal for the past two years. I write in it five or six times a week, and I put down everything that's bothering me. It's great to go back to entries several months after I write them, because I get perspective. The stuff that seemed so bothersome at the time—all that now appears to be just another glitch in the pattern of my life. This journal is kind of like a letter to God—I put in it petitions for what I want and praise for what's He's given me. I write down all my fears, and then I ask for guidance.

"Then I have my Goal Stars program. I have a partner—a woman I met at a church class eight years ago. We help each other with goals we have for the next two weeks—these can be things we want to do physically, mentally, or emotionally. Checking in with a buddy gives me support and doesn't let me slough off the commitment with excuses, as I might do alone. So when I felt I really needed to exercise more, I had a goal to walk every day—and that was on my stars list.

"And then I had a goal to not take every writing job that came down the pike, just because I thought I had to have the money. I got sick of feeling that the money pressure was in charge of me, so my goal that time was to take twenty-four hours before I said yes to anything. I wasn't about to get up at 5 A.M. every day to fit in another writing assignment if I didn't really like it. My partner keeps me on track, and I do the same for her. And we don't *have* to accomplish the goals we set in two weeks—sometimes we'll put a star on hold while we move onto something else that seems more pressing.

"I keep a book with my stars in it, and underneath the goal, I write a list of affirmations to help me get where I'd like to go—and that keeps me on track. So I might put down: Complete new book proposal by June. Can I do it? Yes, because...

I am able to relax easily and as deeply as I wish at any time.
I like myself and my work.
I plan to work for success and a serene present and future.
My purpose is to give you, Kiley, life in all its fullness.

"I'm a very visual person, so it's good for me to have goals right in front of me that I can look at. I made myself a goal board, where I cut out pictures from a magazine that are like whatever I'm aiming toward, and I post them on the kitchen door where I can see the board every day. And when I've passed a certain goal or completed it to my satisfaction, then I change the board. This is so different from the way I used to be, when I would let life just run over me like a Mack truck."

In her early years, Kiley says, she had no will of her own and no sense of what was important in her present or her future life. Kiley finally feels that she knows who she is and what she wants. Planning for the future—even the immediate future—gives her a sense of wholeness and security, and it lets her see the big picture instead of the tiny details, which will undoubtedly diminish in importance as she takes care of the larger structure.

> *... It is not the attainment of the goal that matters, it is the things that are met with by the way.*
>
> —HAVELOCK ELLIS

LEARNING WHAT YOU WANT

If, like Kiley, you've been living under a cloud for most of your life, you may not actually know what you want. Each day seems the same, and the ups and downs you encounter seem inevitable. You are tossed like a shell on the waves, drifting in and out with the tide. You feel impotent and helpless—which causes a lot of stress.

If this sounds like you, you're not making choices. Rather, you're allowing others to choose for you, or you are avoiding choice entirely—you're functioning, but not doing what gives you pleasure and reward.

Initially, you probably won't be sure when to make a choice, which choices to make, or when to stand up for something really crucial—because it never occurred to you that you could make a difference in your own life.

As your self-esteem increases, however (thanks to your attention to other steps in this program), you will wake up to the realization that you are due something in life. And the only person who can give to you is you.

Think about your reaction the next time someone tells you about a new job possibility, or a new man they'd like to introduce you to. If your immediate reaction is "It's too much trouble to apply," or "He wouldn't like me anyway," you have effectively cut off your future at the knees. If you are perfectly happy with your job, and you don't particularly care about dating, that's fine. But if at some level you are ready for a change, you have to allow yourself to do something active to make that change happen.

Life is what I make of it, and what I make of it is up to me.

—ANONYMOUS

POSITIVE RISK-TAKING—LETTING GO OF FEARS

It is frightening to consider what might happen if you ventured forth into some completely unfamiliar area. Let us assume you aren't that happy with your current job and would love to be more motivated to wake up in the morning. This means you have to:

- Get your resume and references together
- Make a phone call to potential new employers (often several calls, to get through voice mail and the various assistants who attempt to block your way)
- Make dates for interviews
- Learn something about the companies you're targeting so that you can talk intelligently—perhaps even come up with some ideas that you might implement if you were hired

- Figure out what to wear to interviews (at least two complete outfits, just in case)
- Prepare a portfolio of your own materials to show what you've done in the past
- Go on second interviews if they're interested
- Deal with rejection if you don't get a job; deal with the anxiety of *can I really do it?* if you are offered a job
- Make a choice to stay where you are or move on

This is a lot of stress (both potentially good and bad) to deal with! You have to overcome a huge number of fears in order to move ahead. If you are terrified at the onset of this process, you'll never get to the point of having to decide if you want to accept a new job. If you can't even figure out what to wear to the interview, you never get past square one.

Most women have been cautioned throughout life that they shouldn't make waves; they shouldn't want more than they already have. If you came from a family where the message was that taking any kind of risk was like jumping out of a plane and hoping the chute would open, you are probably very reluctant to try anything new.

But we can't move ahead unless we can distinguish *positive risks* from negative ones. You can check out the parameters of what you're going to do before you do it. For example, you can find out something about the company you're targeting and the boss from the friend who referred you; you can get a Dun and Bradstreet report; you can talk to people at other companies who do business with the company you're looking at.

Don't be afraid to set challenging goals. The tougher they are, the farther away from you they seem, the more interesting they'll be as you work toward them. Remember that you can always pull back and keep things status quo until you feel strong enough to take the big risk and move ahead.

Exercises in Positive Risk-Taking

1. Make a cold call to someone you consider "famous," perhaps someone you read about in a newspaper article.
2. Ask for a better table in a restaurant when the maitre d' puts you near the kitchen.

3. If the newspaper is always wet or wrinkled, call the vendor and complain.
4. If you don't like the last bunch of parsley left on the supermarket shelf, ring the buzzer for service and ask for a fresh one from the back.
5. Train for a 5K race, and then run in it.
6. Stand up at the next town meeting and offer an opinion.
7. Protest loudly if your partner, parent, or child belittles you.

MAINTAINING REASONABLE EXPECTATIONS

On the other hand, you have to keep a balance. The positive risks you take must be grounded in reality. If you aim way beyond your capabilities or your reasonable progress in a certain area, you will fail—and that way lies a lot more stress.

If you've always loved acting, it's reasonable to assume you could get a part in a local theater company production. It is unreasonable to think you could get a starring role in a Hollywood film.

If you are really good at public speaking, it's reasonable to assume your boss might ask you to introduce the president of your company at the next annual meeting. It is unreasonable to think you might be asked to give the keynote address at the next Democratic Convention.

If you are currently earning $40,000 a year and ask for a raise, it's reasonable to assume you might get another $4,000 or so when you renegotiate. It's unreasonable to assume you'll be bumped up to $80,000.

The "sour grapes" principle applies to setting unrealistic goals for your future. If you are always holding out hope that things will be perfect, you can't appreciate the small steps forward that you've earned. It will cause you a lot of distress if the only acceptable option is your fantasy—and you feel that what you're being offered is beneath you.

Keeping a balance between positive risk-taking and reasonable goal-setting is difficult, and you won't manage it the first time out. If you're patient, however, and learn to weigh your benefits and limitations, you will arrive at a destination that both excites and fulfills you.

KEEPING THE PRESENT AS YOU MOVE TOWARD THE FUTURE

In order to maintain the good things you already have as you set goals for the future, it's important to stay in the moment, knowing exactly what is happening inside and outside you. It's easy to get so caught up in the future that you forget about the daily passage of life, which goes on no matter what you do to aid or thwart it.

You have to pace yourself, too, not racing ahead because you're so antsy about getting to where you want to be. If you push yourself beyond your limits, you'll end up frustrated and may ultimately abandon what may be a very reachable goal. And if you discover along the way that you've selected a goal that just won't work for you, then sit down and do a revision—choose the next most positive alternative and see if you can be content with that.

Finally, always stay alert to your capacity to cope. If one of your goals is sending your child to college, for example, and you start working two jobs in order to save enough money, monitor your stress levels carefully. If you feel overwhelmed, if you're not spending enough time with this beloved child you are working so hard to support, if you aren't taking care of your own needs, then reassess this goal. Maybe your kid will get great scholarship money or get into a work/study program; maybe she can go to a state school that costs less. There are many routes to the same destination—know yourself well enough to select one that works for you.

> *The goal of life is living in agreement with nature.*
>
> —ZENO

SETTING SHORT-TERM, INTERMEDIATE, AND LONG-TERM GOALS

If you suddenly wake up one morning and decide you'd like to be married with children when you've been single all your adult life, there is something out of sync in your expectations. You haven't prepared to change your living situation, so there's no way you can achieve what you desire.

But if you start slowly and make a little progress every day, you may eventually get where you want to go. By setting small goals as building blocks to the larger ones, you will create a foundation for your major structure.

Steps Toward the My Long-Range Goal

1. Spending time alone; spending time with others—learning to be comfortable with both
2. Joining groups with people of similar interests
3. Asking friends to introduce you to other people who aren't partnered
4. Spending time with children and infants—offering to babysit for friends or relatives
5. Reassessing your long-term goal, based on your experiences of Steps 1 to 4; planning ahead, according to your reassessment

Things to Do to be Able to Master Those Steps

1. Examining your motives—are you wishing out of loneliness rather than a serious desire to match your life with someone else's?
2. Working on your self-esteem so that you like yourself better
3. Working on tolerance for others at work and at play
4. Enjoying your friendships with others whether there's any romantic component to them or not
5. Accepting the path that you're currently on by using your personal experiences as goal indicators—allowing whatever happens to happen.

Once you've mastered these short-term and intermediate goals and have a good grasp of what you're aiming at and why, it will be increasingly easy to find your way toward your long-term goal. (Very often, not trying so hard, or not trying at all, gets you where you want to go much faster.)

The learning curve on anything is always harder at the outset, when you know nothing at all, but it gets easier as you acquire skills. The same is true of goal-setting. When you get over the first hump of knowing what you want and going after it, the next rise looks less steep, and the one after that looks even more doable. This is not to say that if you've progressed to dating that it's a cinch to get happily married—however, you will have the structure in place and the confidence of what you've already mastered as you move toward your long-term goal.

Let's look at a few other situations:

Long-term goal: Having a better body image
Intermediate goal: Paying more attention to personal style (type of hairstyle, makeup, clothing you wear); looking in the mirror and appraising good points
Short-term goal: Modifying eating and exercise

● ● ●

Long-term goal: Going on a round-the-world trip
Intermediate goal: Finding the best routes, booking flights and hotels, etc.
Short-term goal: Saving money, planning itinerary, arranging leave of absence at work

● ● ●

Long-term goal: Becoming mayor of your town (or state senator, or governor)
Intermediate goals: Fundraising, enlisting the help of a team of people who want to see you run for office
Short-term goals: Getting known in your community, getting involved in local politics (from school board or zoning board to town council to state house of representatives, etc.)

You can do anything you want. But you have to train for the marathon with two-mile jogs before you can go the distance.

LIFE GOALS

It's a good idea to make yourself a list of the really *big* things you want—if not now, then perhaps someday. The people I interviewed for this book had a lot of very personal things on their lists, but most included the following items:

- Affection
- Expertness
- Parenthood
- Prestige
- Independence
- Service
- Pleasure
- Security
- Leadership ability
- Power
- Self-realization
- Wealth
- Companionship
- Nurturing

If you've lived at least five decades, you undoubtedly look back to see what you have and haven't accomplished, and look forward every once in a while to see where you're going. You may feel some big holes inside—regrets for things and people you've lost; longings for types of experience you've never had. If you are younger, you may not look back as often, but you may be fixed on future goals that seem impossible right now, or just out of reach.

You can *always* develop new life goals and recapture old ones— no door is ever closed to you just because something you wanted didn't work out the first time you tried. Reorganize the above list to your own specifications; add and subtract from it. Put it in your drawer, and take it out again next year for another revision. It's always interesting to see how your life goals change as you change.

> *All paths lead to the same goal: to convey to others what we are.*
>
> —PABLO NERUDA

BE A MASTER

If you have the opportunity, spend some time with a master—a world-class athlete or chef or opera star or a CEO in the business world. You will notice a similar streak in all of them. They appear to be relaxed, interested in others' opinions, willing to change their course if they are shown to be wrong, and very sure of whatever they're doing, whether it's mowing a lawn or being acclaimed as the best in their field.

One way to progress toward your goals is to tell yourself that you are already a master. Once you believe this, you have overcome the problem of doubt. It's easy to take positive risks when you feel you can't fail—and if you're already a master, you know exactly what to do and when to do it.

Close your eyes for a moment and picture yourself engaged in whatever activity you would like to be able to do brilliantly. Think of yourself as having achieved all the skills and passed all the trials that would lead you to being the very best in your field. Notice that you stand a little taller, you have a serene expression on your face, your breath moves easily in and out, and that you can see how effortless the work is because you love it and do it so well. Whether you aim to pitch a perfect game of softball, or win a court case, or get your toddler to stop having tantrums in the supermarket, see yourself having already done it. You enjoy practicing this activity for its own sake—not to gain more fame or to prove anything to anyone. It flows naturally from you, and you can do it perfectly any time you choose.

The more you think this way, the easier it will be to become a master—in your own good time.

YOUR FINAL GOAL IS NOT THE END

We all have the notion that there's one ultimate goal in our future. If we conquered it, we would be complete, at rest, perfectly relaxed and content with life.

That can't be true. No matter what you think you want to accomplish, there is something beyond it. If you climb to the pinnacle, there's no "up" anymore. So you have to go down, around, and up a new path. Otherwise, you stagnate at the top.

If you have a good appreciation of your assets and limitations, you know that right now, you stand above many of your peers in lots of different areas—maybe you're a better mother than some, a better artist, a better accountant, a better listener, a better lover. But you know, even as you grow in experience, that there are those who will always be a little ahead of you. It's great to have a healthy sense of competition, to feel that you just might be able to beat out this or that other person for a promotion, but you still have to understand that you'll never be the best. (Even the world-champion chess player was vanquished by a machine!)

If you had no one to look up to, and no other goal in mind, you'd die of boredom. And your smugness would erode the steady development of your mind and spirit.

Always plan ahead. Change your goals as you meet them. Make sure you re-evaluate your abilities and your needs, as you grow into more challenging feats.

> *Many persons have a wrong idea of what constitutes true happiness. It is not attained through self-gratification but fidelity to a worthy purpose.*
>
> —HELEN KELLER

KEEPING TO YOUR CHOSEN PATH

Just as it's common to reach a plateau when you're working to change behavior, it's also quite normal to get to a place where you've achieved a certain amount and don't believe you can get any higher.

Burnout is something to watch for when you're working your way to a goal, and there are some preventive tactics you can use to keep you from slipping back into old habits that stress you out.

- Keep a journal you can look back at, with pictures if possible. If you see where you were six months ago or even a three weeks ago, you'll be encouraged by what you've done so far.
- Challenge yourself a little every day—the more interesting the goal is, the more you'll stick with it.
- Request feedback from friends who know you well.
- Concentrate more on your inclinations and abilities than what they can get you—spend some time figuring out what you want to be when you grow up.

Even assuming that you have a fulfilling "job," you may wish to take time developing your innate skills. Work on all facets of yourself, whether you think of yourself as primarily artistic, verbal, mathematical, musical, kinesthetic, athletic, spiritual, socially adept, business- or sales-oriented, a legal genius, or a healer. You undoubtedly have a little bit of each of these qualities inside. Get to know them and you'll never be bored with your goals.

> *May this hand ward off your evils,*
> *Gather strength that you have lost.*
> *Display the power you have despaired of*
> *Pick you up from off your feet,*
> *Restore the magic that you lack.*
> *And while this hand shall guide you,*
> *And push you along the way,*
> *It is you*
> *And only you*
> *Who can ward off your own evils.*
>
> —MIA BRUNO

SKILLS TO HELP WITH REASONABLE GOAL-SETTING
Turning Your Fantasies into Reality

If you always wanted to be a rock star, but you never joined a band, and now you're fifty, you can still make use of the goal *behind* the dream. You love music, you love performing with others, so put together a cabaret act, or a weekend blues band, or a barbershop quartet. If you practice and get a few sets together, then record a demo tape on your home stereo and can peddle your act to various clubs in your community.

If you always wanted to build a log cabin in the woods, but you don't know one end of a hammer from the other, you can take a carpentry class and learn skills. You may eventually have to consult with an architect and hire a contractor, but you can at least do preliminary designs and perhaps help with the finish work as your home nears completion.

A fantasy is unreal because it usually goes beyond the reach of what's possible. But you can make it real by taking from it the elements that typify your serious goals and building on them.

Making Yourself a Goal Calendar

Writing down an "assignment" of the week, every week, gives you something to live up to. You might decide to eat better, clean out your closets, start a vegetable garden, or take tai chi classes. Revise your goals as you begin to achieve them and you may be amazed at what you've accomplished at the end of a year.

Make sure you have small goals and big ones—deciding that you will always put the cap back on the toothpaste tube because it bugs your partner when you don't is as worthwhile as deciding you're going back to school to get your Ph.D.

It's also a good idea (although a little daunting) to make yourself five- and ten-year plans. Suppose your kids are still in diapers, but you think you'd like to get back to work when they start first grade. Start reading the want ads now to see what types of jobs are available and what skills you'll need when you re-enter the workplace. Suppose you've been in the work force for decades, but can see retirement down the road. You might begin thinking about whether you want to stay where you are or move; whether to start a new business, adopt a baby from China, or just indulge yourself with your hard-earned pension.

Matching Your Goals With a Partner's

It's sometimes hard to have the self-discipline to do the things you know will profit you in the long run. One of the major deterrents to getting ahead is that we stand in our own way, feeling afraid or inept, procrastinating, or getting frustrated with our own slow attempts at change.

But when you have a buddy to accompany you on this journey, it gets easier. You can pat each other on the back, commiserate when things go wrong, watch each other's progress, goad each other on. It's important that you not have the exact same goals—that way lies too much competition—but it's challenging to pair yourself with someone who is really gung-ho and eager to leap tall buildings at a single bound.

Plan to meet once every other week and share your triumphs and difficulties. Listen and offer guidance, but remember that you are not your friend and she is not you—your own method of getting ahead and achieving your short-term, intermediate, and long-range goals is the one that works for you.

Part II

The Inner You: Relax, Pamper, and Enjoy Yourself

There is just so much you can do on the outside. You can be the most organized individual in the world, with lists of things to do that stretch around the block; you can prioritize until you know the exact order of your day and night. But the exterior is just a house for the person who lives within. If there's no core, no center, your carefully made plans may crumble and prove worthless.

Some women never get around to finding out just what makes them tick. They assume, because they haven't stopped ticking, that they'll go forever. But this isn't true.

In order to manage stress, you have to manage your emotions, thoughts, anxieties, moods, compulsions, desires, and needs. And this means you owe it to yourself to begin a dedicated campaign of retooling the person who often hides inside you, afraid to express an opinion or to enjoy herself because she's not quite sure who she is and what she's entitled to.

In this section, you will learn the steps to take in order to treat yourself well, increase pleasure in your life, breathe deeply, calm yourself with meditation, and explore your sexual potential to the heights.

Enjoy!

Step 5   **Take Time Off and Find a Passion**

A lice was frenzied and frantic. A professional pastry chef, she had a schedule that would turn butter rancid. That morning, she'd gotten up at 4 A.M. to prepare muffins and croissants for a weekend brunch for six hundred doctors at a conference. After that, she had to cut the cakes she'd baked the previous night and start the decorating. The lemon custard filling wouldn't set properly, and it was nearly impossible to get the glacé icing over it before it started running off the marble.

When her assistant (who was never on the premises at the same time as Alice!) called to tell her that she'd run out of chocolate syrup the previous evening and Alice would have to make more, Alice nearly panicked. She still had to bake bread for the dinner baskets and then start plating the cakes.

When she finished work at 10 P.M., she had to clean up and get the kitchen ready for the next morning. There were nights when she didn't think she could stand on her feet another minute, when she wondered what her husband was doing (and with whom), and when she longed for those days long ago when she was a French major at college and dreamed of becoming a translator at the U.N. with a little home-based cookie business on the side.

Luckily, she thought, as she drove home at midnight, Beethoven's Third blasting on her tape deck, the type of life she led left her with a great appetite—not just for food, but for the nicer things in life. When she enjoyed things, she *really* adored them. She loved music, she loved Sunday picnics with her husband, Gary (he unfailingly cooked on Saturdays so they'd have a feast the next day that she didn't have to prepare), and she loved the touch of his hands on the back of her neck when he massaged all the wrinkles out of the week. (He always told her she smelled like vanilla, and that was his favorite scent.)

Alice owed her sense of stability and general good feelings about life to the way that she balanced things—a little sugar, a little lemon, a dash of cardamom; a lot of pressure, a lot of hard physical labor, a lot of great pleasures. If she had a particularly awful day, she would come home, turn on the CD player and soak with bath beads in the tub and a glass of Chardonnay. That really helped. When she could spare it, she would put five dollars in her "mini-vacation" fund in the candybox in the kitchen, and when there was enough there, she and Gary would splurge on a bed and breakfast overnight.

As she mixed a batch of lavender and ginger cookies the next Monday at work, she thought about how good it was to have something to look forward to. There were crises every minute in a hotel kitchen, but she always knew that after she had resolved them (or not resolved them), she would be able to walk away and do something good for herself. Yes, sometimes she felt guilty about her hedonism— her own stash of Teuscher chocolates in the den, her special bottle of tantric massage oil that she'd bought for her and Gary to use, a stack of terrific CDs that she'd either buy or take out of the library each week, if she was feeling poor. But most of the time she allowed herself every pleasure she could jam into her busy life.

"I think baking is like problem-solving," she said. "You have these ingredients—that's the people you have to deal with and situations you get into—and you get to assemble them the way you see fit. Sometimes you use a recipe (that's like going along with all of society's expectations), and other times you wing it (that's like doing your own thing, no matter what anyone else thinks). You improvise and mold and shape stuff and use colors and flavors that shouldn't really go together, like lavender and ginger. Sometimes you make a disgusting mess and you have to chuck the whole thing down the sink, but other times, you arrive at a perfect blend of elements, and that makes you feel important and creative.

"I have moments when I am so totally harried, I'm thinking of seventeen things at once, and I want to cry. Sometimes I let go and scream at the people I'm working with and stalk out of the kitchen. Do I do it for effect? Not really—I just need to get out of the bad scene. I know bakers are supposed to be like opera stars—we're the divas of the food world—but I don't think my emotional nature would be any different if I were a computer programmer. My emotions occasionally run away with me, but at least I have them. I thank God for that. I think the fact that I feel deeply also helps me enjoy all the richness of a violin concerto or the complexity in the scent of a flower. I really appreciate everything that's there—the dreck and the gold."

When you look inside to the type of person you are in your non-stressed moments, you may at first see only a cloudy vision. You may be so accustomed to feeling down and anxious, you've forgotten what it is that pleases you about your life. Maybe you'll have some serious problems determining what exactly does give you pleasure. That's what this step is for. The options and alternatives offered—from music and massage and getting into a flotation tank to food and exercise to enjoying nature to dancing and drumming—can be used to increase your pleasure potential.

> *I take it as a prime cause of the present confusion of society that it is too sickly and too doubtful frankly to use pleasure as a test of value.*
>
> —REBECCA WEST

WHY CAN'T WOMEN HAVE A GOOD TIME?

"Relax and enjoy yourself." Why is this such a difficult instruction for most women? A good many of us were taught from earliest childhood that we had to *do* something worthwhile before we were allowed to go out and play—clean our room, take care of our little sister, practice the piano. So by the time we finally were free, we'd lost the impetus to have a ball.

America is, by and large, a puritanical society. Our ancestors denied themselves, scourged themselves, and subjected themselves to public as well as private humiliations in the name of freedom of worship. Yes, of course, we're beyond all that—and yet the strict maxims of those harsh men and women of long ago are still imbedded deeply in our hard drives. We tear apart the private lives of our politicians and celebrities, and we gossip about those who sit around on their duffs and succeed without the requisite hard work. We have a feeling that life isn't good unless it hurts.

There's another factor here that is even more significant for many women. We don't believe we actually *deserve* to have a good time and experience pleasure. This is not just true of women who were always criticized and nagged as kids—it is also true of those who were praised for their diligence and conscientious approach to life and began to set unreasonable expectations for themselves that had to be met, every single time, in every single situation.

Deep down we may be uncertain as to how much we have to perform, how many problems we have to solve, how much time should be spent doing for another individual or a cause before we feel comfortable accepting a reward. And the nature of the reward itself may become a difficult decision. A new blouse on sale that can be worn to work or to church might seem appropriate, but a massage or facial—or even an evening spent alone in a bubble bath with a glass of wine—might seem frivolous and a waste of time.

Most women are excellent list-makers—if we accomplish twelve chores during a weekend, we feel we're allowed a break. But as soon as we're asked to pitch in and help at a community fair or we have a sick parent in the hospital, we feel we have to set the pleasure aside for later, and go do some more work.

When is later? When it is too late? If we feel that we are basically unworthy and must *earn* merit badges throughout life, we are doomed to an existence that measures behavior and intention as either "good" or "bad." But when we get out of the tit-for-tat rut that keeps us from being kind to ourselves, and begin to see that our rewards are just as important to us as our obligations, then we are better able to care for our inner selves.

BOOST YOUR SELF-ESTEEM BY NURTURING YOURSELF

If you've always been a terrific helpmeet, if you can manage a home, a family, and a job, if you're always thinking about what has to be done next for others around you, then you are a nurturer.

The dictionary defines *nurturing* as "providing food, nourishment, and protection." When you nurture someone else, you take care of all their most basic needs. If you are like most women, you are usually excellent at this task.

The only one you forget to nurture is yourself. And that's a big omission. If you don't protect your interests, if you are always hungry for the nourishment you never provide for yourself, how can you get the most out of each day? How can you do all the boring, tedious, unpleasant tasks and not balance them with exciting and pleasurable ones?

DEVELOP MAD PASSIONS

Joseph Campbell described it as "following your bliss." He suggested that the individuals who are most at peace with themselves have arranged their lives so that they can surround themselves with those things they love best. Their purpose in life, in fact, is constantly to expand their capacity for pleasure.

But in order to feel pleasure, we must abandon ourselves to pursuits that really delight us rather than profit us anything specific. It's wonderful if you grow up with a passion for collecting butterflies and it stays with you forever. But many of us lose our childhood enthusiasms and never replace them with anything else.

This is the time. When you are most stressed, when you feel you can't cope, this is when you need something that takes your mind and spirit to a comfortable and joyful place.

Engaging in pleasurable activities can be difficult emotionally if you feel too guilty, so start small, practicing with small delights. That way you can learn to tolerate feeling uncomfortable at first, not expecting to love what you're doing right away. Then, as it feels easier to take that bubble bath or buy yourself flowers, you can work your way up to more extravagant pleasures, like a night at a bed-and-breakfast all by yourself, or a class in stained glassmaking.

So what *do* you like to do? If you have one passion—gardening, quilting, singing, practicing *aikido*, collecting Hummel figurines— you are one step ahead of the game. If you feel strongly about some activity you are involved with, you have a place to go when your children act rotten and the bills are piling up. It's vital to know that even when you feel so pressured you have no time to go to the bathroom, you can still dream about, think about, and look forward to your terrific other pursuit.

If you are managing an exceptionally busy life, as so many of us are, it's possible that you have no extracurricular activities. You probably can't even think what you'd like to do if you decided to embark on one. Although you undoubtedly say you couldn't fit in anything else in the twenty-four hours you're allotted each day, it's nearly a requirement for a stress-reduction program to have one thing that you don't *have* to do but *want* to do.

How do you find a passion? Usually it finds you, but you must be open to it. Glance through adult education brochures, and read notices on the supermarket or health-food store bulletin board for classes or workshops. Go to your library or surf the Internet, starting with general subject areas and moving to more specific ones.

GETTING YOUR ENDORPHINS UP WITH EXERCISE

If you are still of the opinion that physical activity is drudgery and just makes you sweat, huff, and dehydrate, let me try to change your mind. Exercise is an all-purpose tonic that:

- Elevates mood by triggering the production of endorphins in the brain, those natural opiates that give us a sense of well-being
- Gives us a better self-image and boosts self-esteem and self-confidence
- Facilitates better use of all the organ systems in the body
- Enhances the quality of life as we age by increasing aerobic fitness, strength, flexibility, and endurance

There are dozens of books on the market that purport to give you *the* clue to picking an exercise program and sticking with it. My suggestion is that you simply use the instructions above about following your passion. If you think you like walking, then walk every day. If swimming makes you feel free as a fish, go jump in a lake. You may have to experiment a little—try a day of hiking, one of biking, one of racquet sports, one of dance, one of martial arts, one at the gym or Y so you can use the machinery and do the step classes. Eventually, you'll find the one or two activities that support the type of person you are.

Sticking to the exercise regime you've finally settled on is a challenge for every individual, no matter how much you love it. Most women find that if they can get up a little earlier, they can fit in half an hour before the family wakes up—if they wait too late in the day, they will undoubtedly come up with a dozen other time-consuming events they absolutely have to pack in first.

Some women find that signing a promise and putting it where they can see it (maybe plastered on the bathroom mirror), is one way to keep moving; others find that the answer lies in selecting a partner (a spouse or friend) who will engage in this activity with you.

There will be a time when you get sick or have a house guest and just can't manage your daily routine. Don't make those few days off an excuse for stopping completely. Instead, spend a few minutes on each of the days off imagining yourself doing the exercise. Studies have shown that athletes who visualize themselves involved in their sport in addition to practicing actually do better in competition than those who just get out there on the field every day and don't have a mental connection to the activity.

So think about yourself being active. Tell yourself how great you've felt since you started. Tell yourself that you deserve this wonderful experience, and the sooner you can get back, the better. Eventually, you will.

ENJOYING—NOT ABUSING—FOOD AND DRINK

The body needs fuel, but food and drink is a lot more than just the gas to make your car go. Food is a comfort, a distraction, a temptress, and a social event. For many people, it is the bane of their existence, and they are never happy with what they put into their mouths because they feel too guilty to enjoy it.

You can turn food into a major pleasure by practicing the following health-conscious approach to food and diet. Food will no longer be an obsession, a craving, or a reward, but instead a delightful corollary to your exercise program and life in general. You will start to taste food rather than ingest it. You will no longer think about restricting calories or types of food, but rather will experiment with expanding your food repertoire, using food like the colors on a palette to create an extraordinary work of art that is ever fresh, ever changing.

If you examine what you eat, when you eat it, how and why you eat it, and how much of it you eat, you will never need to consider the word "diet" again. In addition, you will enjoy and savor everything that goes into your mouth.

What You Eat

Select a well-balanced menu based on the Food Pyramid put out by the Department of Agriculture. That means you should go heavy on complex carbohydrates such as pasta, cereals, and breads, eat lots of vegetables—both starchy and nonstarchy, consume legumes more than meat for your protein, and go lightly on fats and sugars. Remember that your weekly allotment of food can include a little of everything: hollandaise sauce as well as bean sprouts, potato chips as well as oat bran.

Be sure that you always put foods you absolutely adore on your shopping list. When you get home from the supermarket, repackage them into small containers so that you have just the right-sized portions at hand when you're hungry for them.

Try one new food a week, just because it is fun to have a new taste sensation. Eat a mango, have some wheat grass, taste a cannoli, make a tempeh burger. Your tastebuds will really wake up and in addition, you'll undoubtedly come up with a healthier regimen than the old routine one you have now.

When You Eat

If you eat at set mealtimes, you are eating to live, not to enjoy. The breakfast, lunch, and dinner routine we've all grown up with was invented purely for convenience; the body actually needs nourishment when it burns (or is about to burn) calories. If you can reschedule, even for a few weeks, you should consider eating five small meals a day as follows: a cup of herb tea and a few crackers when you wake up, a midmorning bagel or muffin, a midafternoon pasta salad, a late afternoon portion of vegetables and beans with a green salad, and a midevening snack of fruit and cottage cheese. You will find that you don't get hunger pangs and feel satisfied with less when you know the next meal is coming soon after.

How You Eat

Don't eat standing up, in front of the refrigerator, or in front of the TV. If you're eating alone, prepare the meal just as you would if you were having a party. Turn on some pleasant music, set the table, use a cloth napkin. If you have a family, make a new rule that mealtime is for eating. That means no phone calls, no homework or reading at the table, no jumping up to go to play practice. The less stressful the eating environment, the better you assimilate your food, and the more healthful it is for your body and mind.

Why You Eat

Do you eat when you're hungry and stop when you're full? Probably not. Often, we eat because we're bored or annoyed or feeling sorry for ourselves. If your mother typically solved your problems with the cookie-and-milk solution, you undoubtedly feed yourself emotionally the same way now.

Think before you consume the quart of Häagen-Dazs. Why are you really so ravenous? You can probably get by with a scoop of ice cream, a glass of water, a good cry, and a walk around the block in the fresh air.

Try this interesting experiment in hunger and satiety, pioneered by Dr. Phillip Sinaikin, a bariatrician in Longwood, Florida, which will teach you to renegotiate your relationship with food. Prepare a regular meal—perhaps a sandwich, a pickle, a few chips, and a glass of juice. Eat exactly half the meal, then take fifteen minutes to answer your e-mail, make a few phone calls, or take a walk. When you come back, ask yourself if you're still hungry. If you are, divide the half-meal in half again, and consume the next quarter. Wait fifteen more minutes, and see whether you need any more food. You may in fact finish the entire meal, but it will take you longer and you will feel more satisfied because you will have allowed the central sensations in your brain to catch up with the hunger receptors in your stomach. Another benefit of this experiment is that you always have some more food to look forward to!

The same principles apply to consuming alcohol and caffeine in moderation. A glass of wine or a cappuccino at the end of the day can be relaxing and pleasurable. You simply have to work with your cravings to know when and why you are drinking these substances—and to quit while you're ahead.

THINGS THAT MAKE YOU GLOW

The "glow response" has been identified as a highly charged positive reaction to an experience or event. You can achieve this type of everyday ecstasy by making a list of times in your life when you've been completely, perfectly happy—even if that feeling only lasted for a moment or two.

When you're glowing, you stay single-mindedly focused on your joy, and you can't be distracted by the numerous things and people that are so annoying and difficult at other times. During this period of emotional arousal, your sympathetic nervous system gets in gear—your heartbeat, blood pressure, perspiration, and muscle tension all rise and then subside within seconds, when your parasympathetic system kicks in. You feel more alive, more capable, better able to meet the challenges that face you afterward.

And the great thing about glowing is that you can get this response without even repeating the experience. Once again, imagination and memory are the key. All you have to do is close your eyes and put yourself back in that deliriously happy setting—very often the image of what occurred will evoke a stronger physical response than the actual experience. Think about how wonderful it was to greet your lover after having been away for a month; or how you felt when you got the job you wanted; or what it was like to give birth to your first child.

You can glow from common daily events (seeing a sunset or hearing your partner say, "I love you,") or from the biggest thrills (parachuting out of a plane or getting a long-awaited promotion).

Glowing not only makes you feel blissful, it also comforts you when you're down and need to patch yourself up. It's the grown-up equivalent of sitting on your mother's lap and having her stroke your hair when you were sad or hurt.

The various "comfort things" that women do are as varied as their own imaginations. Find at least ten items below that have helped in the past, and put them in order so that you can start using them on a regular basis. Then add at least five of your own to the bottom of the list.

Some Common Ways to Glow
- Talking to friends (this was the most prevalent response, bar none, from the women I interviewed for this book)
- Talking to yourself, telling yourself everything's going to be okay (this is not a sign of mental derangement)
- Getting outside, being active (cycling, cross-country skiing, hiking, tennis, swimming, gardening)

- Doing yoga or tai chi
- Quilting, sewing, or knitting
- Surfing the Internet
- Getting a full-body massage or a facial
- Offering a helping hand to someone in need
- Eating—chocolate, cookies, and ice cream top the list
- Reading, sometimes escapist fiction
- Soaking in the tub with fragrant oils or bath gel
- Spending time with those you love
- Getting a new car
- Improving your health by changing diet, exercise, and lifestyle patterns
- Giving presents to someone else
- Christmas
- Coming home to your partner after a hard day
- Kisses
- New clothes
- A spring day
- A friendly puppy
- Finishing your morning run
- Watching the snow come down at the window
- Seeing your child for the first time
- Getting an unexpected card or letter
- Looking at pictures of yourself when you were little
- Climbing a mountain
- Sitting in front of a fire
- Sticking your toes in cool sand on a hot day
- Skinny dipping
- Standing under a waterfall
- Walking in the rain
- Sleeping late on Sunday morning
- Watching the Academy Awards and Grammys
- Not watching any TV at all for a week
- Relaxing in a lawn chair and vegging out
- Going to a park you really love
- Window shopping; occasionally buying something frivolous
- Seeing a movie
- Listening to music

- Spending private time
- Planning a trip
- Masturbating
- Drinking a glass of wine or two
- Singing and playing a musical instrument (for yourself or for others)

And I also love to:

1. _____
2. _____
3. _____
4. _____
5. _____

EXPLORING YOUR SENSUAL POTENTIAL

Women are tactile creatures—we reach out through our senses to enjoy the world. Our eyes grab onto familiar and startling sights. Our ears take in the stimulation of words, music, and other sounds that open up our environment for us. We can heighten our sense of taste as we become gourmands of life—the most ordinary flavors can take on a delicious piquance, and the heady scents around us set the mood for whatever activity we wish to indulge in.

If you become more sensual and spend time *really* looking at a sunset, or tasting one raisin instead of a handful, or listening to the quieter voice in a Renaissance madrigal, you are building yourself up, heightening your appreciation of all those elements that can be too hastily dismissed or ignored. And the more sensual you are, the more you can reap full enjoyment out of the most ordinary things.

We touch when we're sexual, of course, but that's a momentary delight compared to the myriad ways we can touch (physically, mentally, emotionally, and spiritually) when we connect with others who are also sensually aware. The mysterious and powerful pull of our senses keeps what we do and how we do it forever fresh.

FINDING YOUR JOY IN NATURE

A field of wildflowers, a desolate cave, a snowy mountaintop, a pristine beach with the waves lapping at your toes. Any and all of these are

Mother Nature's gifts to us. And particularly in these days, where unspoiled landscapes are becoming few and far between, we tend to marvel at the peace, solitude, majesty and power of settings that are not manmade. Participating in the abundance of nature relieves stress.

If you live in a city, you are accosted by noise pollution, air pollution, electromagnetic fields, and a battery of people who are just as stressed-out as you are. Even if you thrive on city life, it's a good idea to get away from it every once in a while. The pleasure of sitting on a park bench, only a few blocks from the skyscrapers and traffic lights, can change your whole day and give you a new perspective on the places you have to go and responsibilities you have to meet. This time out of time, where you can commune with a bird pecking at a few crumbs, watch leaves being wafted by a breeze, and see the ripples on a pond, offers a vital respite that can make you more able to shoulder the burdens waiting for you at home, at the office, or elsewhere.

If you already live in a rural area, you may be the type of person who reaps the benefits of nature daily, but you may also have begun to ignore the beauty around you. When you have it so accessible at all times, it's easy to forget it's there. Try a different natural setting from the one you're accustomed to so that you'll have beginner's mind about the scent of the air, the stature of the trees, the different color of the light.

There is probably nothing as instructive as growing a garden if you wish to look at nature as a teacher. From the very first hard work of clearing a site and digging beds, to the preparation with soil, mulch, and fertilizer, to the placement of your plants, to the amazing daily progress that occurs without much intervention other than water, light, and air, you get to see what's really important on earth. If you can use the lesson of the garden to treat your own concerns—give them a little push in the right direction and then let them resolve by themselves—you are a very wise woman.

MOOD AND MUSIC

Music has charms to soothe a savage breast,
To soften rocks, or bend a knotted oak.
—WILLIAM CONGREVE

We respond to harmony in sound just as we do to harmony within ourselves. You probably have some favorite song or piece of music that makes you feel that all is right with the world. That may be because you associate it with a particular event or person, or it may stand alone among your emotional resources as a type of comfort that cannot be replicated anywhere else in your life.

Not only does a soothing sound seem to straighten out our rumpled feelings, but the rhythm inherent in any piece and any type of music also gets us back on track. The reason may have something to do with our instinctive response to the heartbeat we heard when we were inside our mothers, before we knew the world and how difficult it could be. When you start tapping your feet or swaying your head to a beat, you have a built-in regulator to help adjust your moods.

It doesn't matter if you can carry a tune or remember which composer wrote the piece. You can use music therapy whenever and wherever you may be, thanks to modern technology. Wear a headset when you walk or pop a CD into your CD-ROM player when you have your computer on. Sing to yourself—make a joyful noise.

Spend some time surfing your radio band for stations that play something that appeals to you. You may find, in different moods, that you crave certain sounds—jazz when you're quiet and reflective, blues when you can't deal with another human being, classical when you're getting organized, rock 'n' roll when you just want to howl. Consciously sit and listen to the music—don't do something else and use it as background noise. Follow its intricate patterns and sequences, and attempt to visualize a scene that it evokes. Bring yourself into the picture and use the musical impetus to resolve some area of dissension or anxiety you may be feeling.

For example, if a Billie Holiday blues number makes you want to cry, let the tears come and see yourself in the situation that is making you unutterably sad. Instead of just wallowing in it, however, know that this sadness ends as the song ends. So as the last bars ring in your ears, find a way to forgive yourself and other people in the situation with you, and move on. You will still have remnants of the feeling of grief within you, but understand that the present moment—the one you're in now that the song has ended—offers you hope and a new beginning. You are now capable of dealing with the present rather than the past distress you've been experiencing over and over.

You can use joyful, snappy, and off-beat music in the same way by aligning your mood to what you're listening to. By focusing clearly on what the music means to you, and paralleling your feelings with the progress of the song, you can create your own program for change and growth.

DANCE AND DRUM YOUR CARES AWAY

> *When you do dance, I wish you*
> *A wave o' the sea, that you might ever do*
> *Nothing but that.*
> —WILLIAM SHAKESPEARE, *THE WINTER'S TALE*

Dance, like music, is one of the oldest known ways to exorcise bad spirits. The body, moving freely through time and space, casts off pain and depression and takes on a self-confident, purposeful energy. The whirling dervishes of the Middle East spin into a trance state where they have no awareness of anything but their gyrating center; the harem dancers of Turkey and the ancient Indian temple dancers joined sensual and erotic postures to spiritual development.

Rhythm is everything when you're dancing. Slow, fast, syncopated, or on the beat, you are subtly drawn into an altered state of consciousness as you obey the regular count of meter. Like exercise, dance is an aerobic activity that releases endorphins and also moves the breath in a healthful way—but the element of rhythm and self-expression adds another dimension of benefit. Paying attention to the beat, you cannot fall back into the old sluggish fatigue and stress patterns— you have to keep up, especially if you're moving with a partner. Dance also releases inhibitions that may have caused the anxiety and stress in the first place.

You can use dance the same way you use music to handle the problem you're wrestling with. You can whirl your head in a circle to get rid of depressing thoughts; you can throw your arms overhead—

donating your bad feelings to the gods. You can stomp on the floor, getting out all your anger.

Another rhythmic stress-reducer is drumming. For thousands of years, cultures all over the earth have explored the communicative nature of the drums—from rocking caribe congas to high-pitched tablas, to the singing dumbek and djembes, to the long birch log drum—to a pot that you bang with a stick. The reason that hitting an object that makes sound is so effective for taking away stress is that you let out a good deal of aggression (through the active movement and striking of a surface) and you also free up the creative, rhythmic impulse that lurks under the surface, usually too timid to come out.

The combination of dance and drumming is a joyous experience and can be done alone, with a partner, or with a huge group of stressed-out individuals searching for a new and different outlet.

THE MYSTERIOUS POWER OF MASSAGE

Massage uses the power of touch to release tension and stimulate certain parts the body. When you feel a set of firm, caring hands on you, you know that you're not alone, and that someone else is devoted to alleviating your stress. You may feel like a baby in her mother's arms, or a helpless animal who's been rescued from a storm. If you decide that you have to take charge, you will soon find that you aren't getting much benefit at all from the experience. It's not easy to let go of old prejudices about invasion of privacy and intimate touch that isn't sexual, but instead offers relief and comfort. Your attitude will tense your mind, which in turn will tense your body.

But by breathing and listening attentively to the instructions of the person tending you, you will begin to enjoy what's happening, even if it's painful to work out all those knots. Once you are able to give yourself over to the hands of the practitioner, whether it's a friend or partner, a professional massage therapist, a shiatsu practitioner, or any other type of bodyworker, you will find that your body tells the tale of whatever's ailing your mind and spirit. The person working on you will be able to zero in on all the various tensions and blockages you've been holding, and with gentle manipulation, help you to alleviate them.

Massage can loosen tight limbs, reduce soreness, and allow your muscles to sit more comfortably beside your joints and bones. It can also make you release some deep emotions that you've been hiding— it's not at all unusual to cry or moan on the massage table. It's also not unusual to laugh.

There are several well-known types of massage. Always ask, if you're seeking professional care, whether the practitioner is licensed:

- Swedish massage involves rubbing and stroking different body parts to alleviate stress and tension
- Shiatsu (acupressure) involves deep pressure, applied with thumbs, fingers, elbows, or feet
- Therapeutic massage (light or deep) is designed to provide healing to afflicted organs and tissues
- Deep tissue massage mixes massage and psychological appraisal of a condition
- Sensual massage is a shared experience between partners to eradicate personal barriers without being overtly sexual.

Any type of touch is healing. In the various studies on stress done on laboratory animals, those who are "gentled" or held by humans during experiments develop a relative immunity to stress. The rats who are handled the most during the first ten days of life usually weigh the most, learn best, and survive longest.

We, who are a lot more sophisticated in our reactions, can benefit just as much as those creatures in cages. By allowing someone else to touch us, we can adapt much better to stressful circumstances.

GO FLOAT

In the 1960s, flotation tanks became yet another way to tune in and drop out. The experience of lying in a darkened room in a big tub filled with Epsom salts was considered a "high" akin to taking hallucinogenic drugs.

The tanks are still around (see the resource appendix for locations), but they offer a great deal more than a wild and wacky experience.

The impetus for developing salt spas came, of course, from history that related the therapeutic effect of lying in the mineral-rich Dead Sea. The mineral components (Epsom salts and magnesium) are absorbed into your bloodstream through your pores and assist in removing toxins from the body. Many spas around the world have included hydrotherapy as part of their regimes—but it's clearly not just for the physical effect.

Flotation therapy takes the stress out of the mind and spirit. It allows you to be weightless in a completely safe environment, as though you are being held by powerful, nonjudgmental arms. Since you are completely supported (it's impossible to sink), you learn an important lesson in relaxation—can you really let go? Are there any parts of your body still holding the tension of the day?

The benefits of this extraordinary experience last far beyond your hour in the salt water. A limited number of studies have shown that repeated floating sessions help to lower blood pressure, improve sleep, improve concentration, enhance creativity, and encourage positive behavior change such as losing weight and quitting smoking.

CONSIDER REIKI

Reiki is a Japanese system of therapeutic or healing touch. The word means "universal transcendent spirit" and involves channeling energy for healing. Although you can be trained to do Reiki on yourself, initially you will study with a Reiki master who has achieved three consecutively higher degrees of training.

The power of touch has been acknowledged for centuries as one of the key elements in healing. Laying on of hands is more than just calming or uplifting in Reiki. It is, rather, a connective force that puts you in touch with all the healing energy in the universe.

It's difficult to describe Reiki without sounding terribly mystical, but that's partly because the training is so secretive, and no one is exactly sure how it works. Within a three-day period, the trainees are "tuned"—sort of like human violins—to a higher vibratory level. As they do the exercises and receive certain words and sounds from their teacher, they become able to draw energy from the universe and apply it in a therapeutic manner.

You feel a lot of heat during your treatments on the afflicted area, whether it's a sore knee or the anxiety in your head. It is not the Reiki therapist who creates this warmth—rather, it's the person they're working on. Your need determines how much heat and healing comes through the channel. The energy you feel is funneled through the channel's body and into yours. If you train as a Reiki channel, you will learn how to draw this healing energy for yourself.

The system was devised by Dr. Mikao Usui in the mid-1800s. Dr. Usui, dean of a small Japanese university, went on a pilgrimage to discover why the type of healing done by Jesus and Buddha was no longer being performed. After a long fast and period of meditation on a mountaintop, he was filled with a vision of light and energy. Terribly excited, he began to run down the mountain, but he tripped and cut his foot. As he bent down to grab it, the bleeding stopped and the pain vanished. After this experience, he devoted his life to teaching others how to use the power he had gained.

During the treatments, your practitioner will stimulate various glands and associated organs of the body with this special touch. In addition to heat, you may feel vibration or sudden release of blockages during the process. At other times, you may feel a great calm settle over you.

As with any other technique that can help you manage your stress, you must do more than simply "be there" in order to receive its healing benefit. You don't have to know how Reiki works as long as you feel open to receiving it. And over time, as you feel more relaxed, you may judge its benefits in an even more positive light.

There are two things to aim at in life: First, to get what you want; and, after that, to enjoy it. Only the wisest of mankind achieve the second.
—LOGAN PEARSALL SMITH

USING YOUR PLEASURE WELL AND WISELY

Doing all the various activities discussed in this chapter is just a start—in order to help you reduce your stress, you must truly feel that the pursuit of your own pleasure is not self-indulgent, nor are you greedy or selfish to feel that you deserve it. If you're really enjoying yourself, you may notice that you feel like a different person, with no room inside for worry.

You will probably feel guilty at first, not knowing just what to make of your new self-kindness. And you may not even enjoy the bouquet of flowers or the massage or the new CD or the extra pillow on your bed. But after a while, nurturing yourself will become as natural as nurturing everyone else in your life, and you may actually bump yourself up to the head of the line. When you take care of number one, you have more to give to others.

SKILLS TO HELP YOU INCREASE PLEASURE

Believe That You're Worth It

One way to build self-esteem is to pretend that you already think incredibly well of yourself. As the lyric from the Rogers and Hammerstein song goes, "Make believe you're brave/And the trick will take you far./ You may be as brave/As you make believe you are."

If you start with the premise that you are a very valuable individual (even if you have your doubts!) and you insist on treating yourself well, you may be amazed at how quickly you start to fall in line with a new attitude. Begin with the assumption that you're good, you're smart, you work hard, and you deserve every benefit you can possibly wring out of life.

Find Out What Gives You Pleasure

If you are uncertain as to what you really want to do that will afford you great pleasure, begin to explore:

- If you've always loved animals, you could call your local zoo or the natural history museum and see what types of programs they offer.
- If you're big on the environment, try the parks programs.
- If you've always liked to cook, take an exotic gourmet or pastry course.
- If you always hankered to be an astronaut, call your local planetarium and see what volunteers can do there.
- Love Paris? There's probably a Francophile club or monthly meeting group in your area. Call a local college or university.
- Is music your thing? Get a subscription to the symphony, chamber music society, or jazz series; if you'd rather play yourself, look in the entertainment section of your paper for auditions for local performing groups.
- If watching green things grow fills you with delight, call the local gardening club or the county agent or agriculture department to find out how you get on a hotline, helping others with gardening problems.

If you have no spare time in which to indulge these passions, you need to go back to Step 1 and think about your priorities. The time you spend doing things you love will increase your tolerance for the lousy moments and give you lots to look forward to.

Step 6   **Learn to Breathe**

"The doctors all told me my spinal injury would heal in two months. I'd been in a terrible car crash, but they weren't worried, because I was so tough. That was a laugh."

Jennifer was grateful to be alive—the accident had left her with six fused vertebrae, and the bones above and below the injury were also damaged. She was practically immobile, so her husband took over all her household responsibilities. Although she had just published her first book and had been set to go on tour, she canceled everything and went to bed.

"My life was on hold. At first I was just frustrated. And in pain. God, I'd never really felt pain before—giving birth was a breeze compared to this! I'd never had any physical limitations, and for 62, I was in great shape. Or I had been. I couldn't believe I was going to be a cripple. I *wouldn't* believe it.

"In a while, the frustration turned to anxiety. What if I was never all right again? What if I didn't get strong enough to put my life back together? I had just written a book about how to look great at any age, and here I was, a mess—not too pretty, I'll tell you. All bloated from taking steroids, and big circles under my eyes from not sleeping. I was too tired to think about working on a new book proposal or querying a magazine about an article. And then, when the doctor allowed me up, and I started moving around again, that's when the trouble really started.

"One day I bent over and felt this pain like an icepick stabbing right into my lower back. I screamed and writhed in agony until my husband took me to the orthopedist for an adjustment. At the beginning of my therapy, I had between four and ten adjustments a day.

"Relafen (an anti-inflammatory drug) took the pain away like magic, but the doctor warned me I could only stay on it two months or risk a bleeding ulcer and other nasty surprises. So even though I felt physically better, I was still an emotional wreck. The stress of what was going on inside my body was still so fresh—I kept reliving the accident and it took my breath away, literally. I could barely inhale. I kept thinking any false moves and I was a goner.

"I don't think anyone who hasn't experienced disability can really understand. Whenever I see footage of Christopher Reeve after that horse threw him, I think, 'Boy, is he brave!' He feels no pain because he's paralyzed, but his whole life revolves around what he *can't* do. Well, that's how I saw what was going on in my life. If I wanted to talk to someone, I needed a speaker phone because it was too much agony to hold a receiver to my ear. If I wanted to eat, I had to plot my way around the kitchen so I wouldn't have to bend or stretch for anything. Putting on clothes was a challenge, and getting into a car was so scary I usually stayed home. What if I fell? What if I couldn't get up? And what would I do when I couldn't take the Relafen anymore?

"It wasn't just the pain. Bad things started happening, and in my frame of mind, it seemed like they were all mystically tied into the accident. My office assistant quit and my daughter's boyfriend was diagnosed with a malignant brain tumor. My son and my son-in-law were both laid off within weeks of one another. The guy who had hit me had no insurance. I found out my literary agent had been withholding money from me, and I had to sue. I knew I wasn't paranoid—there really were awful things happening in my life.

"I told myself that all the other people's problems weren't mine, and that my major job was to concentrate on getting well, but I'm not built like that. I had this image of myself as stoic, able to handle anything—well, turns out I was just the opposite. I was so incredibly depressed, and every additional piece of bad news sent me deeper and deeper. I looked in the mirror and I thought, that's not me. I felt like I was going to be a victim forever.

"It's still not clear to me what pulled me out of this nightmare. I took Prozac for six months because I honestly started thinking about when I should commit suicide instead of whether I should. The drug got me on an even keel emotionally so that I could begin to consider having a future. One that I could control.

"I started doing some self-hypnosis when I read something about how effective it could be with pain. I thought if I could do something to relax my mind and take the stress out of my body and stop the repetitive thoughts that were keeping me awake at night, that would be a start. The technique really worked. But it wasn't enough.

"Someone asked me to go with her and take this class in Tibetan breathing techniques. I thought it sounded strange, but might be fun for an evening. That night, in fact, was what turned me around. The teacher gave me a list of books to read, and then I found other workshops that deepened my understanding of what the breath can do. From being too scared to inhale because I thought it would hurt too much, I really opened up. When I started doing some easy yoga postures with my physical therapist, I remembered how I'd been taught to breathe during my Lamaze training when my kids were born. And from what I remembered, I'd gotten through those births without much pain.

"As I got into the practice, I found that breathing calmed me down, filled me up and gave me a lot of strength. Now I'm doing half an hour of breathing techniques twice a day. It's wonderful."

Breathing in, I calm body and mind
Breathing out, I smile.
Dwelling in the present moment
I know that this is the only moment.
—THICH NHAT HANH, Sutra on the Full
Awareness of Breathing

LEARNING TO BREATHE

The stress of being ill has been shown to magnify and exacerbate the routine life stress most of us carry around. When it hurts too much to laugh, you never really smile inside. When it's too agonizing to move, you can't just walk away from a bad situation. You feel stuck. And this perpetuates the stress cycle—not feeling well enough to care for yourself, you sense a hopelessness about your situation. And then everything, from a shirt lost at the cleaners to a job lost because you couldn't work long hours, can seem like the end of the world.

But Jennifer, luckily, has discovered one of the primary secrets of stress management. Breath is life. In Greek, the words *psyche pneuma* mean breath, soul, air, or spirit. The Latin word for breath, *anima*, also refers to the soul. The Eastern traditions—Chinese, Japanese, and Sanskrit—use the words *qi*, *ki*, and *prana*, which not only refer to breath but also to the "life force."

But when we're under a great deal of pressure, we deny ourselves access to the most healing natural therapy we've got. Our muscles clench, our solar plexus tightens, and we squeeze every bit of air we've got back up through our chest and clavicles. The body feels like it's encased in a hard shell, with barely enough space for a stream of air to squeeze through.

The amount of beneficial oxygen most people take in each day is not enough to feel really good—it's just getting by, surviving. When we're upset and distressed, we keep the breath bottled up, or gasp for air. We may begin to hyperventilate, feeling an excruciating air hunger that just gets worse the harder we try to suck in a breath. And our whole system loses out when there isn't enough oxygen being carried by the bloodstream to the various organs, particularly the brain. You literally can't think straight if you don't breathe right.

But we can learn to recapture the talent we were given at birth. When you practice the various techniques (which can be used instantly, the minute you feel stressed), you have tools at your disposal to make yourself and your surroundings a lot better.

First of all the twinkling stars vibrated, but remained motionless in space, then all the celestial globes were united into one series of movements....Firmament and planets both disappeared, but the mighty breath which gives life to all things and in which all is bound up remained.

—VINCENT VAN GOGH

WHY BREATHING HELPS TO ALLEVIATE STRESS

If you're hurt, physically or mentally, you tend to hold your breath, almost as though you wished to stop the world and your own participation in it. But as soon as you start to inhale and exhale fully, rhythmically, you have an effective distraction from whatever is going on. If you gave birth, and you're within the age range of women who trained long and hard at Lamaze or Bradley techniques, you'll remember that they didn't necessarily obliterate your pain, but they did give you a way to work through the discomfort, to ease your tension and persuade your mind to relax even in the midst of an excruciating contraction.

Think of a yogi sitting on a bed of nails or walking across hot coals—he has no more physical resources than you or I, but he knows exactly how to take his mind away from the nerve stimulus to his skin by channeling all his energy through the oxygen intake and output system. You can do this too, and overcome distress while you enhance your body's ability to fill itself with nourishing oxygen and your brain's ability to trigger comfortable neurotransmitter production.

Proper breathing is also a way for the body to discharge toxins. Just as we dispose of harmful substances through our sweat, tears, urine, and feces, we can also do it with well-oxygenated breath. By freeing yourself of unnecessary waste material, you feel better physically and are better able to cope mentally and emotionally.

The smoke of my own breath,
echoes, ripples, buzz'd whispers,
love-root, silk-thread,
crotch and vine,
my respiration and inspiration,
the beating of my heart,
the passing of blood and air
through my lungs...

—WALT WHITMAN

THE SCIENCE OF BREATHING

It seems easy because it's involuntary; actually, the process of breathing is so amazingly complex that if we had to think about it in order to do it, few of us could master it.

We take a breath, then let it out, take another, and let it out. The oxygen we inhale doesn't last very long, just long enough for it to travel from the nose and mouth to the windpipe to the lungs, branching in two directions to be absorbed into the bronchi. Each bronchus then subdivides in increasingly smaller and thinner branches, which are called bronchioles. When the air reaches the thinnest bronchioles, they lead into small ducts that end in little sacs called alveoli. There are about 600 million of these air cells in the lungs.

Finally, at this stage, the oxygen passes from the air you've breathed in to the bloodstream. It's the intricate capillary system that gets the oxygen to every cell in the body. Once the arteries pick up the oxygen from the alveoli, they pass it on through another branching system. As they move away from the heart, the arteries lead to the smaller and thinner arterioles and from there to the even smaller capillaries. The delicate membranes of these tiny blood vessels allow oxygen to pass into the fluid between the cells. And the cells give back their carbon dioxide, which begins its journey through the capillary membranes to the small veins (venules), to the veins, and finally to the alveoli, where they eject the CO_2 back into the air as you exhale.

The concentration of carbon dioxide in the alveoli determines how fast you breathe—when CO_2 is higher, respiration increases; when it's low, it decreases. If you hold your breath and there's an incredible build-up of CO_2, you'll black out and then start breathing normally. Eventually, you have to let go to let in more oxygen. It's a fail-safe system.

Your lungs are narrow at the top and wide at the bottom, where they are closest to the diaphragm, solar plexus, and abdomen. There are more blood vessels (and consequently more blood) toward the bottom of the lungs than toward the top—and that's one reason we want to learn to relocate our breathing process, relying more on the belly than the chest area for our supply of oxygen.

Now what about the mechanics of breathing? The respiratory system is controlled by the medulla oblongata in the brain stem. This control center, part of the nervous system, is extremely sensitive to changes in carbon dioxide levels in the blood. If there's too much CO_2, the medulla sends a message to the carotid and aortic sinuses, the electrical conduction system of the heart. These heart signals speed up or slow down respiration as well as heart rhythms.

Unlike the heart muscle, the master pump of the body that keeps all systems operational, the lungs are simply hanging sacs without any pumping power of their own. To get air in and out, then, we need the muscles of the rib cage and diaphragm working in sequence to produce the bellows effect we call breathing.

As you inhale, the diaphragm flattens into the abdominal cavity, making a partial vacuum. This pushes the ribs apart so that the lungs can open. Then, as you exhale, the diaphragm pushes up into the rib cage, squeezing the lungs and pushing air out. The rib cage, in turn, contracts inward, hugging the lungs.

USING THE DIAPHRAGM FOR BETTER BREATHING
You don't think very often about exercising your diaphragm, and as a matter of fact, most of the time, you ignore it as you breathe. But to make the most of your breath, and to feel confident using it as a relaxation tool, we're going to practice lifting and dropping this organ consciously. The more you do your diaphragm workouts, the more lung power you actually have, and the more oxygen your body can absorb.

In order to be a diaphragm devotee, you have to do one other thing that's very difficult for most women. You have to let the belly go. Because most of us were trained from our earliest years to stand up straight and make a washboard stomach by pulling everything in, it's very difficult to consciously relax the belly. The suck-in-the-gut look is actually more constipated than sleek, and should be abandoned for health as well as beauty reasons. The effect is to tighten all the essential muscles that help us to relax. If you can't make a big belly and fill it up with air, you can't flatten your diaphragm.

If you need a good role model to show you the intricacies of really effective breathing, go look at a baby.

HOW BABIES BREATHE; HOW ADULTS BREATHE
Babies don't know what they look like, and they don't care. They'll suck on their toes, make funny faces, and spit up all over themselves—

and they're still laughing! One of the most unself-conscious things that babies do is breathe.

When a baby sleeps on her side, you can see the whole mechanism at work. With the inspiration of air, the chest lifts a little, and the belly softens inward. With the exhalation, the chest drops and the belly balloons outward. At the same time, on the rear side, you can see the back and kidney area expand with the inhale, and contract with the exhale. Even the extremities get into the act—the limbs of a relaxed, sleeping child will have a wavelike quality, inching ever so slightly up on the sheet and then down again. The head may tilt and straighten in a rhythmic fashion.

Babies rarely toss and turn, nor do they appear to be rigid in sleep as many adults do. Their whole aspect is soft and receptive, the epitome of relaxation.

Somewhere between our eighth and twelfth birthdays, however, we lose the knack of breathing well. We begin holding rigid postures when we're angry or tense, or we feel embarrassed by our changing body and refuse to let the belly go. The body becomes a hardened shell, the shoulders and hips two fixed clamps above and below the rib cage. As we grow, our habitual breathing (or non-breathing) patterns grow with us, and soon we don't even remember what it was like to soften the torso and make ourselves completely open and vulnerable to the air coming in and going out of us.

Even when we play sports, or when we sleep, we often don't use our breathing apparatus as we should. If you stop yourself right now and concentrate for a minute on where your breath enters and leaves your body, you will probably discover that you're taking in a thin stream of air from your nose and that your shoulders lift to accommodate the activity in your lungs. But there is no apparent life in your back, belly, or genital area. When you block the biggest oxygen-craving areas from getting what they need, you feel numb, frustrated, and really stressed-out.

BREATH-STRESS DISORDERS

When the breath is disturbed, the entire metabolism of the body begins to break down. When we're stressed, we don't take in enough oxygen, and that can affect the synthesis of carbohydrates, proteins, and fats. In addition, we don't manufacture a sufficient number of immune cells to promote healing and growth.

When you can't breathe because you have asthma, you are particularly in need of relaxation techniques that can open your airways. Although you probably wouldn't think of asthma as a stress-related disorder, it is actually a deregulation of the immune system—the body mistakes a harmless substance in the atmosphere for a dangerous one. The mucosal lining of the lungs becomes hypersensitive to any foreign substance—pollen, mold, cat dander, etc.—and our ability to breathe is severely compromised. Although COPD (chronic obstructive pulmonary disease) and emphysema are not stress-related, sufferers find it stressful to try to get air through the diseased lungs and bronchi. The very act of inhaling and exhaling becomes a tour de force, and it's incredibly difficult to think of anything other than the minute-by-minute attempt to grab oxygen before the carbon dioxide build-up becomes intolerable. (Also, when you hyperventilate, the blood pressure increases slightly with the inhalation. The medulla in the brain stem responds to higher CO_2 levels by making the heart work harder to pump blood through the arteries—thus elevating blood pressure.)

You can give yourself a breath-stress disorder by smoking. Nicotine is a stimulant that triggers the release of stress hormones in the adrenals, which means that your respiration rate increases (along with your heart rate, blood pressure, and secretion of glucose into your blood). But in addition, the smoke itself irritates the lining of your throat and lungs and impedes the flow of oxygen into your bloodstream. Even when you aren't puffing on a cigarette, you are working under adverse breathing conditions. And if you're not a smoker, but hang around people who smoke, you've got the same problems.

If you smoke because you're stressed and are having major anxieties about quitting, reread Step 2 on changing behavior. It will feel like a breath of fresh air, quite literally!

> *When you have inhaled completely, you are at one with the universal....You will by then have forgotten your own body and will have entered into a world of nothing but breathing. You will feel as if it is the universal, not you yourself, who is doing the breathing. Finally you will come to comprehend yourself as a part of the universal.*
> —KOICH TOHEI, Ki in Daily Life

WATCHING THE BREATH

You have breathed without conscious effort, you don't even think about it. So now, as you begin to practice the exercises below, you will become *hyper*aware. The mechanics of breathing in and out will start to take over, and you may find that you are more tense as you try to manipulate and order the breath than you were before you knew there was anything the matter with your breathing techniques.

So before and after you work on the exercises, stop yourself and simply sit or lie down, and pay attention to the way in which air comes into and out of you. Don't try to make anything happen, simply be an observer of the process.

Do you breathe quickly or slowly? Are your inhalations and exhalations even, or does one take more time than the other? Do you stop and catch your breath, then inhale some more? Do you draw your nostrils closed in an attempt to take in more air? Does your chest rise as you do this? Do you pause after you've exhaled, getting ready to breathe again? Do you hold your breath? Do you sigh a lot?

You don't need to judge what you are doing—just watch it. Then, after you've completed some of the exercises below, repeat the experience and see how your breath has changed.

WHERE TO PRACTICE BREATHING

Yes, you have to practice, not because practice makes perfect—practice only makes better practice—but because this activity is not as familiar to you as you think it is. Also, because there are so many interesting and different breathing techniques to use, you'll get more versatile if you select one a day and work on it in when you can.

As you learn to work with your breath, you'll be able to direct it where it's needed—perhaps to a sore shoulder or knee, or your throbbing ovaries during a menstrual period. You will find out how to send the breath to your hands and feet to warm your fingers and toes, and how to circulate the breath in your head when you've had a rough day and your racing thoughts seem to crowd out space for anything else, even air.

Fortunately, you don't have to carve out a time of day to breathe, since you're doing it constantly. All you have to do is make yourself aware of how you're breathing, and you can fit it in while performing other tasks.

Use your directed breathing techniques:

- On line at the bank
- While preparing a meal
- While driving or waiting at a light
- In bed if you can't sleep
- While checking your e-mail
- When someone on the phone puts you on hold
- With your partner (see exercise, below)
- While bathing the baby, or taking your shower or bath
- When gardening, playing the piano, playing chess, or doing any hobby
- When taking a walk or hike or engaging in any recreational or sports activities

FINDING A TEACHER OF BREATHING TECHNIQUES

You may find it easier at the beginning to have a mentor who can help you relearn how to breathe. Yoga and tai chi classes spend a great deal of time educating you in specialized breathing techniques, so you may wish to sign up for a course in either one of these practices.

A yoga or tai chi teacher can generally be found through your local Y or health club, at adult education classes, or through word of mouth in your community. Some large corporations offer classes through their health and fitness programs.

Yoga, the ancient Indian system of postures and breathing, is now a sanctioned stress-management technique used by many hospitals for cardiac rehabilitation and pain management. Tai chi, a Chinese moving meditation, may be slightly harder to find, but the search is certainly worth it.

Look for a teacher who is patient and diligent, who is skilled in technique, but who doesn't care as much about perfecting the movements as she does about reaping the healing benefits these disciplines offer both beginning and advanced students. You want someone who does not set herself up as a guru, but rather as a model and guide.

There are many other types of bodywork that emphasize the importance of breathing. Some of these include chiropractic, craniosacral therapy, Feldenkrais therapy, Alexander technique, Rubenfeld Synergy, bioenergetics, Hellerwork, Reichian breathwork, Innertuning therapy, and Trager Psychophysical Integration. Practitioners can be found through holistic health organizations and may advertise in New Age or alternative bookstores.

Emotional and physical states can be altered by changing the breathing pattern.

—WILHELM REICH

GETTING STARTED WITH BREATHING BASICS

Although it's wonderful to have a teacher, you can do a great deal of the groundwork by yourself. First, get as comfortable as possible. This means wearing loose clothing—no constricting belts or tight pants, flat shoes or none—and finding a space large enough for you to stretch out your arms. Begin lying down on a mat or carpet and place one hand on your belly, about three inches below your waistband.

Concentrate on making your body receptive to more oxygen. This means it's important, no matter what type of breathing you're practicing, to keep good postural alignment.

Your head should be in line with your neck, the chin slightly tucked in. Be aware of the natural curves in your back—make sure your waist curves into the floor and your rear end is tucked under. Let your shoulders go slack, draining into the floor under you.

Now release your knees, so that they feel soft and pliable. Finally, release your belly. Mechanically raise and lower your diaphragm a few times before you start the breathing, just to warm up. (You may hear the last glass of fluid you consumed sloshing around in your stomach—don't be embarrassed!)

The hand that's on your belly can push down, to be sure you get all the air out. Then, as you take your first good inhalation, watch the hand rise as the belly rises.

After you have worked on the breathing lying down, you can try the same thing sitting on the floor in a cross-legged position, or in a straight-backed chair. Sit with your coccyx just grazing the back of the chair, your upper back free and unsupported. You want to feel as though your body is suspended from above, as though you had a ponytail right at the crown of your head and someone was pulling it gently straight above you. Once again, place your hands on your belly and push the air in and out. Now you may sense your body beginning to move with the breath, just like a wave coming into shore and then retreating. Loosen all your limbs and allow them to be stirred by the breath.

Finally, you can stand up. Your knees should be released, but not completely bent, since it's tiring for the quadriceps to hold a bent-legged posture for long periods of time. Remember to keep the same good alignment you had while sitting. Remember that ponytail being drawn upward from the crown of your head. The breath can begin in the belly and then spread out to your limbs. Allow yourself to get taller and shorter as the air goes in and out of you.

SKILLS TO LEARN FOR BREATHING

Letting Go of the Stomach Muscles

In order to breathe—really breathe—you have to get loose and allow the stomach muscles to release. Lie on the floor with your hands on your belly, then lift your head off the floor, which will tighten the stomach. When you attempt to get a good breath, you'll find it's impossible. Everything from your xiphoid process (the small bone beneath the sternum) to your pubic bone will feel rigid and immobile.

Now allow your head to relax back on the floor. Roll a little from side to side, yawning as you do so. Come to rest flat on your back with your hands lying at your sides. Begin to fill your belly up, feeling the air entering slowly through your nostrils. See your belly as a balloon, expanding and growing little by little. Exhale at the same slow pace as you inhaled. Repeat this several times, each time sensing your body relaxing more deeply into the floor.

Catching Your Breath

When you're in a stressful situation and feel panicky, your breath will come in short, staccato bursts. Sometimes you feel like you're completely out of air, and that's terrifying. But it's important to know that you can *always* get your breath back, no matter how far gone you think it is. Just to prove this to yourself, put on a watch with a sweep hand and go out and run around the block. Try to sprint, so that you will be "out of breath" very quickly. When you are really panting, come to a stop and begin to walk slowly as you check your watch. If you're out of shape, it may take a good five minutes for your breath to return to normal, but it does come back! This will help calm you the next time you feel you can't get a breath.

Diaphragmatic Breathing

The type of breathing you do every day causes you to take air in as the abdominal muscles expand, and then let air out and release the belly inward. Your diaphragm will flatten and push up toward the rib cage, motivating the muscular activity of the stomach. When you master full diaphragmatic breathing, there is no beginning and end to the breath—it is all one circle.

Reverse Breathing

(This type of breathwork is used in Chinese *qi gong*, below.) According to Chinese medicine, when we were inside our mother's womb, we inhaled and drew nutrients and oxygen inside us through the umbilical cord, then exhaled and let out toxins and carbon dioxide into our mother's bloodstream. So in this "prenatal breath," we inhale and draw everything inward, then exhale and expand everything outward. This is just the reverse of diaphragmatic breathing.

The advantage of reverse breathing is that you have to concentrate on changing your automatic breathing pattern, and focus intently on the process. Because your body and mind are directing all their energy into the breath, there is no room for any stressful, distracting thoughts.

> *Prana is the breath of life of all beings in the universe. They are born through it and live by it, and when they die their individual breath dissolves into the cosmic breath.*
>
> —B.K.S. IYENGAR

TYPES OF BREATHWORK

If you have any concerns about whether you should practice any of the following techniques, check with your doctor before trying them. If you become dizzy at any point during your breathing practice, stop at once, sit down and lean your elbows on your knees so that you can support your head with your hands. Allow your breath to return to normal.

Yogic Breathing

There are dozens of yogic breathing techniques. These six are good either for concentration, relaxation, or stimulation.

Yogic Three-Stage Breathing

Lie on the floor with your hand on your belly. Keep your mouth closed, your tongue lightly resting right behind the upper teeth.

Inhale through your nose and allow only the belly to expand (don't involve the chest at all—don't worry, your lungs will still get oxygen!). Exhale and let the breath out. Repeat three times.

Inhale and allow the belly to expand, then allow the lungs to fill and the chest to expand. Exhale, release the breath from the chest and then from the belly. Repeat three times.

Inhale and allow the belly to expand, then allow the lungs to fill and the chest to expand, then bring the breath up to fill the throat and rise to the top of the head. Exhale, release the breath from throat and top of the head, then from the chest, then from the belly. Repeat three times.

This exercise will focus and relax you.

"Darth Vader" or Roaring Surf Breathing

Concentrate on the breath in your throat. Keep your mouth closed, the tongue lightly resting on the palate, directly behind the upper teeth.

As you inhale through your nose, partly close the glottis. Imagine that you have a small mirror right at the back of your throat, above the tonsils. Constrict the air passages and as you inhale, think about fogging that mirror at the back of your throat. Now exhale, sending the breath in the opposite direction to fog an imaginary mirror in back of your teeth. The sound you make should sound like the surf at the ocean going in and out, or like the *Star Wars* character breathing through his helmet.

This type of breathing exercise will alleviate a painful, hot head and will help balance your appetite. It is excellent for the lungs and may alleviate asthma and speed recovery from other pulmonary problems.

Alternate Nostril Breathing

Place the thumb of your right hand on your right nostril, then inhale and exhale through your left. Close off your left nostril with your fourth and fifth fingers and lift your thumb. Inhale and exhale on the opposite side. This technique centers the mind and actively integrates right and left brain function—this appears to give better electrical conductivity through the brain, which has a stimulating effect. Alternate nostril breathing is used in yogic spiritual practice to raise the *kundalini*, the powerful energy that rises from the base of the spine. (This is also a good partnered exercise during Tantric sex.)

The Cooling Breath

Stick out your tongue and fold it into a tube. Inhale through this tube (you'll hear a hissing sound as you do this) until you can't take in any more air. Then draw the tongue inside the mouth and hold the breath as long as you can without straining. Exhale slowly through the nose. Repeat three times.

This type of breathing really cools you off, no matter how angry or upset you are. It is also reputed to alleviate cravings for food, drink, and sleep.

The Bellows Breath

Close your mouth and inhale and exhale very rapidly twenty times or more from your nostrils. Then exhale completely, letting all the air out, and inhale slowly. When you have completely filled your lungs, hold the breath as long as is comfortable, bringing your chin to your chest. Then exhale, raising the head slowly and evenly. Do not do more than two rounds of bellows breathing.

This exercise stimulates the gastrointestinal system and raises your energy level.

The Stomach-Circle Breath

Exhale and let all the air out. Then muscularly pull in the abdominal muscles. Inhale, and hold the breath as long as it's comfortable without straining. Now lift your stomach muscles and begin to circle them to the right, down, to the left, and back to center. (You will hear a lot of gurgling—that's perfectly okay.) Exhale and let all the air out. Do only two of these a day.

This exercise relaxes the stomach muscles and massages the internal organs.

Sound and Breath

Usually, we want the breath to be silent, contained inside, but sometimes, it's a good idea to vocalize, especially when you're feeling strong emotions. The explosive *ki-ah* in martial arts practice emphasizes a punch or kick (and also scares your opponent!). If you're ever in a dangerous situation, or approached by a mugger, let out a *big* sound as you breathe. You'll be amazed at the power you emanate when you use the breath and the voice together.

Bravery Breathing

You can make yourself feel strong and secure with your breath. Stand with your feet hip-width apart and inhale into your belly. As you exhale, pick up your right leg and lunge forward, lifting your arms and squaring your elbows. Keep your shoulders down. Make your body very heavy and press downward with your shoulders, chest, and back. Let out a sound as you lunge forward: "*HAAAH.*" You should feel massive, like Atlas holding up the world. Repeat on the left leg.

The Sigh

Sighing expresses longing and regret, two feelings we often have when we're stressed about the present and nervous about the future. It's vital that we get our sighs out—and you'll be astounded at the transformation in your whole physical attitude after you've done this exercise.

Sit comfortably on the floor or in a straight-backed chair. Close your eyes and feel your body resting in space, supported by the air around you. Allow yourself to summon up whatever is inside—your joy, rage, compassion, fear, sadness—and go with those feelings, no matter how painful they may be. You may sense tears behind your eyes, or you may feel blank inside—there is no "right" way to react.

Begin by summoning one deep inhalation. Hold the breath for a brief moment, then let it rush out of you with a sighing sound. Take another inhalation, deeper this time, and hold it a little longer. Let a long, pure, moaning sound come from your gut as you exhale. Continue this until the inhalation, breath-holding, and exhalation seem like one wave-like experience.

When all your sighs are spent, come back slowly to regular breathing. You may feel a little tremor or shudder in your body—this is a normal reaction to the welling up of all the emotion inside you.

Qi Gong Breathing

In this type of breathwork, you develop your internal "elixir," that magical brew that offers life and energy. In Chinese theory, the *qi* or life force accumulates in the *tan tien*, a point three fingers below your waistband and three fingers inside. When you build up a good reservoir of *qi* in this location, it can circulate through the twelve meridians or energy channels of the body. Ideally, you can use these exercises to send healing breath to areas that are injured or weak. You can visualize moving the breath upward into your head and clearing out all the stress and worry with each exhalation.

Standing Pole Exercise

Stand with your feet hip-width apart and bend your knees. (This is known as "horse-riding stance.") Allow your arms to rise in front of you as though you were holding a large beach ball. Drop your shoulders and elbows. Feel as though your arms are supported on a cushion of air.

Do the reverse breathing (see above) as you concentrate on building energy in your *tan tien*. You can coordinate the inner rotation of your body with the movement of your belly and breath. Stretch your fingers out in front of you and as you inhale, pulling the *tan tien* back toward your spine, turn your palms upward. Now let the belly come to a "neutral" position in the center and let the palms face each other. Then exhale, expanding the *tan tien* outward, and rotate the palms to the floor. At first, you will only be able to do this exercise for a minute or so, but over time, try to work up to ten minutes.

Candle-Blowing Exercise

Sit at a table and place a lit candle about two feet away from you. Press your tongue against the upper gum ridge of your palate and gently blow through your pursed lips to make the candle flicker without blowing it out. You can increase your distance from the candle as you grow more proficient.

This exercise will teach you patience and steadiness.

Eight Pieces of Brocade

This series of exercises, designed by a twelfth century Chinese general for his troops' daily workouts, moves the breath through all the meridians of the body.

1. *Head turning.* Stand with your feet hip-width apart. Inhale, then exhale and turn your head as far as you can to the left. Inhale back to center, then exhale and turn the head to the right.

2. *Arm stretching.* Interlock your fingers at your *tan tien*. Inhale. As you exhale, lift your entwined arms directly above your head.

3. *Single arm raising.* Hold your hands palm up in front of your waist, third fingertips touching. Inhale. Exhale and extend your right hand overhead, palm up and fingers pointing left, and at the same time lower your left hand below your waist, palm down and fingers stretched forward. Come back to center. Repeat on the other side.

4. *Drawing the bow.* Inhale. Make fists and hold them at your hips, palms up. Exhale and step toward the left with your left foot and bring your hands to your left shoulder. Continue to exhale as you draw back your right arm and extend your left as though drawing a bow. Come back to center. Repeat to the opposite side.

5. *Swaying hips and buttocks.* Stand with feet a little wider than hip-width apart and bend over with hands on your thighs. Inhale and shift your weight forward onto your arms. Exhale and sway your hips as far to the left as you can. Inhale, then exhale and repeat to the other side.

6. *Forward stretching.* Stand with feet about shoulder width (two feet) apart. Inhale. Exhale and bend forward to touch your toes. Go as far as you can with your legs straight. (**Caution:** *If you have high blood pressure, skip this exercise and go onto the next.*)

7. *Slow punching.* Stand with feet in horse-riding stance (see "Standing Pole," above.) Inhale. Make fists and hold them at

your hips, palms up. Exhale and slowly punch up and to the right with your right fist. As you extend your arms, let your eyes and breath follow the fist until it is level with the top of your head. Return to starting position. Repeat on the left side.

8. *Rising and falling on the toes.* Stand with feet together. Inhale. Then exhale as you rise to your toes. Lower your heels as you inhale again.

Tibetan Breathwork

The philosophy of Buddhism takes many forms, and one of the most powerful traditions comes from Tibet. One of the precepts of this way of thinking is that we are an integral part of our physical world. Our bodies and breath are part of nature and emanate from the earth, water, fire, air, and trees around us.

Nature Breath

In this exercise, you will visualize the elements and yourself as part of them:

- Sit or lie on the ground. Inhale the strength of the earth beneath you. Exhale the difficulties in your life that you cannot change right now.

- Drink water and quench your thirst, nourishing yourself as the earth is nourished by the rain. Then inhale the essence of the pure liquid you have taken in; exhale the toxins you no longer need.

- Focus on a fire or a space warmed by the noonday sun. Inhale the light; exhale the dark.

- Allow the wind to caress your face and hair. Inhale the ever-changing movement of the wind; exhale the stagnant moments that keep you from reaching your goals.

- Stand beneath a tree's sheltering branches. Inhale the age-less wisdom of this rooted but flexible shelter. Exhale the flimsy, surface problems that will vanish when you stop dwelling on them.

Step 7 **Get Centered with Meditation**

Nancy is forty-seven, attractive, and a little overweight. This never used to bother her, but lately, she's been very down about everything—her body, her mind, and certainly her spirit. She used to handle single parenting and work just fine—now she feels overwhelmed juggling her bookkeeping job and after-school activities for her eight-year-old, Sylvie. She used to love getting up in the morning; now it's hard to pull herself out of bed. She never used to yell at her child; now she gets rubbed the wrong way by the slightest infraction of house rules. What's going on?

Since her divorce from her husband, Nancy has been in a relationship with Sam, a married man she met in an adult-ed home repair class five years ago. "It was such incredible chemistry," she said. "He just *smelled* right to me. He wasn't that gorgeous or brilliant or anything, but I fell like a boulder for him. He would brush against me and I'd practically have an orgasm. It was so different from the way I felt about my husband, to whom I was still married when the affair began. With him, it was this-is-Friday-it-must-be-sex-night-ho-hum.

"But with Sam, well, even my pores opened up to him. Oddly enough, although we've been sleeping together for two years, I still feel the same, and so does he—our bodies make the perfect jigsaw puzzle together. Unfortunately, everything else about the two of us together causes me grief. He's says he's really in love with his wife, and she inspires him, but personally, I think she calls all the shots and when she says 'jump,' he does. With me, he feels a basic man/woman attraction, and he craves that.

"What do I get out of it, besides great sex? He feeds my ego. He tells me how much he loves my body and what a great sex partner I am. He can sit across a room from me and his eyes open wide and I feel engulfed by his attention. No, that doesn't make a relationship. Obviously, we don't do couple stuff like going out for meals or movies, or spending time with our kids, so on some level, it's always a disappointment. Very often, sex is the whole date—he calls, says he has only twenty minutes but he really wants me, and we do it right on the floor in the hallway or against the dishwasher. What a rush. With him, I have moments of intense physical pleasure like I've never felt before. Then he leaves, and I think, is this any way to run my life?"

Nancy's stress and depression stems from her ambivalence about putting all her emotional eggs in this particular basket. She is unsure that this situation, which can't grow into a relationship, is enough for her and whether staying in it means that ultimately she's denying herself the ability to be a more giving, caring person with a fuller, richer life.

"My daughter wants a father—I can see that every time we're with men friends of mine. Sylvie has met Sam and doesn't particularly warm to him. Of course she has no idea who he is in my life, since when we're with other people we have this disguise of complete nonchalance toward one another. But since part of me is stuck to this man, I can't get interested in other men. And if I'm not dating, I feel like I need the thing with Sam. It's my escape from real life—I never have to think when I'm with him. He treats me like a goddess in bed. How could I give that up?

"Sometimes I get real guilty about what would happen to Sam if this ever came out. His wife's a real ball-buster—she'd take the kids, file for divorce, and leave him living out of a box. I know, he's a big boy, and it's his problem. He's always told me he knows he's nuts for taking the risk, but he can't give me up. And crazy me, I really care about him, and I'd be devastated if his life were torn apart. By the way, we'd never marry if he were thrown out of his house. We're too unalike to be together. As a matter of fact, our thing would probably end if he were free because part of what holds it together is the mystery and thrill of undercover sex.

"So I look at what I'm getting from this and I think, there's something wrong with me. I think I'm hiding from having a real relationship—one where you have to deal with issues and money and kids and where you're going to live and how. As long as I avoid it, I stay in this little cocoon that's safe and easy. You know, sex is feelings and ecstasy and fun. But living your love is hard work."

Nancy had read about every self-help book she could about the addictive nature of sex and was aware that she had a compulsive need for Sam. The kind of stress he added to her life was unnecessary, and yet she found it unavoidable. It distracted her at work and very often made her change plans she'd had with her daughter. She was annoyed that she let Sam call all the shots—she was supposed to be available whenever he asked to see her, but not beg him for a date. The powerlessness she felt in the relationship made her wonder about her lack of self-esteem.

Nancy wanted out, but didn't know how to get out. She wasn't a person who could consider therapy. "I didn't want to be told I was a 'bad' woman or too neurotic to feel real love. I just wanted to work out the problem myself, and try and alleviate some stress in the bargain. I figured if I made some physical changes—ate better and went running every day—I might find some outlet for my energy that wasn't sexual. And those things were somewhat helpful, but I still found myself fantasizing about the relationship when I was out exercising. The little changes didn't really make me *want* to stop the destructive behavior. I needed something that would temper my desires and take care of my need to be adored. I had read a lot about meditation and how it helps you detach from your ego. So I decided to try it."

WHAT IS MEDITATION?

Meditation is a process by which you shut out the noise and busy chatter of the brain and concentrate all your attention on one element—a sound, an activity, a concept, or your breath. By mindfully directing your energy toward this focal point, you can begin to appreciate life—and yourself—in a new way. Meditation does not teach you to *think* more clearly. Rather, it shuts down the habitual thinking process so that you can achieve clarity. It's then easier to understand the various faculties that make you human—your emotions, your will, your spirit. It takes discipline, but by practicing regularly, you can open up new avenues of awareness.

> *Can you keep the spirit and body without scattering? Can you concentrate your mind to use breath, making it soft and quiet as an infant's? Can you purify your contemplation and keep it from turbulence?*
>
> —LAO TSU, Tao Te Ching

IS MEDITATION RIGHT FOR ME?

The *Tao Te Ching*, a great work of Chinese philosophy, probably written in the sixth century B.C., beautifully expresses our frustration as we search for the right way to handle stress. We all want insight and understanding, we want to learn to be patient, to give ourselves a chance to act in accord with life's harmonious plan. But it's so difficult.

Still, it's useful to ask yourself these questions when, like Nancy, you feel you want to use your own resources to handle the stress in your life. In the normal course of life, there are so many "you's"—the mother, the child, the worker, the piano player, the chief cook and bottle washer. None of those alter egos matter when you are quietly sitting, listening to your body and mind, getting in touch with the parts of your spirit that you don't usually contact during the daily grind.

The word "meditation" scares some people. It seems foreign and esoteric. It conjures up the image of a robed figure sitting cross-legged, his hands resting on his knees, eyes closed, his face a blank mask. Actually, this is only one of probably hundreds of accurate images of what meditation looks like, feels like, and is like.

There's a wonderful parable told about a young, ambitious Japanese monk who came to visit a great master, begging to be allowed to study with him. The master invited him inside and listened as the young monk recounted all the hours he had spent in hard work, reading, silence, and meditation. He told of all the various teachers he'd learned from, and the martial arts and spiritual skills he had.

"Well, now," said the great master. "Let us take tea."

He went into another room and returned with cups and a steaming pot. He set a cup on a low table before the young monk and one at his own place. Then he began to pour tea into the monk's cup. He poured and the cup filled up, but he kept pouring.

"Master!" cried the monk. "Stop! The tea is spilling all over the floor."

"You see now," said the master, "how impossible it is to get any benefit if your cup is already full. You must empty your cup, and then come to me."

Meditation is the process whereby you empty the cup. When you are an open vessel, only then can you be filled with insight and self-knowledge and creativity.

The process also allows you to slow the pace of life and take a break from yourself and others. Whether your meditation is formally organized in a group class or an impromptu moment of sitting by a river and allowing the mind and body to let go, it can offer enormous benefits. When practiced daily, it can go a long way to healing the stress in your life.

Basically, there are two major types of meditation. You'll probably want to experiment with both to see which feels right to you.

Contemplation

This variety of meditation involves conscious, directed thought. You may contemplate a prayer or a saying (the Lord's Prayer, Sh'ma Yisroel, Hail Mary, Hare Krishna), an object or picture (a drawing of Jesus or Buddha), a philosophical problem (a Zen koan such as "What is the sound of one hand clapping?") or an unanswerable question such as "Who am I?"

In the contemplative form of meditation, the mind is busy working, focusing on a series of thoughts that lead inward. If you think of the mind as the ocean, you begin meditating on the surface, and as you practice, you plunge down a little lower each moment.

Concentration

In this type of meditation, you avoid thought by riveting your attention on the practice itself: counting breaths (Zen Buddhism), moving energy to various points (the Taoist microcosmic orbit), staring at a candle flame that induces a trancelike gaze, repeating a mantra ("Om" or "One"), or focusing on a state of bliss (the Sanskrit idea of "nirvana").

When you focus deeply on any of these elements, the mind becomes quieter. It's as though you've removed all the furniture from your room so that you can really feel the energy of that room, stripped of all decoration. You might also see your focal point in color, and everything around it in black-and-white.

No matter which type of meditation you select, you don't have to try hard in order to "get" it. Meditation doesn't involve "doing"; rather, it involves "being." There is no intention—it's just a process that allows you to learn where you are at one point in space and time. If you feel exhilarated and secure at the end of your session, fine. If you feel solemn and spaced-out, well, that can happen, too. If you feel vague and unsure of where you were, you may simply need a guide point to bring you back to the present moment. Meditation has been likened to a shepherd herding sheep. Those lost lambs are your thoughts, and the shepherd is your will, gathering them back home.

HOW CAN MEDITATION TEACH YOU ABOUT YOURSELF AND YOUR RELATIONSHIPS?

Nancy is ambivalent about giving up the one relationship in her life that seems fun, exotic, and thrilling, because she doesn't feel she has anything to replace it with. It feeds her ego and makes her feel important and cherished. But once she starts prioritizing and figuring out what is *really* vital to her in the long run, this affair may seem small and petty.

Like Nancy, when you start your practice, you may find yourself visualizing a person you want to be with, or wondering why you feel stuck like a bug on a pin, flailing around for purchase in a whirlwind of thoughts. You may feel frustrated and edgy—that this is silly and pretentious, and you want to give up and go make a phone call.

All of these feelings indicate that you are currently too dependent on your attachments—and what you can do when you meditate is to give up one unprofitable bond at a time. You don't need to feel proud of yourself because you're actually sitting there for twenty minutes; likewise, you don't need to be dejected because you keep thinking about your tax bill and whether you need new snow tires. Meditating is like peeling an onion—you sit and take off a layer of thoughts, then a layer of feelings, then another layer of thoughts and another of feelings, and so forth. When you have reached a point where you can let go of all the joys and problems, you may be amazed to find what's at your core.

Some relationships that you hold so dear may be even better than you believed they were; others may be crutches that impede your own personal progress. But when you meditate, they all fall away so that you can really truly be alone with yourself and discover your potential. You may be a lot bigger than you thought, and more capable than your friends and lovers give you credit for. When you bring with you to these relationships the insight and wisdom you have gained during meditation, you'll find that you have a far greater capacity to handle anger, disappointment, jealousy, neediness, and all the other negative elements we often take from and impose on others.

When you see yourself clearly, you don't imbue everything someone says to you with overwhelming importance. You can detach from the anxiety about pleasing someone else or the fear that you'll be lonely if you don't bend to their wishes. So your good connections with people can improve as you concentrate on the love and respect you share; your bad relationships can also improve—or, as you find you don't need them anymore, they can evaporate painlessly.

DEALING WITH YOUR BODY

The body isn't used to sitting still. Since toddlerhood, we are acclimatized to movement. We crave the ability to explore, to roam around and stretch and scratch. People do sit for long periods of time in front of a television set or a movie screen, but they are being entertained while sitting. And sitting in a car isn't the same at all—think of all the tension you feel when you're strapped into a contraption going sixty miles an hour trying to avoid other drivers.

So sitting during meditation is unnatural. We feel itches and cramps, we need to cough or sneeze, we develop a terrible backache.

Actually, it's not so much the body that rejects being still as the mind, which is in charge of that body. When your mind pays attention to the itches, tingles, and yawning, it can't possibly hold to one point like the breath. So it's an out for the body when the mind says, wow, look how your foot fell asleep, or your hands got cold.

To calm the body, you need a posture that becomes increasingly relaxed the longer you hold it. If you're in a chair, feet should be flat on the floor and back lightly supported. If you're on a cushion, you can sit cross-legged (tailor-style), with your legs folded one in front of the other. If you're very flexible, you can place one leg on top of the other (half-lotus) or intertwine them (full lotus). You'll want to sit on the edge of the cushion, so that only your coccyx actually rests on it. (Special meditation cushions can be ordered through the catalogues listed in the resource appendix.) You can also kneel and put the cushion between your legs.

Tuck in your chin and tilt your head down a bit so that the crown reaches for the ceiling. Rest the tip of your tongue on your palate right behind your front teeth. Place your hands in your lap, facing upward, one cradled inside the other. Or you can rest both hands on your knees, either palms down or facing up as your thumb and index finger form a ring.

When you are first starting to meditate, the most important thing is comfort. So if your hip is screaming in agony, adjust it so that you can get your concentration right back again.

After a few months of practice, however, it's a good idea to start training the body as well as the mind. Now when the legs or back protest, ignore them. You can always get the circulation going again after you finish meditating. And it's very comforting to find that your itches vanish when you don't cater to them.

HOW MEDITATION CAN FOSTER PATIENCE, FORGIVENESS, AND POSITIVE MIND

We all carry around a voice inside that is super-critical: "Why don't you get more done? Why don't you make more money? Why don't your relationships run smoothly? What's the matter with you, anyway?" And this voice, over time, erodes our self-confidence and ability to make the kinds of decisions that can lead to a more centered, less stressed feeling. If you're always self-critical, you leave no room for getting to know and like yourself.

Meditation teaches forgiveness. Our old grudges don't mean much when we are clear about why we developed them. What's more, we can forgive ourselves for not being perfect. Instead of stopping in the middle of meditating and saying, "Oh, I'm not doing this right," we can enjoy the experience for what it is. Who's to say what's right? Do you imagine some incredible epiphany every time you meditate—a vision of heaven or a resolution to your long-term problems with your mother? If so, you have a great imagination! It just doesn't happen that way.

If you have no goal but sitting, quietly paying attention to whatever thoughts and feelings are flickering through you, then you are getting the idea. Even if you find that you are distracted and your mind keeps wandering and you have to bring it back—to your breath, your sound or image—that means you're working on the process. There is no right or wrong. Whatever you do—and don't do—when you sit down to meditate is what you do or don't do. More or less than that is impossible to achieve.

Then there's patience. Patience used to be a virtue, but it's been replaced in our society with efficiency. You don't have to wait for anything if you get things done so fast it makes your head spin. But for the sake of your soul, let's rethink patience.

Can you be patient? Can you wait for the mud to settle and the water to clear so that the right action can arise by itself?

——LAO TSU, Tao Te Ching

It is really true that all good things come to she who waits. We grab some junk food instead of waiting for a real meal; we buy the pricey dress in the window instead of waiting for it to go on sale; we take the aspirin to get rid of a headache instead of trying to breathe it away. If we jump at the first thing we're offered, we may miss out on the real gold, which turns up much later. But if first impressions aren't always accurate, why do we trust them so much?

Because they're easier, and we're all looking for a quick fix that assuages the anxiety level. The faster we can quell that desire, the speedier we are about making that commitment, the more we tend to feel that we're in control of the situation. We really aren't—it's only an illusion.

Meditation teaches patience. You can't get anywhere by trying, so each day, as you sit, you just accumulate experiences. It takes as long as it takes—usually many years—to feel comfortable when you sit and have no goal other than being with yourself. After enough time under your belt meditating, you start to understand why you do it. In fact, some people tell me that they don't like to miss their daily session because their whole day gets off to a better start when they meditate. But they *can* miss it, and do occasionally, because they have the security of knowing that this practice is theirs whenever they want it. They have the luxury of all the time left them on this earth to do their sitting. That's the reward of being patient.

As you become more patient, it's easier to manage stress in the rest of your life. You can sit in a traffic jam without drumming your hands on the steering wheel and imagining that the world will end if you don't get to your meeting on time. You can allow other people to get in front of you in the supermarket checkout line every once in a while. (They will look at you as if you're out of your mind.) You can listen to a difficult tirade from a boss or a relative without feeling you have to jump in to make your point. You realize that you have all the time in the world, and it goes by moment by moment. You can catch the next available moment, or the next.

Meditation is also good for developing positive mind. We are bombarded with everything that's wrong from the minute we wake up each morning until we go to sleep at night. The TV news reports horror stories, our friends' marriages are breaking apart, our tax situation worsens yearly, our friend got mugged in broad daylight, the planet is overcrowded and polluted—and on and on. Yes, there is a lot of bad stuff going on, but there's a great deal of good as well. When our eyes are really open and we take the time to enjoy a sunset, to watch a kid help an elderly neighbor, to see the joy on people's faces when they meet after a long absence, then we realize what we're here for.

And when we meditate, we get to enjoy every moment. We can stop and tune out the hubbub of life so that we can relish the fullness of our own inner space. It feels good to know that we're centered and together, that we have given ourselves the gift of a pause in daily life that truly refreshes us. Meditation builds a positive mind out of thought and lack of thought—out of feeling and detachment. The sense of relaxation that comes from daily practice is rewarding in and of itself.

Your mind will learn. Today you may have to bring it back fifteen times, perhaps thirty. But in three years, you may bring it back only a few times…in ten years, not at all.
—EKNATH EASWARAN, *MEDITATION*

MEDITATION CAN BE USED IN CONJUNCTION WITH DRUGS AND THERAPY FOR DEPRESSION

In the late 1960s, Herbert Benson of the Harvard Medical School began a series of clinical studies on long-time meditators and discovered ways in which the body can heal itself from the stress response. These individuals, who were able to summon involuntary reactions that calmed the mind and body, achieved what Benson began to call "the relaxation response." He published these findings in a popularized version in 1975, by which time meditation had become a growing phenomenon in America.

As we know, when we're stressed, we go into physiological overdrive—our metabolism and respiration escalate, our pupils dilate, our gastrointestinal and salivary functions decline. In addition, the excitation of our endocrine and nervous systems has a severe impact on our cardiovascular system. Heart rate and blood pressure escalate with stress. Serious emotional conditions, such as depression or bipolar disorder (manic depression), may lead to heart attacks. In a 1996 report of a study at Johns Hopkins School of Hygiene and Public Health, people who had been diagnosed with a mood disorder thirteen years earlier were found to be four times as likely to have suffered heart attacks as those who had a good sense of well-being. These individuals undoubtedly weren't motivated enough to eat right, exercise, and stop smoking, but in addition, they may have had a biochemical predisposition to heart disease. Depressed people may have stickier blood platelets, and therefore a tendency to develop clots that can block blood vessels leading to the heart. The sympathetic nervous system can do a lot of damage when it's activated nearly all the time.

But when we relax, our parasympathetic system comes into play, and all that detrimental revving up of the body vanishes. Benson learned a great deal from practitioners of TM (transcendental meditation) and Zen monks in Japan. The practiced meditators were able to slow their metabolism, consume approximately 20 percent less oxygen than normal, and lower their heart rates. In the practiced meditators, blood pressure was incredibly low (90/60 or lower) before meditation and remained so. (It has since been shown that novice meditators can lower blood pressure over a period of months of practice, and then keep the pressure low. They may also be able to boost the immune system, which in turn may protect them from cancers, heart disease, and other life-threatening illnesses, autoimmune diseases, and possibly problems of the reproductive system such as infertility and PMS.)

Benson and his colleagues also charted changes in the electrical activity of the brain—the monks were able to switch from beta waves (the usual fast-amplitude waves we create during the day) to slow-amplitude alpha waves, which give a sense of well-being. A third physiological change for the practiced meditators was a decrease in blood lactate, a substance made in the skeletal muscles that is prevalent when we're particularly tense or anxious. The meditators' muscles easily let go and relaxed during meditation.

If you are currently on medication for depression or panic attacks, meditation can be used in conjunction with medical treatment. This is particularly helpful at the beginning of treatment when you may feel too low to commit to a daily session of sitting. When you have been under a physician's care for a few weeks and the drug that's been prescribed is starting to give you a feeling that you are capable of climbing out of that black box you've been in so long, that's the time to start a meditation practice.

When you feel the calm assurance that meditation can bring, you may discover that the beneficial effects of the drug are now extraneous, and you may be able to work with your physician on weaning yourself off it slowly. Week by week, you will be able to adjust to having good days and bad days—as we all do. But meditation will encourage you on the good days and help you over the humps on those days when you feel particularly overburdened and challenged. (Even if you need to stay on the medication—as many people do—you should find that meditation still adds a beneficial effect to your treatment.)

By the way, meditation can engender a great many emotions that we never suspected were there. It's not uncommon to feel deep fear or sadness, and to cry or shake—these are ways that the personality has of asserting itself even in the midst of trying to blend into its surroundings. So without meaning to, you may begin to tackle a lot of problems you thought you had buried long ago. It can be unsettling to handle this by yourself—you may want to call a good friend or a mentor and share these feelings when you've had a chance to process them yourself.

Society should sanction the time for the relaxation response. Is it unreasonable to incorporate this inborn capacity into our daily lives by having a "relaxation response break" instead of a coffee break?

—HERBERT BENSON, M.D.,
THE RELAXATION RESPONSE

LEARNING THE DIFFERENCE BETWEEN BEING ALONE AND BEING LONELY

Even if you're in a group of fifty, you are always alone when you meditate. For some people, this is a radical departure from their overpopulated life. Some individuals can't bear to be alone. They have to turn on the radio or TV immediately to hear another human voice when they come into an empty house. Some people who have previously lived with others find that the quiet after the death of a partner, a divorce, or a child going off to school or getting married is unbearable.

Single motherhood, in Nancy's case, can bring with it a sense that you are adrift on a life raft and your only hope of survival is running into another life raft—regardless of who's on it. When you grasp at the only available relationship you see on the horizon, you don't always relieve the stress of being alone, as is apparent in Nancy's case. And by jumping onto someone else's raft, you don't fully investigate your own potential to get back to shore safely on your own.

But meditation will take you there. As you get to know yourself better during the process of sitting and simply being in one place at one time, you start to feel a sense of freedom and independence you never had before. As you go through your day, you can separate yourself from people and events that might cause you distress or involve you too deeply in their own hassles. You can explore friendships and love relationships with a saner eye because you will have learned to be more self-sufficient during meditation and won't feel so needy.

You can train yourself to focus in the present moment the same way you train yourself to jump off the [diving] board, or lift weights, or do anything else. The mind that has not been developed or trained is very scattered. That's the normal state of affairs, but it leaves us out of touch with a great deal in life, including our bodies.

—JON KABAT-ZINN,
interview with Bill Moyers

THE BASICS OF MEDITATION

The only ground rules are to remove all distractions and be quiet for a while.

Here are some easy tips for starting out:

- Create a meditation area in your home—perhaps a corner of the bedroom or living room that's not used for much. Make this your personal spot. (You can select a place outdoors, like your porch, if you can use it year-round.)
- The room should have good ventilation and be a comfortable temperature.
- Use a chair, backjack, or cushion. The idea is to feel good when you're meditating, not to concentrate on your aching back. You can always start in a chair, and as your practice proceeds and you can sit with your back unsupported, you can switch to the floor.
- Select one time of day to sit. Most people find that first thing in the morning, before anyone else is awake, is most conducive to meditating. You've just opened your eyes from sleep and your brain is not on fire with all the hundreds of tiny things you have to think about. You may also try meditating before bed, as long as you're not very sleepy before you begin.
- Don't worry about how long to meditate. You'll find your speed. At the beginning, five minutes may be all that feels

comfortable; after a while, fifteen minutes may go by in a flash, and even an hour may seem short. You should sit just as long as you want or need to in order to relax.

- Experiment with standing and walking meditation as well. You don't have to sit every day, although it is the most steadying position, especially for beginners.
- Don't lie down to meditate. Although it's great for relaxation, it is very easy to fall asleep in that position.
- If you feel very pressured and frustrated, come out of the meditation for a moment. Stretch your legs, take a few deep breaths, and then start again. It may just take you a while to settle down.
- Don't try to *do* anything. Rather than feeling passive, you want to be alert and responsive. If you allow the moment to come to you rather than trying to make the moment happen, you'll feel much more in sync with the process of meditation.
- If your body is tired and cramped as you meditate, relax your mind. As soon as your mind lets go of the idea of being uncomfortable, your body will settle down. On the other hand, if your mind is restive and annoyed and wants to do something else other than meditate, relax your body. When your shoulders and chest soften and your breathing becomes even and harmonious, your mind will settle down.
- Do your best to practice every day, no matter how busy or sick you are. Even if you're confined to your bed with flu and fever, you can shut out the illness for a few minutes by meditating.

If you've never meditated before, you may wish to start with a group. You may find it easier to achieve a calm awareness when there are others around you—since emotions and feelings tend to be contagious. On the other hand, it's also nice to discover meditation on your own. If you happen to be a competitive person, you might be tempted to open your eyes and gaze at your friends wondering if they're doing it "better" than you.

Either way—or both in combination—can work just fine.

WHAT EQUIPMENT DO I NEED TO MEDITATE?

The less the better. Other than your space and a comfortable sitting arrangement, you need nothing at all.

Some people do use simple decorations so that their area really feels special to them. You might want to put a flower in a vase, or hang a picture that means something to you. If you focus on a candle during your meditation, obviously that's one object you'll need in your space. Some people choose scented candles or incense to establish a mood; others feel that particular smells are too distracting.

It's also possible that you might want to use a Tibetan bell or "singing bowl" (it looks like a round black or metal bowl with a wooden mallet as a striker). In Zen meditation, the bell is rung once at the beginning of the meditation and three times at the end. The sound is a symbol of calling the mind to attention, and it's a convenience when you have a group of people meditating together—but it's not essential.

How do you know what time it is? Most practiced meditators say that they always know when their time is up. If you keep a clock in your space, and your mind is restless, you'll be tempted to look at it. If you absolutely have to end your meditation at a certain point because you have to be somewhere, you might set a timer in an adjacent room. But the best way to meditate is at a time of day when you have no pressures or constraints, so that if you go over, you can simply enjoy the luxury of that extra time with yourself.

SKILLS TO LEARN FOR MEDITATION

Being Quiet

We are constantly bombarded with sound—inside and outside our heads. In order to learn what quiet is, you first must understand what a state of nonquiet is.

Concentrate first on exterior sound. In a city, it's nearly impossible to hear the quiet, what with the traffic, doorbells, phones and faxes, radios and TVs, and general hubbub of people talking. In the country, in a wooded grove or a big field, it can be just as noisy. The rustle of the wind in the grass, the chirping, humming, and buzzing of bugs, the cries of birds and squirrels can be deafening after a while. But it's only at that point, when you perceive each individual sound outside you, that you can start to make a distinction between what's going on out there and what's happening inside you.

As humans, we are amazingly capable of balancing dozens of different thoughts and feelings at once. Your mind is like a monkey, constantly roving around looking for stimulation, eager to jump onto the next thought, or group of thoughts. Always excited or bored, your monkey mind can't decide what to do first, so it does everything at once (often, not very well).

When you learn to be quiet externally, you have a chance to keep the monkey from chattering. Over time, he'll quiet down too.

Focusing and Centering

You need a focus in order to meditate. It can be your breath, a candle flame, a word, a visual image, or a visualization. If you have nothing at all in mind—a void—it will undoubtedly fill itself with all the various thoughts and worries you've been carrying around the rest of the day. (You may find points in your meditation when the brain really does clear out and you feel a "hole" or nothingness. This can be unsettling for novices—suffice it to say, the hole fills up quickly enough. Don't worry about it! When you feel secure with this sense of nonthought, you can begin to enjoy it. Eventually you can appreciate it as the state of pure awareness.)

The process of focusing and centering is like a loop. First you get right into your one point, then you move away from it as thoughts enter. Then, as you allow the thoughts to pass by and bring yourself back to the point, you begin a new loop. When you sit every day, you'll find that the loops are smaller, and that there aren't as many of them. As you pass each loop, you will feel yourself becoming more grounded.

See your focus as right in the center of your being. You may want to picture your breath or your word as located in your middle, a few inches down from your belly button and a few inches inside. Every time your mind wanders, train yourself to come back to that one point.

The discipline of having a focus will strengthen your own feeling of being centered and rooted. Think of yourself as a tree with roots that go down as far as your branches reach up. These roots tie you to your humanity and to the rest of the universe. As you meditate, you grow those roots deeper.

Learning Alert Relaxation

Our common conception of "being relaxed" has to do with slumping into a couch or lying in a bed. But there's a different type of relaxation that only comes when you're awake and aware—that's what you're aiming for in meditation.

When the mind fixes on one point to concentrate, the body is often challenged. In an attempt to feel "relaxed," we may start to drift away, and that usually means the body will lean to one side, or the chest will cave in, or you'll have an overwhelming urge to swallow. A sense of sleepiness may descend, from which it can be difficult to drag yourself back. Sleep is actually the opposite of the awake and aware state you want to achieve in meditation, but the action of sitting still with eyes closed may just be too cozy for you. You may feel more relaxed than alert.

But just as you can train the mind to come back over and over, so can you train the body. You may not be aware of your physical habits, so it can be helpful at the beginning to have a friend or partner come in and correct your posture, either by touching you gently or by suggesting with words how you can straighten up. Or, if you find that you start to nod off whenever you sit, you might want to try walking or standing meditation.

Not everyone feels relaxed when they start to meditate, however. Quite the opposite—some people become hyperstimulated. The truth of the matter is that although you have stopped "doing," other things are still going on while you're meditating. The cat rubs against your leg or you hear the whoosh of traffic outside your window. You may sense that you feel *too* alert—instead of easing into the moment, like dipping your toes in a cool stream, you feel as though you'd been thrown in head first. So you are more alert than relaxed.

There's a happy medium where you are both alert—paying attention to your focal point—and also relaxed, allowing the mind and body to let go of concerns and tensions.

When you learn to focus and center, you will be better able to combine alertness and relaxation and feel that they are working together rather than against you to strengthen your meditation practice.

Work with a Teacher

These can be difficult to find, although like those practitioners of yoga and tai chi, they often teach at Y's and health clubs, and may advertise on health food store bulletin boards or at community centers. Many large corporations with health and fitness programs may offer meditation as part of a stress-management course.

Having a good teacher, at the beginning, is far more important than what system of meditation she teaches. A meditation teacher will be able to lead you in guided visualizations. She can bring you in and out of your focused, concentrated states. Since novice meditators may be frustrated or confused, it can be very helpful to have an experienced person of whom you can ask questions—even if you don't get answers!

> *Meditation is any activity that keeps the attention pleasantly anchored in the present moment.*
> —JOAN BORYSENKO, *MINDING THE BODY, MENDING THE MIND*

TYPES OF MEDITATION

It doesn't matter how you meditate—you get the same benefits whether you are standing or sitting, concentrating on your breath or a mantra, staring into a candle or at a mandala. Herbert Benson found that the relaxation response occurred just as easily to those practicing yoga, doing Transcendental Meditation® or doing their own brand of meditation like strenuous physical exercise. You can meditate while painting, writing, gardening, writing, cooking, or working, and ultimately, it can become part of every activity you do.

Remember not to let the meditation, or the "need" to meditate daily, become a chore. It should be joyful, not stressful.

Tibetan Buddhism

The philosophy of Buddhism requires the practitioner to let go of the self. "Self," or the ego, is an illusion according to Buddhism, and it is our karma (or destiny) to work toward a state of peace and harmony by letting go of the external and developing the internal powers of devotion and pure perception. One of the extremely practical Buddhist texts states:

> If you can solve your problem
> Then what is the use of worrying?
> If you cannot solve it
> Then what is the use of worrying?

In Tibetan Buddhist practice, the aim is to go from sickness and negativity (caused by a concentration on the self) to healing and positive mind (achieved by an abnegation of self and striving for enlightenment).

There are two types of mental training in Tibetan Buddhism. The first is inward concentration of the body, using, say, a visualization of the body as a perfect deity, or as a stark skeleton, or as a breathing machine. The outward concentration takes the practitioner out of the body to an image of the Buddha or a pure and beautiful place you've known, such as a seashore or a quiet mountaintop.

In Buddhist meditation, the eyes are half-open with a soft focus, trained on a point about a yard away from you.

Zen Buddhism

This practice is an offshoot of the philosophy of Buddhism and was developed in Japan. The practitioner attempts to focus only on the breath. This is done by counting "rounds of ten." You count, "Inhale one, exhale one; inhale two, exhale two," etc., until you reach ten, and then go back and start over. Most people cannot get to ten without a thought breaking the pattern, so it's recommended that they return to "one" as soon as the count is interrupted by any thought. At the end of your practice, the space around you will be littered with your thoughts—but over time, you'll have fewer and fewer to discard.

This type of meditation, too, uses a soft focus with half-opened eyes.

Mindfulness

Mindfulness also comes from Buddhist practice. It has been adapted by Jon Kabat-Zinn and others to make it relevant to modern-day stressed-out individuals like you and me.

In mindful practice, we pay attention to each moment and what it contains, beginning and always coming back to the breath, the even inhale and exhale that comes without bidding. We sense that the inhalation feels cool as it comes into our nostrils; the exhalation feels warm as it flows over the upper lip. Our focus is always the breath, whatever else may be happening to us.

At the same time, we observe wherever the mind has chosen to go. We sense our mind moving from the sound of the clock to the feel of the floor we're on to the taste of the saliva in our mouth. This type of practice can be done anywhere, at any time—you can wash your face mindfully before bed, enjoying the smell of the soap and the feel of the bubbles on your face. You can eat mindfully, relishing the sensation of being hungry, then the feeling of lifting an apple in your hand, then the smell of the apple, then the smoothness of it on your lip, and finally, the crunch as your teeth bare down on it.

Mindfulness in sitting practice becomes a type of self-observation. As your mind jumps from one subject to another, you can watch it move around, seeing that it's restless. Without asking why it's doing all these things, you simply stay with the breath, always coming back to it even as you observe yourself thinking about other things. Imagine that you are a passenger in a car watching the scenery go by, attending to it but not attaching to any one thought or image.

In this type of meditation, the eyes are generally closed so that your gaze is directed inward.

Taoist Meditation

The Taoists split with the Buddhists over the issue of man's place in the cosmos. Whereas the Buddhists feel that there's an illusory quality to all the external trappings of the world, and that only the inner world of the psyche and spirit count, the Taoists believe in the harmony of nature and man. We are part of the cosmos and it is part of us. The major concept of Taoism is the yin/yang, a perfect circle that contains within it two interlocking teardrop shapes. The white, or "yang" signifies everything that is strong, creative, and flowing from Heaven. The black, or "yin" signifies everything that is receptive, yielding, and flowing from the Earth. But the white half contains a dot of black, and the black half contains a dot of white. Each seeming "opposite" is really the complement of its partner.

The practice of Taoist meditation involves joining the two halves—the body with the mind. As you learn this practice, you become able to quiet "the five thieves" (the eyes, nose, ears, mouth, and mind) that threaten to steal you away from your true self.

One exercise that you may try is to move the body's energy from point to point, by integrating the mind, body, and spirit. The breath is the catalyst. Imagine a dot of light that starts at your coccyx and travels up the spine, over the top of the head, down the front of the body to the perineum (the space between the genitals and the anus). Then bring your awareness back to the coccyx and make the circuit go around again. The focus of this exercise, known as the "microcosmic orbit," is to circulate life energy, which is called *chi* or *qi*. The way you do this, of course, is by using the breath, which regenerates and heals the cells of the body even as it revitalizes the spirit.

In this type of meditation, the eyes are generally closed so that your gaze is directed inward.

TM® (Transcendental Meditation®)

TM® came to the United States from India in 1959, brought by a teacher named Maharishi Mahesh Yogi. (He later became the Beatles' guru, which helped to popularize this practice in the West.) The Maharishi's aim was to help all of humanity attain enlightenment, which they could do by means of study and meditation, and in addition, to start teacher-training courses all over the world. Dr. Herbert Benson's research in America was done with the participation of TM® practitioners.

TM® is a distillation and update of ancient Vedic (Indian) meditative techniques and involves concentration on a *mantra* or word that is selected particularly for the practitioner. The Sanskrit word has no particular power (some of them are meaningless), but the constant repetition of one sound offers a buffer for the mind. Thoughts are not banished in this form of meditation—as a matter of fact, the belief is that if the mantra brings up thoughts, this is simply a sign that the nervous system is cleansing itself, working its way toward relaxation and pure awareness. By meditating, you are allowing the life energy (called *prana* in Sanskrit) to flow freely.

The appeal of TM® for Westerners is that you are "taught" by a professional and given a personalized mantra (but many other people may have your mantra). A basic course doesn't leave you at sea with your newfound practice, but rather includes lots of "check-ups" and follow-up sessions. You are also asked to abstain from nonprescription drugs for fifteen days before beginning your course. TM® is to be practiced twice daily, for fifteen to twenty minutes at a time. A fee is charged for the course.

Most of those who feel that TM® works for them claim that their practice makes them more energetic and optimistic, and that they are less hostile and defensive, even when dealing with difficult people and experiences.

In this type of meditation, the eyes are generally closed so that your gaze is directed inward.

Visual or Tactile Focus

Just as you can concentrate on a sound like a mantra (see the previous section), so you can use other senses as your focal point.

A particularly good visual focus is a candle flame. Set the candle about two feet in front of your cushion or chair and stare into its center. Feel its warmth. Let whatever thoughts come to you flow in and out, without holding onto any of them. You may induce a type of trance-state from this sort of meditation, which can be very relaxing and peaceful.

You can use a tactile focus as well. Take two stones of unequal weights and hold one in each hand, moving them gently in space and trying to equalize their weight with your mind. Be sure to relax your arms and shoulders. As you hold the stones, you will eventually notice that the one which felt heavier to begin with feels lighter, and vice versa. Soon, they feel as though they have equal weight. (One of the reasons for this, undoubtedly, is that we are able to balance the two sides of the brain when we're in a state of trance or ecstasy.) When your mind has balanced the two stones, switch the stones in your hands. Begin again. As soon as they are balanced, switch them again. Do this three or four times.

Your eyes should be lightly closed during this meditation.

Yoga and Tai Chi: The Moving Meditations

The ancient practices of yoga (Indian) and tai chi (Chinese) are in themselves types of meditation. They are particularly useful if you are so stressed you simply can't sit still.

Yoga, which means "yoke" or "union" in Sanskrit, has been practiced since the third century B.C. This system of postures, called *asanas*, stretches the mind and body by alternating energy flow and relaxation. Each posture offers you a feeling of movement combined with stillness, and if the posture is physically challenging, you can make it easier on yourself by breathing into the pose. The longer you remain in the posture, the more alert and calm you feel. When you stop thinking about "holding" a posture and instead, begin releasing into it, you are developing a healing practice that will soothe the mind as well as the body. Yoga, like any other form of meditation, causes a release of neurotransmitters in the brain, those feel-good hormones that fill us with a sense of well-being.

Tai chi chuan (*taijiquan*) developed as a moving meditation that could also be used as a martial art. The tai chi "forms" or choreographed patterns follow the Taoist concept of yin and yang: the external body moves and the internal spirit soars. As you practice the forms, you begin to sense that *they* are practicing you. Tai chi builds strength, endurance, and elasticity in the practitioner, and also allows *you* to find balance and harmony within the various parts of your life. When the the choreographed forms have become second nature, you learn to flow and go with the changes inherent in movement. So, too, you can carry this awareness outside your practice to life itself.

Tai chi forms can be difficult to learn, but your concentration on them, and your patience with yourself as you practice them, can be a meditation in itself. Once you've mastered the patterns, you can go inward to focus on your breath, or the rotation of your limbs in movement, or the circulation of *chi*, or life energy.

The idea of yin and yang (the two seemingly opposite sides that contain within them the kernel of the other and together form a perfect circle) is a wonderful starting point for healing. Balance and symmetry in your forms parallel what you would like to have in your life. It's impossible to feel relaxed if you're working too hard at your practice. However, you cannot progress if you give in and don't devote time to learning your forms. It has to be a mix of the two.

OTHER TECHNIQUES THAT MAY SERVE AS MEDITATION

For some, the idea of meditation will always feel strange and too foreign to be considered, so I'm going to suggest alternatives that will work in the same way to relax the body and clear the mind. Any of these techniques can be used in conjunction with meditation as well.

Body Scan

Jon Kabat-Zinn, director of the Stress Reduction Clinic at the University of Massachusetts Medical Center, suggests the following exercise to become aware of the entire body. Lie down in a quiet room and beginning with your right big toe, concentrate completely on one body part at a time. Move up the right leg, up the left leg, then the torso, then the back, then neck and head. Just bring each organ into consciousness; don't try to change it in any way. The whole scan should take you about forty-five minutes.

Progressive Relaxation

A slightly different twist on the body scan is this exercise, designed by Dr. Edmund Jacobson. This method teaches you to break down tension into workable units—and then get rid of it. Make a fist in each hand and hold it tightly, as hard as you can. Then let go completely. Open the hands and see how different they feel. Move up to the forearms—tense them, then relax them. Now the elbows, the shoulders, the neck, head, and jaw, the face and eyes, the forehead and scalp. Then work the upper back and chest, then down the torso to the hips, legs, and feet. Each time, get as tense as you possibly can and release. At the very end, tighten the whole body, hold your breath, and then suddenly, let go. See how the exercise has changed the way you feel, inside and out.

Autogenic Training

This relaxation technique was developed by Johannes Schultz, a German neurologist who used to hypnotize his patients and then ask them to move their painful limbs. The treatment was so effective that he decided to use it on people who were completely awake.

The following suggestions can be read into a tape recorder and played back, or you can ask a friend to read them to you:

I am quiet and relaxed.
My right hand feels heavy.
My right hand feels comfortable and heavy.
My right hand feels heavy and relaxed.
I am quiet and relaxed.
My left foot feels warm.
I can feel the warmth in my toes.

My left foot is warm, heavy, and relaxed.
I am calm and relaxed.
I am quiet and at peace.
I feel relaxed.

Continue through the body, using these repetitive, calming instructions until each joint, limb, and organ is loose and open. When your external body is relaxed, you can send the suggestions to your heart, mind, and spirit.

Self-hypnosis

Trance is a long-proven method of stilling the worried mind and providing a focus for introspection. When you hypnotize yourself, you smooth out the mental wrinkles and put yourself into a quiet place where you can recuperate and heal.

In self-hypnosis, you summon up the right brain—the intuitive, imaginative side—and put the analytical left brain on hold. Your brain produces alpha waves and halts beta wave production, just as it would during meditation. It requires the same type of concentration and focus to hypnotize yourself as it does to meditate. You don't "blank out"; rather, you are able to gain perspective on upsetting elements in your life. Under self-hypnosis, you can see the stressful event without letting it get to you.

It's a good idea to have one or two sessions with a professional who will be able to instruct you on the technique of getting into and out of self-hypnosis. After that, you will be able to induce this state whenever you like.

Sit quietly and allow your eyes to roll upward. Take a deep breath and hold it. Then close your eyes gently, telling yourself that on a count of three, you will be falling deeply into trance.

One. You are aware of your surroundings and feel secure in them. Two. You are allowing yourself to leave the thinking realm and moving into the state of alert awareness. Three. You are completely, deeply relaxed.

Now tell yourself that your arms are too heavy to lift. When you are able to accept this physical suggestion, you will also be able to tell yourself that you are managing the stress in your life, that you feel comfortable and at peace with yourself, and that this feeling state will last even when you have roused yourself from trance.

Finally, you can come back up to your more routine type of consciousness by inhaling, holding the breath, then letting it out. As you count to three, come fully awake and retain all the harmony that you experienced in a trance state.

Prayer

For those who come from an observant background, prayer is the one of the greatest comforts to be summoned up when under stress. More women I spoke to used prayer as a means to calm down and relax than any other method.

Healing and faith have a long tradition, going back to the Bible. And today, more than thirty medical schools offer courses in faith and medicine. The quiet mind can help the body to heal.

Prayer is quite different from meditation in that it has a goal—when you pray, you are restoring hope in yourself and aligning your feelings and thoughts with some power greater than yourself. The Office of Alternative Medicine of the National Institutes of Health is currently investigating ways in which the power of prayer affects healing, just as Benson did with meditation decades ago. Results so far have been impressive—a 1988 study in San Francisco showed that heart patients who received prayers had fewer postoperative problems than those who weren't prayed for. Another study, this one of 91,000 individuals in Maryland, indicated that weekly church-goers had 50 percent fewer deaths from heart disease than their non-church-going neighbors, and committed suicide on an average of 53 percent less frequently.

There's no mystery here. If you feel that you're not alone in the world, and that someone or something is there to help you in your hour of need, you aren't impotent in the face of disaster or trauma. When you feel peaceful inside, many experts believe, you can actually strengthen your immune system, and this works as good preventive medicine for both body and mind.

Meditation—in all of its forms—is a gift you give yourself. Not only will it start to relieve some of the stress you feel, it will also enhance your practice of all the other steps in this program.

Step 8 **Increase Sexual Pleasure**

T anya was in a pretty good marriage—everyone said so, and she believed them. But she was bored. And being bored made her angry and frustrated. And that was incredibly stressful. Sometimes she thought it was all her fault, that if she were warmer, funnier, more exotic or more *something*, her husband would pay attention. Sometimes she was sure it was his fault, and she just wanted to scream at him and demand whatever it was that was missing. But since she didn't know what it was, she shut up and acted like everything was fine. She and Phil had been together for twenty years, which was something of a feat.

What could it be? They didn't argue; they had stuff in common to talk about; they even had enough money to go on a vacation once a year. But she felt so blah when she thought about her life. She wasn't really the adventurous, risk-taking sort, but she wanted more than she had. And she felt that she deserved it.

Every once in a while, Tanya would stop what she was doing and watch Phil moving around the house. She'd study how he walked, how he sat down or picked his fingers, the way he forgot to button a middle button because he was too rushed and impatient. And she'd realize that she had stopped thinking about him as a sexual being. After twenty years, he was just part of the woodwork of her life—comfortable, nice to talk to, but definitely not a turn-on. The last time they'd made love—was it really a month ago?—she hadn't had an orgasm and he hadn't asked what was wrong. And the time before that—it had to be the night of Corrie's birthday party, when they were both a little drunk. And that time, he hadn't even really been able to get it up. They fell asleep right after and never discussed it.

Sometimes her body felt empty, a hollow rind. It wasn't as good as it had been when she was twenty-five, but she knew that was normal. At forty-eight, she was thicker around the middle and had a fierce case of cellulite on her butt. But she had great breasts (Phil used to kiss them, but he didn't even look at them anymore), and terrific legs. She knew she was attractive, but she didn't *feel* attractive, or much appreciated any more. She was no sex maniac, but she felt an aching need to be touched.

And what about Phil? He had to be as bored and annoyed with their lack of a sex life as she was. She had seen him at parties—women gravitated toward him, flirted with him. She didn't mind that, mostly because she never felt that he would act on any invitation that was extended. He was just not very sexually interested in much of anyone.

"I try to think back to when we met, when we were both working our first jobs. He was selling cars and I was working at a real estate firm, and we used to run into each other at this local diner at lunchtime and chat. One day he called me at work and asked if I'd have dinner with him—he promised no greasy spoon. So we started dating once a week, taking in a movie or going out to a club. I was always aware of when he touched me—like helping me on with my coat (he was such a gentleman!) or grabbing my arm when he was talking about something that really meant a lot to him, like trout fishing. But after our dates, he'd give me a peck on the cheek.

"I think we'd been seeing each other for six months before my girlfriend and I figured that he was so shy that I was going to have to make the first move. I was worried—I told her he'd think I was slutty or whatever they call it these days—but she encouraged me and said I was too sweet for anyone to think I was fast. Which was sort of true.

"That night, we'd gone to a pizza place with some friends and they had a band and we danced. It was so much fun, and I was feeling really great. When we pulled up in front of my apartment, he was about to get out of the car, but I yanked him back and pulled him toward me and gave him a big, deep, juicy kiss. He looked astounded. But he said, 'Hey, that was nice,' and he kissed me back. And we sat there necking for the longest time. I was incredibly excited, like I was going to jump out of my skin.

"It was another month before we went to bed together, and he wasn't very aggressive. I was always a little nervous about being the initiator, but I did it because I was nuts about him at this point, and thought that when I showed him how much I wanted to give, he'd give back. It was always hard for him.

"I guess the best time we ever had sexually was right after we were married—he wanted to do it three times a day, and sometimes he'd give me a surprise call at the office and tell me to meet him at home for lunch. He never said what for—like he couldn't say the words 'Let's make love.' But I didn't mind. It was so tender and loving. Never wild—but we're not like that. I was never awfully comfortable with oral sex—giving or receiving—but I must say I started having terrific orgasms when he would use his hand on me while he was inside me. I felt sheltered and protected when we were in bed together, and that gave me a lot of self-confidence in the rest of my life. I realized that it's important to have someone else say, 'You're beautiful, you're special,' for me to really believe it.

"So when did it fizzle out? I know it was bad after the kids came—we were always exhausted. And when they were school-age, Phil was always saying we'd wake them up. We started doing it less and less often, and we never talked about it. Sometimes it was very good, like when my mother had the children, or when we went away and we were in a nice hotel room. But most of the time, it was about as routine as brushing my teeth. Phil had problems every once in a while, and I was very patient, never critical, but I think he started not wanting to do it because he was afraid of embarrassing himself. I didn't push it, and I bit back all the words—like 'I need to be held and kissed, even if we don't have intercourse.'

"But I'm going to burst with what's inside me now. As I've gotten older, I think, I have more of a need for physical stimulation. So now it's time to say the words, before I stop being in love with my husband. I want to keep my marriage, and I *really* need the physical expression of what we have and can give. And I don't believe that crap like you get too old and eventually you don't want it anymore. I think I could breathe easier and walk taller if I had more sex and more affection. So I'm going to ask, and I'm going to keep asking until something happens between us. It's going to be very awkward, and I'm going to feel awful bringing this out into the open, but you know what? I'd feel more awful sitting on it for the rest of my life. That would be rotten for my mental health, let alone my physical well-being."

Sex and intimacy are incredibly powerful ways to reduce stress. A woman's sense of herself as a person, as a creative force on the planet, stems in great part from her sexuality, as Tanya honestly tells us. And the more comfortable she can feel with her role as an intimate, giving, receiving, caring person, the more self-esteem she can build.

> *The Lover wants to touch and be touched. He wants to touch everything physically and emotionally, and he wants to be touched by everything. He recognizes no boundaries....*
> *Ultimately, he wants to experience the world of sensual experience in its totality.*
> —ROBERT MOORE AND DOUGLAS GILLETTE,
> *THE LOVER IN HIS FULLNESS*

WHAT SEXUALITY MEANS TO WOMEN

Sex is not only something you do in the bedroom or the back seat of your car. You can employ the potential of your sexuality in a boardroom, on the playground, or in the kitchen. The spark that we send off to others as we go through our daily activities, the energy and life force that pulses out of us—this is the essence of sexuality.

We are all sexual beings from the first year of life. Unfortunately, around about our sixth or seventh birthday, we start getting messages from our parents and the outside world that there is something wrong with being sexual. Little girls are told not to touch themselves, not to stand provocatively with their hand on one hip, or to sit with their legs apart if they are wearing a skirt, or to wear a top that comes down too low. They are even cautioned not to laugh too loud when they are really happy. They learn to repress all the daring, exciting, stimulating thoughts and feelings that threaten to bubble up and eventually erupt. For most, this happens at around sixteen or seventeen, for some as early as fourteen. And for others, it never happens because the impulse was squashed in the bud.

Many of us don't like ourselves enough to feel sexy. Having picked up the media's adulation of bodies that are so painfully thin they look like they'd be crushed in a passionate embrace, we have learned to loathe what real bodies with real substance look like. We have to look at ourselves naked in a mirror before we can show ourselves to a lover, and that can be very scary. Our physical body is the house of the spirit struggling to make itself comfortable and loved. And if we don't appreciate the outer person, how can we ever get to the inner one?

But our sexuality is in fact one of the most powerful tools we have for liking ourselves again. Sex is a creative aspect unlike any other—it is the basis of our relationships with others and our ability to fashion strong ties with close companions of both genders. Sex allows us to relate to others in terms of pleasure. It lifts our spirits (even when money is tight or a parent is ill), and this can change our attitude toward life in general. When you think about it, partnered sex is the only time that two bodies actually meld into one. This is symbolic of our being part of something bigger than ourselves.

> *The sole philter [aphrodisiac] I ever used was kissing and embracing, by which I made men rave like beasts, stupefied, and compelled them to worship me like an idol.*
>
> —ARETINO, QUOTING LUCRETIA

MORE SEX FOR BETTER SELF-ESTEEM

When you really like yourself, you know you have something to offer to the world. This means that you expect others to deal with you fairly, to be interested in what you have to say, and to feel attracted to all those qualities (sexual as well as every other quality) that you exude. If you think you're a pretty neat person, you feel comfortable with others. And when you feel comfortable, you aren't afraid to be vulnerable and open with a partner.

One of the biggest issues we deal with when we offer ourselves to a partner, whether it's for a cup of coffee or a lifetime of love, is rejection. None of us can stand the idea that we might open ourselves wide and be completely vulnerable, and get knocked down by the one person we hope to entice. If Joe or Jill doesn't say "yes," does that mean I'm unattractive, unworthy, unlovable? Of course not. And yet many of us, having suffered abuse or humiliation as a child, interpret a lover's casual "Not now" or "I'm busy" as total condemnation.

On the other hand, if you can separate yourself from the need to be wanted, you can develop a much keener and more positive sense of yourself. Perhaps you asked at the wrong time, or you asked in the wrong way. Or maybe—here's a radical thought—the person you asked is the one with the intimacy problems, and you're the one who knows her own mind.

Once you are able to identify those needy feelings, you can stop throwing yourself at people who would prefer to let you bounce off rather than stick. You can wait for others to come to you and develop your own essential personality, one that thrives alone at times and with others at times. When your sexuality guides you toward experiences with others that are comfortable rather than needy, you are well on your way to being a person with high self-esteem.

And when you find a partner who reacts the same way, you can turn sexual experiences into much deeper forms of communicating. Instead of just going to bed, you will be going toward the depths of another's individuality, learning to be part of a whole as well as being all yourself.

MORE SEX FOR BETTER HEALTH

There are indications from recent scientific research that a good sex life can boost your immune system. We know that during arousal and climax, we generate a great deal of hormonal and neurotransmitter activity. Many of these substances have an affinity for immune cells and can promote their growth and dissemination throughout the body. In a study conducted at the University of Pittsburgh on women with breast cancer, it was found that those with the highest T-cell count (white blood cells that fight infection) were the ones who said they had great sex lives. The women with lower counts either had no sex life or said their sex lives were unsatisfactory.

This is easy to understand when you consider the fact that when you feel better, it's easier for you to heal. You may have anxiety attacks and periods when you're down and blue, you may suffer from PMS or arthritis, but when someone caresses you and cherishes your body and spirit, you have a better chance of recovering—because you really want to. There's a reason for you to get up in the morning and a reason to be healthy again.

In addition, sex erases many of our aggressive, hostile tendencies. Developmental and cross-cultural neuropsychologist James W. Prescott has studied cultures with fewer sexual taboos than our own. He discovered that the more physical affection shown and the less repressive the society's rules, the lower the incidence of adult physical violence.

Think of how peaceful and luxurious you feel, lying in your lover's arms after a bout of lovemaking. If we all lived up to our sexual potential, the afterglow could save the world.

Extreme pleasure
Brings bashfulness and languor.
Jade softens,
Blossoms droop.
My hairpin hangs on my sleeve.
My hair flows down my arms.
Mercilessly the slanting lamp stares at me.
I am damp with perspiration,
And my eyes are dim with intoxication.
I am sleepy,
I am sleepy,
Oh, my love, I am sleepy.

—SUNG DYNASTY POEM, CHINESE,
TENTH CENTURY

REAPING THE BENEFITS OF SEXUALITY WITHOUT A PARTNER

It's possible to be a sexual being if you have no one currently in your life. Your sexuality comes from deep inside and is fostered by your own sense of attractiveness. The old longing to bond is hard to break—and if you came from a family where your parents always talked about "When you get married" or "When you bring your boyfriend home," you may feel like a failure when you don't bring anyone for their approval (or perhaps bring a girlfriend, which would not warm the cockles of *most* parents' hearts).

Many women have had terrible experiences in partnered relationships—perhaps they've been subjected to rape or abuse, or a humiliating and degrading daily grind that wears on the soul. Understandably, they may be very turned off to jumping into another situation that might be just as bad. It's a healthy choice for them not to select a new partner right away—but this doesn't necessarily mean they have to turn themselves off sexually. (And it's not even possible for most women to do this—our instincts generally keep desire alive even when we have no specific object for it.)

We don't have to be mated—there is no rule that says it—and we can in fact be very happy all by ourselves. You may choose to be celibate for a while and consider yourself a sensual rather than a sexual person. You may masturbate and get a great deal of gratification from that type of sexual stimulation. Or you may have sequential relationships, choosing to be sexual only when you meet someone with whom you wish to share that experience.

Our sexuality changes as we grow. And whether we decide to engage anyone else in our quest for a deeper awareness of our sexual nature is our own business. The stronger we are as women, the less we feel we have to rely on a partner to give us orgasms, or fulfill an emotional void. It is when we truly understand how much potential we have and can enjoy that all for ourselves that we become ready to include someone else on our journey.

MASTURBATION FOR STRESS REDUCTION

> *Your body belongs first of all to you. Unless you can develop some kind of sense that your body is your territory (which you can choose to give as a gift, share, or keep to yourself), you cannot freely give it in a sexual interaction with another person.*
> —JULIA HEIMAN, PH.D., JOSEPH LOPICCOLO, PH.D., *BECOMING ORGASMIC*

What is it about self-pleasuring that makes us giggle or cringe and look down? Are we really that embarrassed about touching places that make us feel wonderful and getting resolution from the experience? Is it just the old superstition about growing hair on your palms or going mad? Is it the fact that we have never been encouraged to explore our genitalia and in fact may find it difficult to insert a tampon or check for an IUD string? Or is it more? I wonder if it could be a deeper, more terrifying fear of actually enjoying ourselves.

It is okay to be nice to yourself and to tell yourself that you are worth flowers, candy, a delicious meal out, or a new dress. You also deserve to have as many orgasms as you wish. As soon as you can acknowledge that you are the most important individual in your life, you can deal better with the concerns and problems that cause doubt and fear.

Masturbation is one of the best stress reducers around. Just like meditation, it alleviates muscle tension. After climax, it reduces blood pressure, heart rate, and respiration. It stimulates the production of female sex hormones and neurotransmitters that promote a sense of equanimity. All you need is privacy—it's free and you don't need any equipment (although vibrators and dildos can make it even more enjoyable). You don't have to worry about pleasing a partner, or not coming quickly enough, or appearing to be a showoff by coming too much or too often. You are in complete control and get to call all the shots. This in and of itself imparts a lot of self-confidence and independence.

Still not convinced? It could be that you fear you will "waste" your precious juices or excitement and won't have enough sexual energy left for a partner. This is a completely unfounded fear—as a matter of fact, the more you allow yourself to become aroused, the easier it is. It's been found that people who fantasize and think about sex a great deal tend to have more sex, whether alone or with someone else. So masturbation, in fact, warms up the body and mind for partnered activities.

It's important to know your body. Make a date with yourself; turn off the phone and fax and turn on some quiet music. Take the time to undress slowly, feeling your way around unfamiliar landmarks. See if you get a kick out of tickling the backs of your knees or stroking your eyelashes. Look in a mirror and see which breast is larger or which hangs lower. Squat over a mirror and admire the extraordinary flower created by the inner and outer vaginal lips, with the clitoris standing at attention inside them. Enjoy the flow of warm liquid that begins as you gently touch the area or place a finger inside your vagina.

You can learn a great deal about the way you approach life and your problems by comparing it to your reluctance or enthusiasm for pleasuring yourself. Do you rush in, unthinking, and just go at it full force? Do you hang back, waiting hopefully for a change in your feelings? Or do you take each moment as it comes, reveling in your own ability to make yourself happy? Remember that your physical well-being is an integral part of your essence, and it deserves to be cultivated.

HOW TO CONQUER YOUR FEARS OF TALKING ABOUT SEX

For many women, saying it is more stressful than doing it. Things you do in the dark can be forgotten the next day, but when you've stated your intentions and desires out loud, you feel like the world knows all your hidden secrets.

It's difficult to talk honestly with your partner—"nice" girls don't use dirty words or have dirty thoughts. You think maybe he'll make fun of you or won't be interested in your feelings. You don't want to spoil the romantic mood by getting those thoughts out there in the open.

But once you do, you will feel a totally different connection with your partner. The secrets that have been locked inside you are now shared, and you have a two-way street to travel along. When you are able to say what you like and don't like, your communication in and out of bed improves.

How do you do it? If you've never been honest about sex, if you feel too awkward to begin to express your hidden desires, what can you do to open up?

- *Do it indirectly.* You may tell your partner, "I read about two people in a magazine who (fill in the blank for some sexual activity)…what do you think about that?" Or, "My friend Sue said that she and her husband have experimented with _____. I wouldn't feel comfortable doing that with anyone but you, but doesn't it sound interesting?" By putting your thoughts in someone else's mouth, you assuage the anxiety about putting yourself on the line.
- *Do it on the phone.* When no one can see you, you feel safe and not silly. If you have a particular fantasy and have been holding

back, try calling your partner at the office and suggest that when you get together, there's something you'd very much like to try.

- *Talk about your desires when you're not in bed.* If you start in with suggestions right before or after lovemaking, your partner may take it as criticism. Instead, select a time when the two of you can be alone—having a Saturday lunch on the back porch, or going for a long drive in the car. That way, your ideas have time and space to develop.
- *Try saying things that don't sound like you.* If you never talk "dirty," or if you never use baby talk or whisper in a foreign language, the newness of the experience may add spice to your relationship. Also, when you select a way of talking that isn't "you" and select a new persona to get your message across, you can be a lot freer and easier about what you say and how you say it.

LEARNING TO FANTASIZE, ALONE AND WITH A PARTNER

The brain is the most influential sexual organ we've got—if we think sexy, we *are* sexy. It is the idea of intimacy and eroticism that gets us going and allows the body to respond fully. As you imagine your lover kissing you, you can feel goosebumps rise on your skin; as you anticipate what will happen when you are together later, you can sense a rush—physiologically similar to, but a whole lot nicer than a stress response. You are primed and ready for anything, because you've dreamt about the specifics.

If you have trouble making up sexual situations that can pique your interest, there are some visualization techniques that will help.

Give yourself half an hour of private time, and turn off the phone. Sit in a comfortable chair or lie on a mat on the floor and begin to design a scenario that's pleasing to you. Start with the room you'd like to be in with your lover—how big is it? Is it day or night? What kind of furniture is in it? How soft or hard is the bed? Is there music playing? What kind? Think about the smell of the fresh, clean sheets, and the flowers outside the window. Picture your lover's face when he walks into the room and sees you in the scene.

Where would you like to be touched? What words would you like to hear? You are allowed to make up any activities (no matter how racy or unusual). Remember, fantasies are just thoughts—you don't have to realize them.

After you've become expert at dreaming up situations that get you aroused, you can include your lover. Ask first if your partner would like to share some sexual thoughts with you. If you sense that you're the braver of the two, initiate the sharing experience, perhaps by getting into bed with some erotic literature (any of Nancy Friday's or Lonnie Barbach's books of fantasies will get you off to a good start). Read some selections to each other, and then, when you're primed for it, go ahead and relate your own personal hopes and dreams.

Fantasizing together is just another way of cooperating and communicating. When you don't have to hide your feelings, you gain a new sense of relaxation and camaraderie with the person you are closest to. And this kind of open talking can be a model for the rest of your life.

PUTTING STRESS ASIDE SO THAT YOU CAN BE SEXUAL

> *Touching, stroking and caressing should be a gentle, progressive activity just as intimate and affectionate when clothed as it is when you meet flesh to flesh.*
> —RICHARD CRAZE, *THE SPIRITUAL TRADITIONS OF SEX*

When you feel that there's something wrong between you and your partner, it's hard to open up in bed. That's very stressful. If you're terribly busy, and the only contact you have is rolling over on top of each other for twenty minutes once a week, you can't begin to think of the experience as fulfilling. That's also stressful.

Sex can cause stress—certainly an illicit affair that brings on guilt and secrecy can tie you in knots, as can a relationship where the timing and communication is off and neither person is getting what he or she needs. This type of stress can double back on itself—you expect the unpleasant experience that happened last time to happen again, and so it does.

But you can break the cycle and turn agonizing stress that turns you inside out into positive stress that lets you meet the challenge head-on. First, you must see the problem as a problem—not as something that's wrong with you. If you're having trouble in bed, you may need to communicate better *out* of bed, or you may need a few sessions with a sex therapist to set you on the right track. Try to tackle the difficult issues with your partner when you're feeling competent in some other area—perhaps when you've just been given a raise, or praise for a job well done.

Sex can serve as a respite, a time out of time from the hassles of your life. When you are cuddled close in the arms of someone who cares about you, you can let the tensions of the day drain away. And when you rise, refreshed and invigorated, from an intimate afternoon, you will be stronger in body, mind, and spirit, and perhaps better able to handle the difficulties of the rest of the day.

GETTING WHAT YOU WANT IN BED AND OUT OF BED

It's very difficult to talk about sex and sexuality, particularly if you're not getting what you need. But you can't assume that your partner can read your mind—it's hard enough for him to read your body when you're involved in the act of love. This is just as true at the dinner table or in the boardroom as it is in bed. You have to be assertive, even if it pains you to open your mouth and speak. And it's best to start outside the bedroom when you're first practicing.

Being assertive is not "ladylike," so if you were brought up to swallow your words and behave, you are going to have to do a lot of soul-searching in order to change your ways. But it's not impossible. Start small, with some problem where you *know* you're in the right. It can be as simple as returning a carton of expired milk to the supermarket. Express your complaint calmly and simply, and ask if the store owner would be kind enough to replace the item. When you've gotten satisfaction here, you'll see that it pays to speak up, and you'll be able to extend this facility even further—confronting your child's teacher when she's been unfairly critical, demanding better service from a contractor working on your house, talking to your boss honestly about the type of cooperation you feel you deserve at work.

It's kind of sad, when you think about it, that it's easier to work out stresses with people you don't know than with people you do, but then, there isn't as much stake in the argument. When you get up the nerve to tell your co-worker off, the worst that could happen is that you get switched to another project or group. But when you make demands on the person you love, you risk everything. So it takes a great deal to get a great deal. But it's worth it.

If you'd like more time in bed, say so. If you'd like to initiate the action, do so. You will find, as you move along the uncertain ground of relationships, that your footing gets stronger as you act with the courage of your convictions.

Evidently, there are women who have serious sexual dysfunction and get no enjoyment whatsoever out of the sexual act or even sexual thoughts. It is beyond the scope of this book to discuss physical problems such as vaginismus (vaginal spasms that make intercourse impossible) or dyspareunia (pain on penetration), or emotional ones such as lack of desire or anorgasmia (inability to have an orgasm) but professional help can make a very big difference. Don't be ashamed or embarrassed to consult a sex therapist about these problems.

SKILLS FOR STRESS-FREE SEX

As with any other activity that can work as a stress management technique, enhancing your sexuality takes planning and a little work (but what fun work it is!). These elements that you can add to your love play will become second nature, but at the beginning, you must give the exercises some thought and take the time to make them your own.

Erotic Massage for Relaxation

When you learn to let go—really let go of all your doubt, hesitation, lack of confidence, and fear—you don't need to react with the fight or flight response that comes when you're stressed. The techniques of erotic massage allow you to learn to touch and to be touched by your partner without holding back.

Get into comfortable clothes and ask your partner to lie down beside you on a rug or comforter on the floor. Begin by touching each others' faces, exploring the nooks and crannies, the planes and angles. Close your eyes and let your fingers do the "seeing." Now do the same with your partner's head and neck, arms and shoulders, back and waist, legs and feet. You will have to arrange yourself in different configurations to be able to touch the various places one at a time. Talk to each other only when necessary, suggesting when you'd like to turn or move, or perhaps, when you'd like to concentrate on a certain area.

You may find, in your passage across, around and down each others' bodies, that you avoid the genitals. But during this thorough exploration, you want to treat every part equally—the breasts, pubic mound, perineum, vulva and the penis, testicles, and anus should be considered part of the whole.

Which areas feel best to you? Give your partner information as needed with positive comments. "Yes, that's great. Keep doing that. Oh, I love it when you touch me there," are all incentives to keep going.

When you have completed your tours of one anothers' bodies, stop and hold hands as you breathe together. You may feel languid and soporific, or stimulated and on fire—or both! Tell each other what's going on before deciding whether to take off your clothes and begin the process all over again.

You may want to stop here if you're new to the activity and feel that this is about as intimate as you'd like to be. But if you're on a roll, keep going.

The experience of massage when you're naked is even more sensual and delicious, and by using massage oils, getting your hands to slide easily along your partner's flesh, you can enhance the experience. Be sure to use different kinds of touch—gentle and slow, brisk and rough, teasing and playful. See how you can make patterns on one another's bodies with fingertips and knuckles. Cover every inch with your touch. Ask your partner first whether gentle pinching or slapping might be fun to try as well.

When you receive your partner's touch, think of it as a gift, an opportunity to allow someone else to come into your private space. Feel all your tensions dissolve under the loving hand of your partner. You have all the time in the world to enjoy yourself—and you deserve it.

With this shared experience, you are constantly donating good feelings and good wishes to another, and at the same time, you are getting it all back for yourself.

Sensate Focus Exercises

These exercises allow you to play the roles of giver and receiver, one at a time. First you get to give everything while your partner is passive; then you switch roles—your partner is active and you take what's being offered. The purpose of the experience is to get into the physical contact without feeling guilty that you are enjoying yourself at the expense of someone else's pleasure.

During the first week, sit or lie down together with your clothes on. For the first twenty minutes, you are the doer and your partner does nothing. You are allowed to make any type of physical contact with all areas *except the genitals* as long as it isn't harmful or unpleasant. Your partner can give you positive feedback, but should say nothing critical. Then switch places, and you be the receiver for the next twenty minutes. Afterwards, talk to each other about how you felt during the experience.

During the rest of the week, you may remove some of your clothing, but once again, stay clear of the genital area. See whether you surprise yourself in your reactions; perhaps you have erogenous zones you never dreamed of. Talk about your reactions with one another.

When the second week begins, you may do the exercise naked, but try to pay equal attention to all body parts. If you are very aroused, tell your partner to stop the stimulation so that you don't proceed up to orgasm. Allow the feeling to subside; then you may resume the touch.

At the end of the second week, you will have an entirely different focus when you lie down with your partner. When you finally decide to have a full sexual experience, the heightened anticipation and excitement will make your lovemaking infinitely richer.

Quickies

No matter how crammed your day and night are, you can always fit in a quickie. When your lover jumps out of bed and gets in the shower, go join in. When you're raking leaves on a Sunday morning, stop and roll around in them for a while (if you have neighbors, go inside and take a break on the top of the dryer in the laundry room). When your child has soccer practice, sneak home and get in fifteen minutes of rousing sex play. Remember, every sexual act does not have to end in intercourse, nor do you necessarily have to take off your clothes. Whatever you do that's intimate and exciting will get those endorphins going and help stimulate the immune system. And not "going all the way" but experimenting with less conventional activities can add interest and energy to your sexual repertoire.

Dates

There are other times when it's a good idea to plan out an afternoon or evening in advance so you can have all the time you want. Make a date (and put it on the calendar as you would any other social commitment) to send the kids to Grandma's, turn off the phone, and order some take-out. Take a bath together, with plenty of bath oil, and then give each other a long, lovely massage. Spend some time talking about what you'd like to do—do you want music on, do you want to be blindfolded, would you like to use sex toys, how about an erotic video?

As you share this luxurious experience, be open to changing your plans. That way you get to have some organized time together but still feel spontaneous.

Laughter

Sex is funny. If you came from another planet and had no idea what the conjugal act was all about, you would probably split your sides (if you had sides in your new form) over the sight of humans frantically removing clothing and getting into all kinds of different contorted positions as they made strange noises.

None of us is Venus de Milo (and even she was flawed after she lost her arms). Our bodies are frail and often asymmetrical; our technique generally leaves a lot to be desired. The more we don't aspire to be those golden goddesses of love that we see on the screen or in print ads, the better we'll do. It's funny to be so excited that you trip getting out of your underpants; it's laughable when you're standing before your lover wearing nothing but your socks and glasses. But it's *human*. The more we love the intensity and delirious abandon of sex and forget about looking great or acting perfect, the better our sex life will be.

Stocking the Cookie Jar

But not with cookies. Keep an extra jar for spare change and bills. Instead of spending the money on a fancy meal or a concert, use it for a romantic evening at a bed and breakfast or even at a roadway no-tell motel. Having an intimate experience in a place that isn't home adds a note of the forbidden, which can be a lot of fun.

Notes and Phone Calls

It's suspense and anticipation that makes for the mystery of sex, so try enticing your partner before the event. A titillating invitation in his pocket ("Meet me for a naked lunch—I have some chocolate syrup we can lick off each other") is a terrific prelude to something exciting happening. And a sexy phone call to his office with a lot of heavy breathing can be the foreplay you both need to spice up what's to come later on.

When your partner tells you all the things you two might do when you're alone, your own fantasies begin to sprout. There's nothing like a hint of eroticism before the event to enliven and enhance the experience to come.

You can't have sex constantly—when would you have time to work or go for a bike ride or diaper the baby? But you can be sexual all the time by getting your needs and desires in focus.

Part III

The Outside World: Getting the Help You Need from Others

We are more than the sum of external and internal parts—we are also part of the greater world. Part of a family, a community, a universe that has range and scope and potential. No woman can make it alone, no matter how much she values her privacy. The outside world can be a welcome respite from the interior monologues we hold with ourselves, and sometimes, reaching out for help can resolve many stressful problems.

When others care about you, they will be concerned about your well-being, but if you deny them access to your innermost feelings, they'll never figure out what you really want. So ask! It couldn't hurt to ask. And if the answer is "no," get yourself a backup who might say "yes."

Look for opportunities to include others in your journey toward a more peaceful, harmonious existence. Link hands and minds with those who love you and see what amazing results you get.

Step 9 Enlist Family Support

Beatrice is forty-two, a wife, mother, and general tender of the home fires. Her job is secure, but not exciting. As a lab assistant at a pharmaceutical firm, she has to be exact, on her toes all the time. But the work is tedious, and sometimes she has this mad desire to run away from it all.

Instead, she runs home. She does the shopping, picks up the kids at school, and delivers them to their extracurricular activities; she prepares her notes for the town committee meetings and starts dinner. When her husband comes home, she listens to the stories of his day while entering the bills she's paid into the computer. She goes out again to chauffeur the kids back home, finishes preparing and serving dinner, then does the dishes before going out to her meeting. She makes sure to call her mother in Chicago before going to bed at midnight.

By the time she's ready for sleep, she is beyond tired. She's blank, numb, her head buzzing with the sounds and sights of the day and the thoughts of all the stuff she has to do tomorrow. And every day is the same. Weekends, which include cleaning and helping the kids with school projects, are just as harried. She doesn't tell herself very often that she's dissatisfied, because she figures, what good would it do? The only person she ever shares her frustration with is her sister.

"I live like a rat in a maze," she said to Rachel one day.

"Yeah, so do we all."

"No. Not you. You take vacations. Your husband does half the cooking, and when you need a Sunday to go to the mall and pick up a couple of things, he takes the kids. You read books—where do you get the time? I haven't read a book in years. You and Mark actually talk to one another, and he brags to people about how smart and terrific you are. Don't tell me you're a rat, too, because you're not."

"That's because I got my fairy godmother to wave a wand over me and turn me into Cinderella going to the ball," her sister joked.

"Ha, ha, funny." Beatrice took a breath. "You know, what I really envy isn't your reading ability. I'm jealous that I don't have someone telling me I'm good, I'm worth it." She sighed deeply. "I think I'm invisible."

Rachel shook her head. "Boy. I think you made yourself invisible."

"What do you mean? Maybe Bob doesn't know I get scared in the middle of the night, that I worry about how we'd keep this house if I lost my job—which might happen. He thinks I'm superwoman and he doesn't need to pat me on the back."

"Tell him you're not. Ask for what you want." Rachel grabbed her sister's wrist. "Bea, I stood up for myself. I didn't wimp out. I said what I wanted and needed, and I never took less. You can do it too."

"No, Bob isn't like Mark. He's busy with his own life, and probably wouldn't know how to comfort me. But if I want my marriage to last, I have to give him what he needs and stop thinking so much about myself."

"Really." Her sister snorted. "That is the most codependent thing you've ever said." Rachel shook her head. "Men are people, just like us. They can cope and they can be empathetic and they can pitch in when they have to. Guess what—if you said you needed to go away for a week or two, he'd do some laundry, and some shopping, and the kids would go to school and not die of scurvy and actually enjoy themselves.

"And if you asked him to hold you when you cried in the middle of the night, he'd be there for you. He's not a machine; he's your husband, the guy you married because you told me when he looked you in the eye, it was like he became part of you. The longer you treat him like a helpless baby, the longer you don't admit that you can't do it without his support, the longer you will be a stressed-out, miserable, agitated, griping, bitter woman."

Beatrice's face was white. She was in total shock. "Is *that* what you think of me? That I perpetuate this mess that is my life?"

Rachel smiled. "You called it a mess, not I. Give it some thought. Gotta go. Bye, sis."

Beatrice couldn't fall asleep that night. Not because of her usual anxiety about getting everything done. Rather, she wondered at her own opinion of herself, at the way she had carefully structured her world so that only she was capable and smart and everyone else was a dodo. She was neglecting her husband by not letting him be there for her. It was like she couldn't trust anyone—even the man she loved—to take care of business that she considered important.

As she watched her husband blissfully snoring away, she thought about the fact that they'd been together for twelve years, yet she'd never made any demands on how they worked their life. Planning some home renovation? She'd call the contractor. Deciding to see the in-laws? She'd make the date. Dealing with a bad report card from one of her kids? She'd call for the appointment and see the teacher. Worrying about getting older and wanting to hear that she still looked good? She'd choke it back and he'd never know.

Beatrice had always assumed she had to do the whole thing or it would fall apart. But how fragile this relationship would be if it she couldn't rough it up some!

"Bob," she said quietly at breakfast. "Would you do me a favor?"

"Yeah, hon, sure."

"Great. I need help. A lot of help. I need you to talk to me, be there for me, support me. Is that okay?"

"Help doing what?"

"Whatever. Help just living, I guess."

He looked a little puzzled. But he clearly responded to the intensity in her voice. "Whatever you say, babe."

She could see he didn't get it. She would have to teach him about her and tell him every time she needed him. Well, it would make their life more challenging. Anyhow, it was a beginning.

If you have a family, you have a built-in support system that you may not be using—or using properly. Beatrice has just woken up to the fact that she can't go it alone. This is a very important step for you to take, too. Hard as it seems at first, it will mark a huge change in the way that you accept and manage your stress.

My spouse worries or escapes in TV sports. I need to talk about what's bugging me or do something physical.

—PAT, 35, PUBLICIST

I've found that when we do things as family, the routine daily problems don't seem so important and eventually resolve themselves. We use the 'great outdoors' to offload a lot of the stress. Nothing like a good spelunk or river–raft to get those endorphins flowing. I think also that when my husband and I are in physically challenging situations and can work together, it makes me feel supported all around.

—ISABEL, 28,
FREELANCE ADVERTISING COPYWRITER

THE FAMILY BALANCING ACT

A family, like a tree, has roots and branches. It sits in the middle of the world's anonymity like a little island, not quite self-sufficient, but at least producing its own fruits and trying to govern itself.

But when one family member assumes all the responsibilities, this tree starts listing to one side. The other family members forget or are allowed to ignore the fact that one person is keeping the entire structure together. Over time, those roots wither and decay. They can no longer send out new shoots to support the life of the entire tree.

It is most commonly the woman in the household who either takes the whole burden on her own back or refuses to allow others to handle the load. Has this happened to you?

When you first made a life with a partner, the two of you were gung-ho to share, to do things together, to make nice to each other and congratulate each other on a job well done. And then, somehow, things fell apart. Who can tell what subtle alterations happened during the years of your relationship that made one side pull harder and faster?

Maybe you started doing all the work because it just sat there and never got done if you didn't do it. Or maybe you felt you were the only one who could accomplish it to your satisfaction. And that led to your unconscious decision not to ask for help or even to get credit for what you do. It's possible you don't let people appreciate you the way they might because you have some impossible standard of the kind of praise you'd like. And so you settle for nothing rather than the gift they could give but you won't accept.

Why do women always feel responsible? Why do they often insist on working in a vacuum, isolated from those they love, who love them?

Part of the answer is that most women are extremely capable and can do lots of jobs at once. There is such satisfaction in being a competent whirlwind that the roles add on and on. How many women do you know who say "no" when asked if they can take on just one more chore? The more we do all by ourselves, the more self-esteem we gain. Except when we turn around and see that no one cares.

> *I don't talk about my problems too much to my spouse because I have so many, and he can only handle one thing at a time. If he has to think about more than that, he gets terribly nervous, and communication really breaks down.*
>
> —GILDA, 46, MANAGER,
> EXECUTIVE ACCOUNTS FOR CHEMICAL COMPANY

LOTS OF ROLES MEANS LOTS OF STRESS—AS WELL AS SATISFACTION

As it happens, numerous studies haven shown that the more roles a woman assumes, the greater her chances of being physically healthy, more satisfied with life, and less depressed. This concept, known as "expansion hypothesis," is based on the premise that as you expand what you do in life, you feel useful—that there's a reason for your being here.

But this theory isn't true across the board. Too many meaningless roles are draining—and women more typically take these on in addition to their more important roles. For women, it was traditionally assumed that the feelings of success came from playing the wife and mother roles. Today, that's no longer the case. Single, divorced, and childless women can be just as happy and well-adjusted as their nurturing home-and-hearth peers. You can eliminate the domestic front entirely, be a bear in the marketplace, and feel like a satisfied woman.

However, once you add on those traditional roles, something happens. For a man, being husband and father as well as paid worker have profound personal, emotional, and spiritual benefits. For a woman, the reverse is statistically true. Yes, it's fine to be a wife and mother, as well as being a worker, but suppose you spend a great deal of time and energy on your job, more than you do at home? If you travel on business and leave the house and kids to a sitter, you start worrying about the role you've left at home. The psychological distress inherent in trying to make things run smoothly on the home front is compounded by the fact that this stuff is supposed to be a cinch for any woman. Your core roles of wife and mother should offer stability and substance to life—as they do for men.

But playing those roles to the hilt involve a lot of domestic scutwork that is exhausting and debilitating. (The stresses of actually thinking up and performing all these chores are frequently lost on your male partner, who would never have felt obligated to tackle them in the first place.) And when you compare it to managing a department, speaking at a convention, or writing the great American novel, it sure doesn't measure up.

Why don't women ask for help as well as the recognition that they're doing an extraordinary job? Aren't those home-based roles just as important, and shouldn't they be acknowledged as such? Many women apparently worry that their place in the family structure is to be the supreme manager, and to change that would be to topple a house of cards.

It's time to change that attitude.

Face it: you need support. Everyone feels better when she is told that what she is doing is worthwhile and has purpose. Your motivation increases with each pat on the back, and consequently you are able to do more. But support, to be valuable, should be more than emotional. It has to be concrete. That means that you need a backup system that will fall easily into place if you're not around or if you're not well and can't manage your usual load. Or if you have finally come to your senses and decide that you don't have to carry this burden any more.

> *The husband of plus-sized model Emme Aronson is her*
> *height (5'11") but thirty-five pounds lighter (she weighs*
> *190). When asked by* People *magazine to comment on*
> *his feelings about his wife's size, he said, "When I'm*
> *tired, she can give me a piggyback ride."*

HOW TO TALK TO YOUR PARTNER ABOUT YOUR STRESS

The women I interviewed for this book typically had trouble discussing their stress with their life partner—some just clammed up and kept quiet about it, and others made a lot of noise and whined and complained, but never seemed to get results.

What do you want from your partner? To tell you you're doing well, that he is astounded that you fixed the carburetor because he wouldn't know where to begin, that you're smart, funny, an inspiration to him and your kids, that you're doing great on your diet and look wonderful. Well, that would be fabulous, but only if it's heartfelt. Phrases like those above are easy to say, but not always easy to mean. The person who only pays lip service to who you are and what you believe in is still taking you for granted.

If you aren't getting what you need, you have to ask for it. Demanding will get you nowhere, and for many men, those let's-fix-our-relationship-talks are a real turnoff. You need an approach that is subtle but firm, honest and not manipulative.

The Ostrich method (sticking your head in the sand and hoping no one will notice) is counterproductive—nobody wins here.

The Bull method (ramming your opinion down your partner's throat) can only work if you can make your anger into a creative challenge as opposed to a brutal club.

The Cat method (wait a while and then pounce) is the one I advocate. Let me tell you why.

Patience is a misunderstood virtue—most people interpret it as wimpy or too ambivalent to work. But, in fact, patience takes great strength of character and an ability to seize the moment. So when you want to be told you are luscious and desirable or brilliant and capable, you may have to come up with several occasions where you become what you wish to be praised for. Make yourself a big target and express yourself clearly. When he is clearly aware of you, your virtues may shine brighter.

This also goes for support when you're stressed-out or depressed. Make the time to ask his advice on whatever concerns you and be sure you give him your own feedback—"You've made me feel better," "You're the only person I can tell this to," etc. When you support him, you may find that the seesaw works in the other direction as well, and he may find it easier to support you.

Another excellent tactic is to employ a traditional method used in writing fiction. When you want your reader to cheer for the heroine, you get other characters to talk about her in glowing terms. If you can get a friend or relative to talk you up in front of your partner, he may see your worth in a new light. Understand that you will have to ask your pal for the initial support, but that may be a little easier than asking your spouse.

The question remains, why are we afraid to ask for support from the person who is supposedly the most close and intimate of anyone we know? In great part, it's embarrassment—we've been doing without this truly essential element so long that it feels funny to make a big deal of it.

But we have to, in order to retain our self-esteem and to improve the quality of the relationship we've worked on long and hard, as well as to ease our stress burden. You may be surprised to find that your partner likes helping you out and telling you you're good. Good feelings multiply and double back on themselves—the more positive you can be as a couple, the more benefits you both receive.

My spouse is in total denial at times, and then at other times, he looks to me to fix the stressful situation. I have always been the "fixer." UGH.

—ELAINE, 49, PART-TIME
BENEFITS MANAGER IN MD'S OFFICE

*I initiate talking more, but then he opens up.
When he's upset, he rarely (if ever) talks to a
friend, but he'll talk to me if I start it. So I feel
good about that.*

—JILL, 38, MANAGER OF VOLUNTEER
PROGRAM FOR COURT SYSTEM

TALKING TO YOUR KIDS ABOUT YOUR STRESS

Children can be incredibly selfish. And if you help them to remain so, they will grow into incredibly selfish adults. Instead, start them off right with a healthy dose of awareness about their connections to other people.

When my daughter was five, we joined a Y swimming program. As we were getting dressed in the locker room after class one day, an elderly lady in the next booth was struggling to bend over and put on her shoes. I asked if I could help and she gratefully agreed. As my daughter looked on, I slipped them on her feet.

On the trip home, my daughter asked why I had helped a stranger. "Because she couldn't do it alone, and I was there and could do it for her. And it made me feel good to know that I was there when she needed someone."

The next day, I watched through the window as my daughter assisted a four-year-old friend who was having trouble tying her shoelaces. The lesson was mastered. I didn't have to say, "You should do this," but rather, "I did this, and I feel great about it."

It's not a terrific idea to burden your kids with your problems, because if they are highly sensitive, they will assume that they are to blame for everything that's happening to you. But depending on their ages, you can teach empathy by saying, "Mom's a little down today, could you give her a kiss?" or "I really hate it when that happens, don't you? I'd really feel better if you'd just stand by me and hold my hand" or "Do you mind if I scream and vent some hot air? I'm really mad and I need you to understand why I'm grumbling today."

If your children are older, they may not learn by example—as a matter of fact, they may want to do just the opposite of what you'd like them to. When you say you have too much to do and need them to pitch in, they will claim homework, a date with a friend, or cramps. Without being a real meanie, you can emphasize that a family is a cooperative venture, and their participation is essential.

So ask them to sit with you over a glass of iced tea and tell them you need their advice. This will put them in the driver's seat and turn the mother/child power thing around. Talk about your stress in concrete terms, and ask for precisely the kind of help you want. For example, "I've got a load of work from the office and I'd really appreciate it if you'd throw together a salad for dinner tonight." Ask, and at least once in a while, you shall receive.

> *When there's something going on between me and my husband that bothers him, he won't say why he's moody. He just walks out of the house when he's upset and comes back when he's better. At this point, he's not interested in my problems—which he wouldn't see as problems anyway. So we never talk about us, just about the kids.*
>
> —JANE, 39, HOUSEWIFE AND MOTHER

UNRAVELING THEIR STRESS FROM YOUR STRESS

If you assume all the jobs, and then on top of that, you assume the headaches and anxiety and stress of everyone around you, that will compound the difficulty of your task. You are dealing not only with your own stress, but with everyone else's.

A study conducted as part of a National Institute for Mental Health grant by Ronald Kessler, Elaine Wethington, and Jane D. McLeod found that women are more affected emotionally not only by their own stressful experiences, but also by the stressful experiences of those they care about. Kessler states, "Women's roles *obligate* them to respond to the needs of others."

We are all bound up in our family's angst. If our child gets a rotten report card, we feel we fell down on the homework job. If our spouse doesn't get a raise, we may beat ourselves up about not inviting the boss over for dinner. Why is this our fault? Naturally, we are involved in emotional concerns of the people in our lives, but they are not us. The more we can separate from their difficulties, the more we gain perspective on our own place in the family structure.

Interestingly enough, it's the roles we play and not our personalities or some particular "female" gene that makes us hypersensitive to others' troubles. As little girls, we played with dolls and fussed over their real and imaginary injuries and insults. We didn't necessarily try to solve their problems (except to patch them up with Band-Aids). Rather, we commiserated with them, put them to bed, made them special foods. And this type of behavior continued in our peer play and in real life, when we were old enough to look after our siblings. We were rewarded for being empathetic—our mothers praised us for thinking of someone else before we thought of ourselves—and this type of socialization becomes ingrained over time.

Men tend to worry about taking care of business. Their method of attack is generally, "How can we 'fix' the problem?" In contrast, we women usually approach with the attitude of "How can we 'understand' the problem?" This leaves us open to hours, days, and months of anxiety and worry on our behalf and on behalf of anyone we love dearly.

So in order to get out of this pattern, we have to be more assertive about including others in our quest for peace and harmony. Instead of mulling over suggestions for our spouses', parents', and childrens' difficulties, it's time we started thinking of ourselves. This does not mean becoming selfish. Rather, we want to be *self-filled,* learning to weed our own garden rather than immediately going to extract the mess from someone else's.

And the thing we can do is figure out what forces we can enlist in order to help us out during a time of trouble. The curious fact is that if we spend the time on our own development, we will end up stronger and therefore able to help others when they really need us.

I'm very outspoken; my husband holds everything inside and won't talk about it. I never feel supported—I'm like a balloon hanging in the air.

—JANET, 45, CLERICAL STATE WORKER

> *When there's a problem, my husband and I dis-*
> *cuss family matters and then we compromise.*
> *We've learned to do that very well so that the*
> *problems never get a chance to escalate.*
> —DORA, 53, MOTHER OF SIX, SECRETARY

REMEMBER WHAT YOUR MOTHER DID, RIGHT OR WRONG

The last generation handled things differently. Up until the early 1950s, an American woman's roles were very well defined. What was important for her took place in the home.

If you remember your mother's way of handling family disputes and agonies, you may come up with some interesting permutations on old family dynamics. Maybe she appeared to the outside world to be a wimp, doing whatever your father said, whereas in actuality, she manipulated everything behind the scenes. Or maybe she was top dog, and no one took a step without her approval. Roles were bigger and clearer then, which could be good or bad for the children. It was easier to know your limits than it is today, and yet many of us felt too restricted because what Mom or Dad said was so influential in our lives.

As a partner or parent today, it's a wise idea to think about all the things your mother did in the household and see how she accomplished them.

Was she directive and forthright? Did you know when you'd overstepped your boundaries, or did punishment fall out of the blue? Did your father back her up, or did he fight with her about her decisions?

Was she wishy-washy and ambivalent? Did she never know exactly what she wanted—or what she expected from you or your father? Did she surprise you occasionally with a decision that seemed completely unlike her? Did your father support her in these unconventional mandates?

Did you ever see your mother and father hugging and kissing? Did he tell you how terrific he thought she was, or did he criticize and nitpick?

The most important question to ask yourself when you're thinking about how much you'd like to borrow from your mother is, did she get what she wanted? Was there a sense that she was important in the family structure? How were you aware of the kudos and accolades your mother accumulated during her lifetime?

Finally, how much are you like your mother, and what facets of her can you bring to your own household? What traits of hers would you like to wipe out of yourself?

By looking backward in time, you can see yourself coming around the bend. And when you arrive in the present, you'll be ready to assume the roles you've got with a great deal more authority.

I tend to want to face the common stress elements head on—confront them, question them, try to eliminate them. But my spouse tends to ignore them in hopes they'll go away.
—MARY, 47, FUNDRAISER FOR A MAJOR UNIVERSITY

I have a lot of anxiety about one thing—these stray cats that live outside our apartment house. In the winter, I'm terrified they'll freeze, and I'm a mess because we can't bring them inside. This probably sounds crazy, but it's how I feel. My husband thinks I'm overreacting and tells me to forget about them, which is not what I want to hear from him. But he's behind me on everything else.
—OLIVIA, 42, GRADUATE STUDENT

SUPPOSE THERE IS NO FAMILY TO SUPPORT YOU

Being a woman alone means you do have all the jobs and play all the roles by yourself. The good part of this is having your own little fiefdom—you get to be messy or neat, you get to buy and prepare whatever food you like—you owe no allegiance to anyone unless you choose to. The bad part of this is that you can become very lonely, dependent only on your TV for solace, and habituated to mindless activities that seem crucial but are only time- and stress-producing.

Even if you're alone, you can still summon support from others around you. If you have a birth family somewhere nearby or at a distance, it's a healthy idea to establish a mutual support system. So you don't always get along with your parents or siblings—still, there's probably one area you have in common that you can use as the basis for your family support network. And when you're talking computers, stock options, dance lessons, or gardening, you can slip in information about what you're doing and how you feel about it. If you're in sync with your family members, you can ask for moral support. If your relationship is more ambivalent, don't demand too much. Be patient and let whatever is growing between you continue to grow. See whether you eventually get more help than you bargained for.

You can create a family out of friends. Invite people over for a meal once a week; offer to split a share in an organic food coop or to go out to a coffee bar together. Make a regular custom out of seeing people. Involve yourself with others and they will involve themselves with you.

HOW TO PLAN A DAY OF GIVE AND TAKE

Look at a typical day. How much do you do? How much do those you share your life with do? How can you get more support than you have right now?

Household Tasks

Make sure you not only divide up the duties, but rotate them. Have periodic talks about who likes to do what chores more, for a change of pace. During these talks, explain that you'd like feedback about what you do—in return, you'll give family members feedback about what they do. (Obviously, you'll all get some positives and some negatives—don't expect total praise.)

Work and Career

Share the activities of your day with your partner and kids if they're around. As you tell them what happened, ask for support for what you did or didn't do in any particular situation. If you're getting a lot of criticism, weigh it fairly, then ask, "But what did I do that had merit?"

Your partner can help you in your profession even if you aren't in allied fields. Networking counts for a lot, after all. Expect your partner to make introductions for you or mention what you do and how capable you are. It's possible he may know someone (or that someone may know someone) who might be able to help you out. For example, you might be looking for a new job, which your husband could mention to his co-worker whose wife was in a similar field. Through that contact, you might get an entry into her company.

Personal Endeavors

Bring up everything that's going on, even if you feel it's incredibly personal. What about your mother going into a nursing home? What about your wanting to lose ten pounds or go on an all-women's sailing trip to the Azores? What kind of support could your spouse and children offer you if you're depressed over the death of your high school English teacher? How about your anxiety over taking a new job or going back to finish your Ph.D.? None of these issues are easy to deal with, and the more you can discuss them with people you love, the more solidarity you feel behind you, the clearer your choices will become.

The Future

Sometimes we don't think about what's ahead, and we just put one foot in front of the other. But there are times when we think about what it might be like to change careers midstream, or to have a baby at fifty, or what we'll be like when we're very old. It's at times like this that we particularly need to bounce our hopes and fears off someone who knows us really well. Because we can move ahead in hundreds of different ways, it can be terrifying to select one path. So we need a partner or mentor who can cheer for the dreams we'd like to realize. Even if those dreams seem unrealistic, a helpful supporter will encourage us to try and move toward a place where we can do all those things that seem so ephemeral and impossible right now. (See Step 4 on goal planning if you have trouble imagining what your future could be like.)

When thinking about what lies ahead, you need the perspective of someone who loves you and sees all your potential, and who can laugh and cry with you over the ridiculous hurdles you'll have to surmount to get where you're going.

It's a brave partner, too, who can allow you to take a course that doesn't include him. Because women outlive men by approximately six and a half years in this country, it's likely that some part of our futures will be spent alone. And even if you and your partner live long and fruitfully together, you may still have certain goals to reach that are all yours. When your partner can spur you on to fly alone, you can get even higher.

SKILLS FOR GAINING FAMILY SUPPORT

In order to get everyone on your side, you may have to do some work with yourself and then with the people you live with or are close to.

Skills You Need

- *Being assertive.* Tell people how you feel and tell them you'd like to know how they feel. Don't bottle up your anger or it will eventually spill over, either in passive–aggressive or in hostile behavior.
- *Being proud of yourself.* If you aren't, who else will be? If you think you've done something great, acknowledge it. If you've gotten on an exercise program or begun to meditate daily, admit that you have the self-discipline and self-respect to stick to some new good habits.
- *Give your emotions free play.* If you think too much, you get stuck in mental patterns. Too many head trips and not enough feelings make you dizzy with "should haves" and "if onlys." When you're struck by the horror of a newscast about a rape or the wonder of a perfect sunset, give yourself leeway to express everything that's going on inside you. You can do this in front of those you love—even if it initially embarrasses you (and them).

Skills Your Family Needs

- *Listening.* It's important to have a good ear when you just want to wail. It's also vital that your audience be sympathetic to your side, while offering constructive comments that might help you accept why things didn't turn out your way. A good listener is also someone who can sit with you in silence, hearing your intention rather than your words.
- *Responding.* You want your family members to give you the goods. That means cheering you on when you think you can't go any farther, congratulating you on meeting your goals, introducing you to the experiences you need to get

ahead. If your partner and kids don't respond the way you need them to, I suggest you institute a family meeting once a month or whenever any member wants to call it. At this meeting, each person gets a chance to say what they want from the others. This doesn't mean that everyone has to give exactly what's been asked for—but the request is a jump-off point for negotiation.

- *Giving you freedom when you need it—even when you don't ask for it directly.* This will take time, and you will have to ask at the outset. But when you're fed up with chores, when you just can't handle another activity, pass the buck to them. You might institute a rotating chart where everyone gets to do certain chores on certain days. Everyone should have a day off with no obligations, and everyone is allowed to trade. So when you're particularly stressed and you really need a break, you can switch with someone else.

- *Offering support even when they don't understand why you need it or don't really approve of your decision.* This is something you'll have to bring up in a family meeting. Otherwise, it's unlikely that you'll get it. You might want to explain that sometimes, the best way to help is to give it without feeling it's warranted. Remind your husband about the time you sent him a box of cigars at the office even though he didn't get the new account. You could point out to your sixth-grader that when he was bummed out about not making the team, you took him for ice cream and a walk by the river. You could tell your teenage daughter that she didn't have to say she'd broken up with her boyfriend—you just knew. And then explain that you expect them to figure out when you're sad or angry and support you.

DON'T FEEL GUILTY ABOUT ASKING FOR FAMILY SUPPORT

Do you think that if you ask for what you want, you're imposing? Unless you're an incredibly demanding, greedy individual with very little concern for those around you, it's unlikely that you are. And imagine how much stress you're loading on yourself by believing you're not worth their consideration. In fact, you can reduce your stress by taking more and giving less.

There are couples who rededicate their marriage vows after half a lifetime of being together. It's as if to say that they want to acknowledge the dedication they've always had to each other and admit that maybe it's gotten rusty over the years and needs a little emotional polishing. If you were really in love and completely committed to one another when you were twenty, then perhaps if you repeat the process fifty years later, you can recapture the excitement that comes with a new relationship. It wouldn't be such a bad idea for all of us to consider periodically the reasons we're with our partner instead of with someone else. If we've worked this hard on a relationship, we owe it to one another to be there all the time, in sickness and health, depressed or happy.

Asking for support is just part of remembering why we came together in the first place. We were there for each other so we wouldn't have to be lonely, or meet the challenges of life without a buffer. We can be as independent from one another as we like, we can have our own friends and take our own vacations and spend our own money, but when it comes down to it, we have partnered up for a reason, and we must never let that part of the relationship founder. A good balance means sometimes being the giver, and other times being the taker. It's just as vital to develop your receiving abilities as it is to work on your giving.

And when you need something, usually someone else needs to give back to you. The gift of shoring up those we love involves many facets—we might give time, money, understanding, love, or humor. Taking the support that's offered isn't greedy—actually, by asking for assistance or confirmation, you are making the other person feel highly important and valued.

Even if you still feel a little guilty, keep up the good work. Getting that support from your partner, children, and other family members is essential to your survival, and to theirs.

Step 10 **Get Professional Help**

Marla wasn't making it. She felt anxious and unsure of herself a great deal of the time, and it was increasingly tough for her to concentrate on her work. Her elderly mother in Atlanta had just had a stroke and was living with her even more elderly sister, which made Marla incredibly guilty. Not that she'd ever gotten along with her mother, but still, she was an only child, and who else could Mom count on? Her husband was increasingly critical of her coldness to him ("I'd like some sense that you know I'm here. Remember what a husband is?" he asked one awful night), and Marla took his sarcasm badly. Her life was a mess, period.

She had thought about therapy before, but she was wary. In her family, people didn't bare their souls, and she couldn't imagine trusting anyone enough to be able to get any benefit from the experience. But one day, she woke up from a dream she couldn't remember, crying profusely. She realized that she wasn't doing herself any good just sitting around being unhappy.

She didn't know anyone who'd ever been in therapy (or she didn't *think* she did—she'd never ask), so she called her family doctor and asked him, confidentially, if he could give her a name. The psychologist he recommended wasn't taking anyone new, but after talking with her briefly on the phone about her situation, this therapist gave her the name of a social worker he felt might be helpful.

So one rainy Thursday night, telling her husband she was going out with some co-workers for dinner, she started therapy. Her practitioner was about her age, about her height and build, and had almost the same shade of red hair, although hers was much shorter. It was funny, sort of like seeing a copy of herself sitting in the opposite chair. The room was comfortable, lit by cozy lamps, and there were interesting masks hanging on the walls. There were double doors on the office, so that people in the waiting room couldn't hear anything. It was like a little warren, tucked away and safe. Marla felt good about it.

But she didn't know what to say. The therapist, Sandy, asked her a few basic questions about her reasons for considering therapy, and then asked her to talk about herself. She wasn't used to it—it felt awkward, like learning in-line skating (which she had tried once, but she had been too scared to continue). At the end of the first session, Sandy asked if Marla had some questions for her.

"I'd like to know if I'm really sick, I guess," she said softly. "And I'd like to know if I'll ever get better."

The therapist was silent for a minute, and then said, "As to whether you 'get better,' that all depends on your own definition of 'better.' But as to being 'sick,' no, I wouldn't say you are. You may be confused and upset a lot of the time, but many people feel that way. The fact that you're motivated to come here and talk to someone means that you'd like to find your own way out. And I'll try to help you with that. Do you think you'd like to continue?"

Marla was shocked. The therapist was asking her if she approved of their session. She'd assumed it would be the other way around. "Yes, sure," she answered abruptly.

They met once a week. At first, Marla found that she was very nervous on Thursday afternoons, distracted and worried that she wouldn't have anything to bring to the table. But over the weeks, as she was able to open up and talk more about things that frightened her or got her furious, she started looking forward to Thursday nights.

"I hardly ate dinner tonight," she said to Sandy after their sixth session, "because I really wanted to talk about Jim, and I couldn't just sit across the table from him and think that I was going to blurt out all these personal things.

"Why don't you tell Jim you're coming here?" Sandy asked.

"Oh, God, he'd laugh so hard, he'd split a gut." Marla looked disgusted.

"Does he do that? Laugh at you?"

"All the time. Like the other night, I was getting out of my jeans, and I tripped and kind of fell over. And he called me a klutz."

"Are you?"

"No!" Marla nearly yelled the words.

"You sound angry."

"He's a pig! I feel awkward around him, like I physically don't belong in the same space. And he's always jumping down my throat—he doesn't think I'm hard enough on our son about his homework and chores, so he yells at Bobby for no particular reason. It's like he wants to drive a wedge between me and my son."

"And how do you react to that?"

"I used to clam up or walk out of the room."

"Avoiding what might come."

"Right! But he'd come after me and pick and pick, and it was just intolerable. So one day, I stood up for myself. He backed off. And lately, I've been saying, 'If you want to pick a fight with me, don't go through our child.'"

"It's difficult to be in a situation where everyone's on trial."

"You said it! He is just so critical. Like when I was little and my mother used to make a big deal out of my not—"

She suddenly stopped talking.

"What did your mother do?"

"It's weird, how we were talking about Jim and then I flashed back to her. They really are very much alike."

That revelation was the beginning. And from then on, Marla began to explore her own reactions to other people—her husband and mother, her boss, her best friend who also put her down a lot. She learned to wait patiently in any situation where she was feeling criticized until she thought of a reasonable comeback, or a way to react that didn't seem like wimping out to her. It was terrifying, at first, to tell people exactly what she wanted from them. But in about three months, it was a little easier, and at this point, she told Sandy that she didn't feel sick anymore.

"I think I'm basically okay now, and I can make it on my own, but I don't want to end therapy because it feels so good to come here and find out that my feelings are normal. That I'm normal. But I'm going to anyway. End therapy."

Sandy was silent.

"Aren't you going to say I should or I shouldn't?"

"I think you've already made up your own mind about that. It's a sign that you are making progress, and you'll continue to do that. You can always call if you have to."

There were days when Marla wondered why she'd quit so soon, and she did call Sandy a couple of times, but she realized she didn't *need* to be tucked away in that safe little warren anymore. She was starting to like taking care of herself.

> *We would rather be ruined than changed*
> *We would rather die in our dread*
> *Than climb the cross of the moment*
> *And let our illusions die.*
> —W.H. AUDEN, "Age of Anxiety"

WHAT'S THERAPY FOR?

It's hard to change—it doesn't feel good. You like doing all those old familiar things, even if they make you miserable.

And it's even harder to admit that you can't do it all by yourself. But the truth of the matter is that sometimes, you need more than a friend who will listen to you ramble on about what's bothering you. Very often, it's difficult to see the problem clearly because you're too close to it. And even if you are aware of it, the techniques outlined in this book that might help you deal with it might be too hard for you right now to understand or to use. If you don't have a determined attitude toward change because you're just too stressed-out, you may need guidance from the outside. Allow that to happen, and you will feel less alone, more confident that others can help you make a difference.

A therapist can be a vital adjunct to your own self-growth because he or she is trained to open up the possibilities for the type of changes you find difficult to make. You also might consult a professional if you have taken care of a certain problem to your satisfaction, but it returns and you have no new methods at your command to cope with it. During the process of therapy, you will find out how to cope with your stress on your own and make yourself into a healthier individual.

Let me tell you about how useful and interesting therapy can be. I myself have experienced many "fifty-minute hours," sitting in a chair across from a compassionate, talented, insightful person who was able to get me motivated to end destructive behavior and begin a healing process that only I could do for myself. In great part, because of my time in therapy, I am today a happily married woman with a delightful and rather well-adjusted thirteeen-year-old daughter. I am able to cope with elderly parents and in-laws, and a stressful freelance lifestyle. I learned about myself through therapy; I know enough to see when I am slipping into old patterns and uncomfortable habits. And I learned that I am capable of handling all the pressure I give myself—even more than the pressure others lay on me. I highly recommend the process, although it is sometimes painful and often frustrating. At the end, however, it is a new type of self-knowledge and freedom.

HOW DO YOU KNOW THAT IT'S TIME TO TRY THERAPY?

Stress can be annoying and upsetting, but it can also be debilitating. If your condition is so uncomfortable that you feel weighed down and anxious all day, every day, some therapy may be necessary in order to get yourself back on track. Very stressed women can also suffer from depression, panic attacks, or obsessive–compulsive disorder, and having multiple problems means that it's harder to know where to begin to take care of yourself.

When you're feeling truly miserable, it is sometimes tempting to think about taking a pill to alleviate the bad feelings. Our society sanctions the "quick fix" for any type of mental or emotional problem. As a matter of fact, many women find that when they go to their physician feeling down or fatigued, the very first suggestion for a remedy is Prozac, Xanax, or any one of the various mood-altering antidepressants on the market.

There are certainly disorders (manic-depressive or bipolar disorder, for example), that react effectively to medication. There are other disorders where both medication and talk therapy should be implemented. Taking medication when you're in a very fragile state is sometimes but not always warranted. A few weeks—or a minimum of six months on an antidepressant if you are in a serious depression—can allow you to start working through some problems on your own. However, long-term drug therapy is not meant to be a substitute for talk therapy and the various healing strategies I cover in this book. A pill, while responsive to the symptoms, may bring on many unwanted side-effects such as dry mouth, dizziness, hair loss, joint pain, and loss of libido. If you're pregnant and on antidepressants, you risk having a low birth-weight baby. Also, your physician will discourage you from nursing your child when she's born, which means missing out on one of the most wonderful experiences you can share with your baby.

But if you need medication, it's important to be compliant with your dosages and your schedule. You and your therapist may find that you respond quickly to medication and can then get down to the deeper work of getting insight into your problems so that you can come up with solutions. It's vital to find a caring professional therapist who will do more than simply write you a prescription.

By answering the following questions on page 215 honestly, you can get a basic assessment of whether or not you have a problem. If you feel you do, you can ask your family doctor for a referral to a therapist. You can also call your local hospital and ask about outpatient mental health services, or check the Yellow Pages under "Psychologists," "Social Workers," "Pastoral Counselors," or "Counselors—Human Relations."

ARE YOU DEPRESSED?

Depression is one affective disorder (a disorder that deregulates mood), that can be effectively treated with both medication and some form of psychotherapy.

Answer the following questions to determine if you are depressed:

1. Are you preoccupied by one or several issues, so much so that you can't concentrate on anything else?

2. Do you feel that your problem will never reach a conclusion?

3. Have you lost interest in activities and people?

4. Are you sad and pessimistic about everything?

5. Do you have trouble enjoying yourself?

6. Are you often irritable?

7. Do you have difficulty concentrating?

8. Have you noticed changes in your appetite, weight, and sleep patterns?

9. Do you burst into tears for no apparent reason?

10. Have you lost interest in sex?

11. Is it hard for you to make any type of decision?

If you find that at least three of the first eleven statements are true for you on a regular basis, you should consider getting an evaluation to determine whether you are depressed and get a recommendation for treatment.

12. Do you feel unworthy of anyone's attention or respect?

13. Are you exhausted all the time and find that it's hard to drag yourself out of bed each morning?

14. Have you abandoned responsibilities at work and at home?

15. Have you let your personal hygiene slip because you don't care how you look?

16. Do you find it impossible to communicate with anyone, even your friends and family?

17. Do you have feelings of impending doom and utter hopelessness?

18. Do you dwell on thoughts of death or suicide?

If you have answered "yes" to any one of the last six questions, make an appointment to talk with your doctor. You could well be in a severe depression. You should get help as quickly as possible.

DO YOU SUFFER FROM ONE OR SEVERAL ANXIETY DISORDERS?

General anxiety disorders cover a great range of problems: phobias, obsessive-compulsive disorders (OCDs) including eating disorders, and post-traumatic stress disorder (PSTDs). People with any one of the anxiety disorders may also suffer from panic attacks.

If you are the type of person who feels she has to take care of the world and every detail in it, you may be particularly prone to anxiety disorders. It's been shown that this condition is more likely to occur to people who are very self-critical and feel they must do everything perfectly. These are women who need to be in control all the time—to let something slip is unforgivable. But as you see, underlying these feelings of keeping things tightly reined in is a fear of taking any sort of risk and a basic lack of self-confidence.

The range of problems and treatments is beyond the scope of this chapter, but following are some specifics about just a few of the anxiety disorders.

DO YOU HAVE PHOBIAS?

Phobias are fears that may be completely irrational, but that are just as terrifying as a mugger coming up behind you with a knife. You may have a simple phobia to any number of specific things, such as snakes, dogs, blood, heights, driving at night, or flying in a plane. Or your phobia may center on social situations, such as speaking in public, or using a public toilet. Most phobic individuals cope with their fears by avoiding them, and yet the amount of anxiety that develops around possibly confronting these situations or objects can fill one with dread.

According to the National Institutes of Health, one in nine Americans are dealing with some sort of phobia. This is such a common problem, and yet many people are ashamed to admit to it. Phobias are difficult to manage on your own. Therapy for this problem usually involves desensitization, where you are introduced slowly to the object or situation you dread. Behavioral and cognitive awareness techniques have proved very helpful in the treatment of phobias.

DO YOU SUFFER FROM PANIC ATTACKS?

If dealing with your phobias or stress becomes overwhelming, the pressure may escalate to an intolerable level. The feeling of terror that overwhelms you may seem to come on without any apparent cause, or it may be an accumulation of problems that have been building up over time. Panic shows itself in a variety of ways. You may have heart palpitations or an inability to catch your breath. You may experience dizziness, numbness, hot and cold flashes, trembling, and nausea. You may also have a feeling that you're about to die. An attack like this takes you out of the realm of everyday reality and into a nightmare world where there is no promise of waking.

DO YOU SUFFER FROM PANIC DISORDER?

Panic attacks are usually brief, leaving you shaken but relieved to be back in a more balanced world. But if you have these attacks often (four attacks within four weeks, according to most experts) or if the attacks last longer than ten minutes, they may constitute a disorder.

If you have a cluster of the symptoms listed above, and they have become so overwhelming that you purposely avoid other activities, you should get an evaluation by a professional. It is important to be reassured that you are fine, you are not going to die, and that you will find a way out of your distress.

The most common and debilitating symptom of panic disorder is agoraphobia, which actually means "fear of the marketplace," and technically what this means is a fear of the outside world. Agoraphobics may dread any object or situation that takes them from the comfort of what they know—and the fear can become so overwhelming that it relegates the sufferer to staying at home, or even in one room in their home.

Panic responds very well to several types of therapy. If you see a cognitive/behavioral specialist, you will be given "homework" desensitization exercises in your sessions. It's important to do these on a regular basis. Medication may be another avenue of care to explore for panic.

DO YOU SUFFER FROM OBSESSIVE–COMPULSIVE PROBLEMS?

Obsessions are thoughts or images that take hold of us, distracting us from work, relationships, and activities. Compulsions are rituals we perform that reinforce our obsessions. For example, if you are certain that your house isn't safe, you may go back repeatedly to see if you've locked the doors. Or if you feel dirty and soiled a lot, you feel you have to wash your hands repeatedly. Many women with eating disorders are compulsive about the way that they handle or consume food; others with an obsession about a relationship may repeatedly call or drive past the desired person's house.

If you're nervous, tense, and apprehensive about life, you may be more prone to developing OCDs than those who have a forceful, take-charge attitude and those who are more comfortable about allowing life to take its own course.

When you're on your own, it's tough to stop doing the behavior that fulfills some need, because as soon as you perform your secretive or repetitive activities, you alleviate the anxiety. But with a therapist, you have guidance, and a specific program to help you out of the old behavior into a new healthful one.

The healing of the spirit
Has not been completed
Until openness to challenge becomes
a way of life.
—M. SCOTT PECK, *THE ROAD LESS TRAVELED*

HOW TO PICK A THERAPIST

The range of help you can get is nearly as wide as the number of therapists in practice. There are compassionate "friend types" who empathize with your distress, and there are detached professionals who might seem as comfortable offering you tax advice as ways to manage your intimate problems. There are those who tell you exactly how to change patterns of behavior, and those who let you do your own thing until such time as you see fit to change it. Whomever you feel comfortable with is right for you.

Referrals are usually the best way to get a therapist you click with—a satisfied friend or family member is a good advertisement. Your family doctor may refer you, and your local hospital will have a listing of people in your community whom you can contact. Holistic centers and community affairs bulletin boards are additional sources of names. It's not a particularly good idea to find a therapist through the Yellow Pages unless you have a reference to that person from somewhere else.

Once you have decided to pursue therapy, you have taken one step in the right direction. But let me caution you not to act hastily. It's tempting to sink into the first couch you come to, because you feel you need help so badly. But this puts you in a position of weakness and the therapist in an untenable position of power. You should see several people before you make your decision, particularly if you've never had any experience with the therapeutic process before. One therapist may be too didactic, another not warm enough, a third too emotionally overbearing.

When you come to a conclusion about which therapist you'd like to see, you can suggest that you re-evaluate this relationship after a finite time—say, six sessions. (A good therapist will suggest this him or herself.) This way, you can be sure that things are working out the way you want them to. Remember, you are buying the services of a professional and you deserve to get the *right* professional. Don't be afraid to terminate the relationship because you think you're going to hurt someone's feelings. You have the right and obligation to act responsibly in finding a professional who will be your partner—not your Svengali—during your course of therapy.

But if you've chosen correctly, you can do yourself a great deal of good. The person should be a good listener, open-minded and not judgmental, and able to both lead and follow in a discussion.

How do you know what credentials your therapist should have, or which type of professional you'd be most comfortable with or what type of psychotherapy you may need? Here are some particulars about the various specialists you might consult.

Psychiatrist

A psychiatrist is a medical doctor with a specialty in psychiatry. The most qualified will have done a psychiatric residency after their internship and will be board-certified. If they have the additional certification of psychoanalyst, their training will include a psycho-analysis of their own, so that they can be aware of their own input in a therapeutic relationship. These doctors have usually treated severe-ly ill patients during their internship and residency, and they are familiar with medications that will alter moods and relieve depres-sion. It is not essential that you take drugs when you see a psychia-trist, but you should know that your doctor may suggest a course of Prozac, Xanax, or some other medication to work in tandem with talk therapy.

Psychologist

A psychologist has a Ph.D. or Psy.D. in psychology, which includes the range of psychological disorders and dysfunctions. He or she might alternatively have an Ed.D. in education. A psychologist must also pass a state licensing or certification exam in order to prac-tice and may also be trained in psychoanalysis.

Psychologists might offer any type of therapy from behavioral and cognitive to gestalt (see below). They may treat you alone, or with your partner or family. Since psychologists are not doctors and therefore can-not write prescriptions, they will have to refer you to a psychiatrist or a psychopharmacologist for a consult and a course of medication.

Clinical Social Worker

A social worker receives a master's degree (MSW) in social work, usually after two years of training in welfare, child advocacy, and place-ment after hospitalization. They must also be state licensed (LICSW) or certified (CSW). These days, social workers may have additional cre-dentials that allow them to offer psychological counseling, sex therapy, family therapy, therapy following incest or abuse and battering, and therapy for eating disorders. Look for a social worker with extensive experience in psychotherapy rather than in social services.

Sex Therapist

A sex therapist may come from any of the above fields and will have additional training in human sexuality and dysfunctional sexual behavior. The sexual component of your problem is generally just a small part of the relationship or personal problems you may be having. In this type of therapy, you'll be given exercises to do alone and as a couple to raise your level of comfort with one another and bolster your feelings of intimacy.

Counselor

This rather catch-all phrase refers to individuals who have taken advanced training in some form of psychological therapy—although, unfortunately, many people without any credentials at all hang out a shingle calling themselves "counselors."

A qualified counselor usually has a master's or doctoral degree and may have specialized training in certain settings—for example, in schools or substance abuse programs.

A *pastoral counselor*, who is a priest, minister, or rabbi, may take additional courses in seminary to enable him or her to work with parishioners in trouble. This is often a good choice for individuals who have no experience with therapy but who trust their clergyman or clergywoman to give good advice and offer solace in times of need.

SHOULD YOU BE ALONE, OR IN A GROUP?

The process of therapy is quite different when you are one-on-one with the therapist as opposed to working with a partner, your family, or a group of people you don't know.

Your particular problem may determine whether you want to be alone—obviously, if your major stresses come from your partnered relationship or your family dynamics, it can be very useful to have the appropriate people in the sessions with you. Often, your therapist will schedule time for you alone, and then time to work with you and your family members.

Group therapy, no longer as popular as it was in the 1970s and 1980s, is a phenomenon all to itself. Although there is a therapist who acts as the leader, the group itself becomes the catalyst for change. Everyone is entitled to make a contribution that may assist in the therapeutic process. Sometimes, it will happen that certain people in the group bond, but others don't, and they feel like outsiders. Sometimes one person takes off after another, or one individual acts as another's protector. The group becomes a "family," with all its various quirks and problems. It's the therapist's role to try to bring all these disparate threads together—and sometimes that works beautifully.

A support group, on the other hand, is different in that there is no authority guiding the sessions. Although there may be a facilitator who makes sure that each person gets a turn to talk, this is more a do-it-yourself process. Support groups can be wonderful if you are experiencing a particular type of stress (eating disorder, mother or father loss, violence in the home, etc.), because all the members have walked in your shoes and know intimately how serious your problem can be.

It is always possible to combine one-on-one therapy with the compassion and concern of a support group.

DOES THE ORIENTATION OF THE THERAPIST MATTER?

Your therapist will have been trained according to a certain philosophy of psychological thought, which means that he or she will conduct your sessions along certain lines. Many therapists these days are eclectic—that is, they may work according to psychodynamic lines when you appear to need that kind of help, and may suggest behavioral changes when you have moved along in your therapy. As long as the two of you are in sync, it doesn't really matter what type of orientation your therapist has.

Here are some of the possibilities:

Psychoanalytic

This school is derived from the work of Sigmund Freud. The philosophy is that we don't change by thinking about our problems; we change by understanding the rationale for our unconscious thoughts. In these sessions, you lie on a couch and "free-associate"—that is, you say whatever comes into your mind. The doctor usually sits out of your view and makes no comment on your statements—although he or she may repeat what you say or ask questions about what you've said. The focus is on your past, and how it affects your present. This type of therapy can take many years.

One type of psychoanalytic approach that may be part of other work done in sessions is *Jungian* therapy. Carl Jung felt that only through our dreams can we connect with the larger forces of life and death. The *anima* or soul, is thought to be present in the representations we give it as we sleep. The patient is asked to record dreams and, with the help of the therapist, interpret them based on the larger issues of her life.

Psychodynamic

This is the most common type of therapy practiced in America. You sit and face your therapist and discuss together your various conflicts and problems. You may talk about the past, but the present really becomes the focus of the work. You will be helped to see how your various relationships and your feelings about yourself help or hinder you in your growth and potential. The therapist is not directive, but rather, asks leading questions about your statements. He or she will point out when you're angry, sad, or ambivalent. The self-knowledge that you gain during these sessions can help you to change your future behavior.

Gestalt

In gestalt therapy, you remain firmly fixed in the present. The innovator of this philosophy, Fritz Perls, decided that since the past was over, it was more important to get on with the work of the present—the "whole thing," which is the translation of this word from the German. In this type of therapy, the client expresses, or acts out, his or her feelings. You may be asked to have a conversation with your mother, for example, where you switch back and forth from one chair to another, playing both parts. This way, you learn how to confront your feelings with immediacy.

Behavioral

This type of therapy is derived from the work of B. F. Skinner, who trained rats and dogs to respond to various stimuli. Although people are far more complex than laboratory animals, they can be motivated to change their interior feelings by altering their exterior actions. This is very useful for people with phobias and compulsive behavior problems.

Behavioral therapy involves a variety of exercises, including desensitization (you work in slow steps toward the behavior or situation you dread), behavior modification, flooding (you dive into the experience you dread), modeling (your therapist role-plays the situation in your place so that you can mimic what he or she is doing), and assertiveness training.

Cognitive Therapy

The idea behind this therapy is to reorder the way you think about yourself in the world. The idea is that emotional problems come from negative and distorted thinking, and that you can overcome unpleasant feelings by changing negative thoughts into more positive and realistic ones.

Frequently combined and called *cognitive-behavioral therapy*, this dual approach has proven effective when used for depression, anxiety disorders (including OCDs, phobias, and compulsive gambling) and eating disorders. (See Step 2 for a full discussion of how this type of therapy works on stress.)

WHAT HAPPENS IN A THERAPY SESSION?

When you call for your first appointment, you'll be asked what the general nature of your problem is, how long it's been going on, and why you think you're not able to handle it yourself. The therapist might also wish to know if any other relatives are involved, and whether you'd like private or family sessions or both.

Remember that you are engaging the services of a professional. You have every right to know that this person is qualified to treat you. When you speak with the therapist on the phone, you can ask where she or he went to school and what her or his degree is in, whether she or he is licensed to practice and has any advanced degrees, whether she or he is affiliated with any hospital or treatment center, and how long she or he has been working with clients suffering from stress and related problems. You should, of course, inquire about the therapist's fee schedule, when payment is due, whether you have to pay if you miss a session, and whether he or she accepts any insurance assignments.

At your first appointment, you will introduce yourself, giving all the history you think is relevant to your problem. At the same time, you should ask about the way the therapist works—what can you expect during a session? Is it one-sided, where you do most of the talking, or will it be interactive? Will there be exercises you're expected to do at home? Does the therapist take phone calls between sessions, and is there a charge for a telephone consultation?

Also, you should find out as much as you can about the therapist's feelings about treatment. Does he or she believe that people can get better—and, based on the experience of this practice, how long does that usually take? (You will probably want to steer clear of someone who initially tells you it takes years to get well.) Does the therapist encourage the use of medication (antidepressants and mood-altering drugs), or does he or she feel it's better to let the therapy itself act as the healing agent? Finally, after you've both gotten these basics out of the way, you might ask for an initial response to your problem—what does the therapist think you can accomplish during treatment? What goals can you set together for change?

How do you know if this is going to work? Obviously, other than the hope that the two of you start making headway on your issues, you don't know. A lot of it is instinctive—you can feel when it's right if you trust the person who's sitting across from you, and if you feel you're getting support and encouragement. Ideally, your therapist will model the kind of self-expression and self-awareness that you hope to be able to achieve. The therapist should be an example of how a person can get along in the world on her own. You may know very little about this individual's personal life, but you will understand from your sessions together how he or she thinks and feels. That can be very helpful to you at a time when you are particularly confused and anxious. The single best predictor of how well therapy is going is that you feel confident about your therapist and the work you're doing together.

If you say something outrageous, the therapist shouldn't react in a hostile or accusatory manner. He or she might ask why you feel that way, or might try and delve into the meaning behind your angry or bizarre words, but always without judging you. This is your stress, after all, and you have your own way of reacting to it.

During each session, which may be once or twice a week or more, you will come in with something that's been on your mind since you last met. This area of concern will be your jump-off point for the rest of your fifty minutes (some days, you may never leave the topic you started with).

Each form of treatment has a particular pattern, although a good therapist will never play the numbers by rote, but will improvise around the client's needs. The rhythm and content of the session, the progress, and the outcome of therapy will all depend on your problem and the type of therapy you select.

It may be helpful to follow the course of one patient suffering from general anxiety disorder to get a feel for what her sessions were like. The type of therapy was dynamic, although it was also somewhat eclectic, incorporating several different disciplines:

At the onset of therapy, Evelyn got her emotional cards on the table, and the therapist asked directive questions to help her sort those cards into order and find out which ones were most troubling. The therapist knew the rules of this game and Evelyn didn't, which meant that sometimes she felt tricked into a response, and as if stuff was being dredged out of her that she never wanted to see the light. But the therapist's reason for broaching difficult subjects is that she or he feels that the client is ready to deal with more difficult material.

To get this particular type of therapeutic process started, the therapist has to take charge. This means that initially, Evelyn felt that her therapist was stronger and more powerful than she was. After all, she was feeling pretty rotten when she decided to make that first appointment, and when she walked into the office for the first time, she felt helpless and desperate to be taken care of. (The overwhelming feelings of love and dependence that many people experience in therapy is called *transference*, where you transfer feelings you've felt with your parent to the therapist. In many schools of psychotherapy, it is believed that transference is a crucial element in a successful therapy. In time, as you feel less needy, these feelings mature into a partnered relationship.)

As therapy continued, Evelyn discovered that she was going in directions she never imagined. She found that she left the sessions even more upset than she was when she came in. But this meant that something was happening. It's often been said that the old self must die to make room for the new one to be born—and this is often an unpleasant process. She had to trust herself—since she could see that change was happening in her life despite the bad feelings and rage and frustration, she figured she was on the right track.

One of the turning points in this good therapeutic experience happened when Evelyn began to add her own interpretation to the comments the therapist had made about her behavior, her thought process, and her emotional states. Over time, as she began to look more closely at her stresses and how she managed or didn't manage to deal with them, she found that she talked more and the therapist talked less; that her therapist became less directive and she became more assertive. She was even able to take the lead when she wasn't in a therapy session to start restructuring her life. As she started making daily changes when she wasn't anywhere near her therapist, she knew she was getting better on her own.

> *A blissful trustfulness on the patient's part*
> *makes the relationship at first a very pleasant*
> *one; one thanks him for it, but warns him that*
> *this favourable prepossession will be shattered*
> *by the first difficulty arising in the analysis.*
> —SIGMUND FREUD, *COLLECTED PAPERS, V.2*

HOW WILL YOU FEEL AS THERAPY PROGRESSES?

This is such an individual experience that it's difficult to generalize, but there are certain landmark events that occur during almost everyone's therapy.

At first, you want to present your story. You want to look good and smart and on the right side of any emotional debate. You want the therapist to like you—just as you want to like and trust the therapist.

But as time goes on, you begin to find the cracks under the surface. You are not as noble as you think—sometimes you're self-serving, sometimes jealous, sometimes manipulative. You may start to dislike the therapist for statements he or she may make that indicate you're holding back. Eventually, you may cry and rant and rave—that's all part of the deal.

But if you never get under the nicely manicured exterior of your feelings and actions, you never get anywhere. The maxim "No pain, no gain" is applicable here. On the other hand, you should not feel brutalized by the experience. If your therapist is making you uncomfortable in any way and you feel threatened physically or emotionally, you should seriously consider terminating.

But in most cases, your pain is part of the healing process, and you do come out on the other side, knowing yourself and liking yourself better. You may also be surprised to find that you don't dislike the darker side of your personality, either.

HOW DO YOU KNOW WHEN IT'S TIME TO QUIT?

You don't "need" your therapist anymore when you can take care of your own emotional ups and downs. But there's the rub. We *always* long for a parent figure to lean on, no matter how independent we are or how well we were loved in childhood. So if you transfer a lot of your dependence onto a therapist, how do you get rid of it?

The answer is that when you are able to make decisions outside that therapy room without asking permission first, when you can actively alter destructive patterns you've been stuck in for a long time, when you can make rational judgments about previously irrational behavior, then you're functioning on your own and can probably make it without the support of your therapist.

As you are drawing close to the end of therapy, you will want to consolidate the work you've done and see whether you've met the goals you began with. It's perfectly possible that your reasons for going into therapy in the first place turn out to be insignificant now that you've done the hard work of self-examination. So your initial goals may have vanished long ago, and your new ones may still be in their fledgling state. That's fine, as long as you can sum them up for yourself and see that you're headed in a healthy direction.

In some types of therapy, the insurance company determines when you stop—if you wish to continue, it's on your nickel. Sometimes, your therapist will suggest that it's time to wind down. You may feel hurt and abandoned; you may fight against the decision—and then realize that you're holding onto something that you used to need but don't anymore. When you can see this, it's a clear indication that you're ready.

It's best, of course, when the two of you decide together on a quit date. With some practitioners, you stop cold turkey; with others you may wean yourself from once a week to once a month, with a promise that you can always call and come in for a "refresher" session.

WHAT IS THE GOAL OF THERAPY?

For most people, there is no blinding flash of realization. There is no one moment in therapy where it all comes clear, and suddenly you see the wonderful possibilities of life lined up before you. It is far more common to terminate therapy feeling that you've made some progress—a little—but that nothing radical has changed.

Your personal goals become the goals of your therapy.

Generally, there are three types of goals:

- Change
- Insight/understanding/acceptance
- Choice/life decisions.

If you are most interested in change, you would probably select behavioral therapy; if you are looking for insight, you would be best off picking dynamic therapy; if you are struggling with choices, you might want to explore gestalt therapy.

With behavioral therapy, the results come pretty quickly, as soon as the behavior changes. But sometimes the deeper issues that caused the behavior take many years to resolve. With dynamic or gestalt therapy, again, you will see the benefits sometimes only after you have been away from the sessions for a while. It is only in the weeks, months, and years after therapy has formally ended that what you have learned in your sessions comes into focus, kind of like those pictures on the Internet that start fuzzy and slowly, very slowly, appear in fine resolution.

You can't erase the past. All the lousy, rotten memories, the people who hurt you, the ways in which you abused yourself—they'll always be there. But you can make sense of the past and integrate it into the present—and then you can take control of the present and enjoy it. You can look forward to good days and bad ones knowing that you'll be able to handle them. Once you can understand what happened to you and how you used to act, you don't have to repeat your behavior. And this symbiosis among past, present, and future is the goal of therapy.

Therapy should teach you compassion and forgiveness for all things you used to beat yourself up about. No, it doesn't feel good when you fail, but unless you take risks and experiment with reactions, you'll never change the way you look at stress.

Eventually, however, the forest won't look so scary, and the monsters won't come around so often. And if you haven't achieved the goals you originally thought were important when you started therapy, you can say that you have found something much more vital—your ability to stand on your own two feet, even when a hurricane threatens to blow you over.

HOW YOU CAN INTEGRATE THERAPY WITH YOUR TEN-STEP PLAN

If you care about yourself, you won't treat therapy as though it were a magic bullet, some pill you can swallow twice a week to make all the bad stuff go away. Therapy is a growth process, just like prioritizing, goal setting, behavior change, and meditation. It is life-affirming like breathing and sexuality. It makes you part of the world and makes the world part of you.

So if you want to have a lasting effect from the hours you have spent getting to know yourself, you will adopt it as your tenth step and use it daily, regardless of whether or not you are still seeing your therapist. The cumulative effect of taking care of yourself externally, internally, and with the support of others will grow as you do. Eventually, you won't remember a time when you thought that you couldn't make it, or that you hated everyone, or that the world was bleak and sad.

When you have assimilated all this deep feeling and keen wisdom you've gained and allowed it to penetrate your spirit, you cannot help but like yourself more. And if you can do that, you're almost home.

Afterword   **Letting Go, Going On**

A s we explore what we want for ourselves in the future, we will find that the amalgam of everything we've learned—prioritizing, behavior modification, delegating responsibility, setting goals, learning to relax and pamper ourselves, breathing, meditating, increasing sexual pleasure, getting family support and professional help when necessary—makes us more capable of dealing with tragedy, comedy, and the banal everyday routine that can be stressful in itself. Not only are we more capable, we're also more relaxed, so there's less effort involved in every venture we approach, from a new job to a love affair. We'll find that we have increased patience for ourselves and others, and that perhaps for the first time in our lives, we feel that our bodies, minds, and spirits are truly and happily integrated.

A WOMAN'S BILL OF RIGHTS

I have the right, capability and responsibility to:

- Control my own life
- Refuse a request without guilt
- Express my anger
- Ask for affection
- Ask for help
- Figure out what's really important
- Question authority
- Choose when to assert myself
- Indulge in healthy competition
- Not be perfect
- Change my mind
- Be treated with respect
- Get what I paid for
- Make time for myself
- Live in the moment
- Be content

—and finally, and most important of all,

- Be myself.

Appendix **Resources**

RESOURCES TO EASE YOUR STRESS

Women who are in the midst of stress need help fast, and there are a variety of groups and centers around the country to come to your aid in taking care of yourself. The more you know about your reactions to difficult situations, the more easily you can stop a panic attack or a series of headaches in the bud.

Don't feel you have to "tough it out." Call a hotline. Join a support group. Start your own circle of friends in stress.

STRESS CENTERS

The various centers around the country offer a variety of services, including workshops, seminars, group sessions (usually ten to fifteen in a course), classes in yoga, tai chi, and other bodywork, cognitive and behavioral training, skills training, and problem-solving. Most have a hotline you can call in an emergency. The centers may be staffed with psychologists, psychiatrists, social workers, nurses, massage therapists, or yoga, tai chi, and other bodywork teachers.

Although most insurance does not cover stress care, it may cover the manifestations of stress (headaches, backaches, high blood pressure, extreme fatigue, eating disorders, gastrointestinal disorders, infertility, etc.) that can be treated in such a clinic. Some companies (Oxford Health Plans on the East Coast; Kaiser Permanente and several smaller West Coast plans) do offer coverage for alternative and complementary medical care.

Center for Anxiety and Related
Disorders at Boston University
648 Beacon St., 6th floor
Boston, MA 02215
(617) 353-9610

Center for Applied Psychology
Rutgers University
807 Hoes Lane
Piscataway, NJ 08855
(908) 445-2704

American Psychological
Association
Office of Women's Programs
750 First Street, NE
Washington, DC 2002-4242
(202) 336-5500

Division of Complementary
Medicine
University of Maryland School
of Medicine
Kernan Hospital
2200 Kernan Dr.
Baltimore, MD 21207
(410) 448-6871

Duke Center for Living
Box 3022
Duke University Medical Center
Durham, NC 27710
1-800-235-3853
(919) 660-6600
Dr. Martin Sullivan

Behavioral Medicine Clinic
Stanford University Health
Services
401 Quarry Rd.

Stanford, CA 94305
(415) 462-9111

Stress Reduction Clinic
University of Massachusetts
Medical Center
55 Lake Avenue N.
Worcester, MA 01655-0267
(508) 856-2656
Dr. Jon Kabat-Zinn

Mind/Body Medical Institute
Deaconess Hospital
1 Deaconess Road
Boston, MA 02215
(617) 632-9530
Dr. Herbert Benson

The following organizations
are affiliates of the Mind/Body
Medical Institute in Boston:

Mercy Hospital and Medical
Center
Stevenson Expressway at King
Drive
Chicago, IL 60616
(312)567-2600

Center for Anxiety and Stress
Treatment
4350 Executive Drive, Suite 204
San Diego, CA 92121
Shirley Babior, LCSW
Counseling (619) 542-0536 or
e-mail:health@stressrelease.com

Federal government hotline:
1-888-8-ANXIETY

CATALOGUES OF STRESS-RELIEF MATERIALS

Living Arts
P.O. Box 2939
Venice, CA 90291-2939
1-800 254-8464

Stress Less
P.O. Box 52164
Atlanta, GA 30355-0164
1-800 555-3783

Dharma Crafts
405 Waltham Street
Suite 234
Lexington, MA 02173
(617) 862-9211

INFORMATION ABOUT DISORDERS AND ALTERNATIVE STRESS THERAPIES

Smoking Cessation

Smoke-Enders
4455 E. Camelback Rd., Suite D150
Phoenix, AZ 85018
1-800 828-4357

Eating Disorder Treatment

National Association of Anorexia Nervosa and
Associated Disorders
P.O. Box 7
Highland Park, IL 60035
(708) 831-3438
Hotline: (847) 831-3438

Headache Treatment
National Headache Foundation
5252 N. Western Ave.
Chicago, IL 60625
(800) 843-2256

Depression Therapy
National Foundation for Depressive Illnesses
P.O. Box 2257
New York, NY 10116
(800) 248-4344

Obsessive–Compulsive Disorder Treatment
Obsessive–Compulsive Information Center
Dean Foundation
8000 Excelsior Drive, Ste 302
Madison, WI 53717-1914
(608) 836-8070

Flotation Therapy
The following are professional and commercial providers of float hydrotherapy. There are many more centers around the country; ask those on this list to refer you to a float near you.

PA, Levittown:	High Tech Flotation Spa
	Andy Vendetti, 888-SALTSPA
NY, New York:	Blue Light Flotation
	Sam Zeiger, (212) 989-6061
FL, Orlando:	ALAR, (407) 352-7741
IL, Chicago:	Relaxspa
	Goodie Jocis, (773) 736-9388
CA, San Francisco:	Susan Verde, (415) 789-7874

Reiki
Center for Reiki Training
29209 Northwestern Hwy #592
Southfield, MI 48034
1-800 332-8112

RECOMMENDED READING

Babior, Shirley, and Carol Goldman. *Panic, Anxiety, and Phobias.* San Diego: Whole Person Press, 1996.

―――. *Working with Groups to Overcome Panic, Anxiety, and Phobias.* San Diego: Whole Person Press, 1996.

―――. Calm Down Audiotape.

Barnett, Rosalind C., Lois Biener, and Grace K. Baruch. *Gender and Stress.* New York: The Free Press, 1987.

Benson, Herbert. *Your Maximum Mind.* New York: Random House, 1987.

―――. *The Relaxation Response.* New York: William Morrow, 1975.

Borysenko, Joan. *Minding the Body, Mending the Mind.* Menlo Park, Calif.: Addison Wesley, 1988.

―――. *A Woman's Book of Life.* New York: Riverhead Books, 1996.

Chopra, Deepak. *Ageless Body, Timeless Mind: The Quantum Alternative to Growing Old.* New York: Crown Publishers, 1993.

Cooper, Phyllis. *Euthenics for Stress Reduction.* Dubuque, Iowa: Kendall Hunt Publishing, 1994.

Domar, Alice D. *Healing Mind, Healthy Woman.* New York: Henry Holt & Co., 1996.

Easwaran, Eknath. *Meditation.* Berkeley, Calif.: Nilgiri Press, 1991.

Farhi, Donna. *The Breathing Book: Good Health and Vitality Through Essential Breath Work.* New York: Henry Holt & Co., 1996.

Girdano, Daniel A., George S. Everly, Jr., and Dorothy E. Dusek. *Controlling Stress and Tension,* 4th ed. Englewood Cliffs, N.J.: Prentice Hall, 1993.

Goleman, Daniel. *The Meditative Mind: Varieties of Meditative Experience.* Los Angeles: J.P. Tarcher, Inc., 1988.

Hager, W. David, M.D., and Linda Carruth Hager. *Stress and the Woman's Body.* Grand Rapids, Mich.: Fleming H. Revell, 1996.

Hay, Louise L. *You Can Heal Your Life.* Santa Monica, Calif.: Hay House Publishers, 1989.

Hoffman, David. *An Herbal Guide to Stress Relief.* Rochester, Vt.: Healing Arts Press, 1991.

Jackson, Ian. *The Breathplay Approach to Whole Life Fitness*. New York: Doubleday & Co., 1986.

Kabat-Zinn, Jon. *Full Catastrophe Living*. New York: Delta Books, 1990.

———. *Wherever You Go, There You Are*. New York: Hyperion Books, 1994.

McMinn, Mark R. *Making The Best of Stress: How Life's Hassles Can Form the Fruit of the Spirit*. Downer's Grove, Ill.: InterVarsity Press, 1996.

Maccoby, Eleanor E. *The Development of Sex Differences*. Stanford, Calif.: Stanford University Press, 1966.

Money, John, and Patricia Tucker. *Sexual Signatures: On Being a Man or a Woman*. Boston: Little, Brown & Co., 1975.

Murray, Michael T. *Stress, Anxiety, and Insomnia*. Rocklin, Calif.: Prima Publishing, 1995.

Pelletier, Kenneth R. *Mind as Healer, Mind as Slayer: A Holistic Approach to Preventing Stress Disorders*, 2d ed. New York: Delta Books, 1986.

Prochaska, James O., Ph.D., John C. Norcross, Ph.D., and Carlo DiClemente, Ph.D. *Changing for Good: The Revolutionary Program that Explains the Six Stages of Change and Teaches You How to Free Yourself from Bad Habits*. New York: William Morrow, 1994.

Sachs, Judith. *Nature's Prozac*. Englewood Cliffs, N.J.: Prentice Hall, 1997.

Sapolsky, Robert M. *Why Zebras Don't Get Ulcers: A Guide to Stress, Stress-Related Diseases, and Coping*. New York: W.H. Freeman and Co., 1994.

Selye, Hans, M.D. *The Stress of Life*, rev. ed. New York: McGraw-Hill, 1984.

Smith, M.H. *When I Say No I Feel Guilty*. New York: Dial Press, 1985.

Thondup, Tulku, *The Healing Power of Mind*. Boston: Shambhala Publications, Inc., 1996.

Williams, Juanita, ed. *Psychology of Women: Selected Readings*. New York: W.W. Norton and Co., Inc., 1979.

Witkin, Georgia, Ph.D. *The Female Stress Syndrome: How To Become Stress-Wise in the '90s*, 2d ed. New York: Newmarket Press, 1991.

Woolf, Virginia. *A Room of One's Own*. New York: Harcourt Brace Jovanovich, Inc., 1957.

Index

About the Author

Judith Sachs is a health educator, writer and speaker. She is the author of seventeen books on preventive healthcare, including *Nature's Prozac*, *The Healing Power of Sex*, and *What Women Should Know About Menopause*.

She has served as an adjunct professor at the College of New Jersey in Trenton teaching stress management, and conducts workshops at holistic centers, schools, and women's organizations throughout the tri-state area on preventive healthcare, stress, sexuality, and midlife issues. An HIV/AIDS educator for the American Red Cross, she also consults to various corporations, including Johnson & Johnson, Ortho-McNeil, and Warner-Lambert, on many aspects of wellness care.

Sachs lives in central New Jersey with her author husband, Anthony Bruno, and their thirteen-year-old daughter, Mia.

$9.95 (Canada $13.95)

WHAT EVERY WOMAN NEEDS TO KNOW IN ORDER TO RELAX

Engaged in the ultimate juggling act of keeping home, job, relationships, and parenting in the air simultaneously, most women live in a constant state of stress. While most men can relax as soon as they finish their day's work, studies show that women's stress levels actually increase after work. For them, home life and all of its responsibilities constitute a second full-time job.

Break the Stress Cycle offers women a proven program for lowering their stress levels and promoting well-being through the following steps:

- Identify the major stresses you face
- Focus on changing one behavior at a time
- Learn to delegate responsibility and get help and support from your family
- Learn meditation and breathing exercises
- Increase your sexual pleasure
- Know when to get professional support

LEARN HOW TO CONTROL THE STRESSORS IN YOUR LIFE AND ONCE AGAIN ENJOY LIFE TO THE FULLEST!

JUDITH SACHS is a bestselling writer on the subjects of women's health and sexuality. She is the author of *The Healing Power of Sex*, *Nature's Prozac* and *What Women Should Know about Menopause*.

0 45079 20007 4

50995

9 781580 620079

ISBN 1-58062-007-8

ADAMS
M E D I A
CORPORATION

http://www.adamsmedia.com